THE CHARGE OF THE BULL

JEAN BRISSET

THE CHARGE OF
THE BULL

The Battles of
11th British Armoured Division
for the Liberation of the Bocage
Normandy 1944

Originally published as
LA CHARGE DU TAUREAU

Translated by Thomas J. Bates

BATES BOOKS
Norwich, England & Berkeley, California

1989

First English edition
published in 1989 by
BATES BOOKS
120 Hillcrest Road, Berkeley
California 94705, U.S.A.
and
Wensum Point, 32 Whiffler Road, Norwich
Norfolk NR3 2AZ, England

ISBN 0 9512349 0 0

Printed by
Tas Offset Printing Services
Wensum Point, 32 Whiffler Road, Norwich
Norfolk NR3 2AZ, England.

DEDICATION

A l'Abbé Amiard, mon guide

This photograph was taken in 1976 at the time of Father Amiard's Golden Jubilee. On that occasion he was created a Knight of the Sovereign Order of St. John of Jerusalem, the last of many honours awarded to him.

ACKNOWLEDGEMENTS

The publication of this book would not have been possible without the generous cooperation of many official organizations in England. The Directors and personnel of these organizations greatly facilitated my researches. I would, therefore, like to offer my thanks to:
• the Imperial War Museum, who put so many important documents at my disposal, including nearly all the photographs used in this book;
• the Public Records Office where I was allowed to consult the War Diaries of the various units that appear in this story;
• the War Office Library which was an inexhaustible source of information;
• the 11th Armoured Division Committee who gave me constant support and encouragement;
• various British writers and editors, in particular Major-General H. Essame, who allowed me to read and reproduce large extracts from the histories of his Division and the various units in it;
• and, last but by no means least, the Old Soldiers, *les Anciens Combattants,* who sent me personal accounts of their experiences.

On the French side my thanks go to:
• first of all, Father Amiard, without whose help and encouragement much would never have been accomplished;
• the Committee in Flers for the twinning of the cities of Flers, Normandy and Warminster, England;
• the Committee for the 11th Armoured Division Monument at Le Pont-de-Vère;
• the officials who helped me prepare and submit the application for a grant to meet the costs of writing and publishing the original, French edition of this book;
• the Conseil Général de l'Orne who very kindly approved the grant;
• the Societies and Associations of Old Soldiers;
• those who replied to the questionnaires I sent them including Madame D. Morel, Messieurs Bertrand, Bessac, Coulon, Grandin, Laignel, Pierre, Ricordeau and Salles;
• the many other witnesses I interviewed, both in person and by correspondence, who were kind enough to confide their memories to me;
• all the others, from near and far, who contributed to making the writing and publication of this book possible.

Finally, I must express my delight at having the Prefaces to this book written by the famous Commander of 11th Armoured Division, Major-General G. P. B. Roberts, CB, DSO, MC. Legion d'Honneur, Croix de Guerre.

TABLE OF CONTENTS

FOREWORD

The inspiration for this English edition of Jean Brisset's book, *La Charge du Taureau,* originated in a remark made to me by Bill Holden in Normandy in 1985.

In 1944 Private Holden was a Bren-gun-carrier driver in 'S' Company of the 1st Battalion Royal Norfolk Regiment. He was lucky to get through the war unscathed and in August 1984, accompanied by his friend, ex-Corporal Ernie Seaman, MM, formerly a stretcher-bearer in the same Battalion, he went back to Normandy with me. The three of us went there primarily to find the exact place where their comrade, Corporal Sidney 'Basher' Bates, VC, had made his last stand.

We met Jean Brisset for the first time on that 1984 visit. I had been introduced to M. Brisset, through letters, by Miss Rose Coombs, MBE, a retired librarian formerly with the Imperial War Museum. Rose had always taken a motherly interest in 'Basher' and had written one of the first articles I read about him for the magazine, *This England.*

Knowing that I am writing a book about Corporal Bates to be titled *Sidney Bates VC — A True Camberwell Boy,* (incidentally, as far as I know, I am not related to him) and how anxious I was to pin-point exactly where he fell, she referred me to Jean Brisset's book and gave me an introduction to the author. This was a most useful introduction for not only did M. Brisset know a lot about the battle in which Sidney fell but he also spoke and wrote excellent English. With his help, the three of us, who spoke little French, found the exact place where Corporal Bates, standing alone in the middle of a field near Pavée at the western end of Perrier Ridge, turned back the attempt of 10 SS Panzer Division to overrun the 'NorMons'. The 'NorMons' were a composite force, hastily assembled during the battle, made up of the 1st Norfolks of 3rd British Infantry Division and the 3rd Monmouthshire Regiment of 11th Armoured Division, the 'Charging Bulls' of this story.

In late May 1985, Bill Holden and Ernie Seaman went back to Normandy, this time with a large group of ex-soldiers of both the 1st and 7th Battalions of the Royal Norfolk Regiment. The 7th

1

Battalion had also fought in Normandy in 1944 and their Captain David Jamieson had been awarded the Victoria Cross for his bravery during the battle of the Orne bridgehead near Grimbosq, just south of Caen. That was on 7 August, one day after Corporal Bates' action.

Again, the Norman author helped the Norfolk soldiers make a great success of their pilgrimage. Looking for a way in which to show the appreciation of his group for M. Brisset's assistance, Bill Holden had the happy idea of presenting him with a copy of his book, *La Charge du Taureau,* inscribed with the signatures of all the members of the party. It was a nice thought but, unfortunately, they could not find a copy of the book in any of the book stores in Caen. It was out of print. So, instead, they presented M. Brisset with a plaque commemorating the visit. Jean was delighted with it, especially when he noted, with quick Gallic perception, that they had spelt his name "in the English way, with two tees!"

Bill Holden told me all about this and also said, in passing, that it was a pity there was no English edition of Jean's book because the brief but vital part played by the 1st Norfolks was described in it. And thus a seed was planted.

A few days later, when I returned to England, I went to Mayfield, in Sussex, to interview General 'Pip' Roberts, the former G.O.C. of 11th Armoured Division. I was anxious to meet him because I had many questions to ask him about the climactic (as it was for the Sidney Bates story) Battle of Perrier Ridge. As is well known, in 1944 'Pip' Roberts was the youngest Major-General in the British Army. It is less well known that, in the same year, I was a 21-year-old subaltern in the Royal Corps of Signals laying battlefield telephone lines around Imphal, on the Burmese border. It is not surprising, therefore, that even after 40 years old army instincts reasserted themselves. I realized, in a panic, for time was running short, that before I went for my interview with the General I had to do something about my rather casual California hair style, even though there is not much hair left to style. I looked around the village for a men's barber shop but there was not a striped pole in the place. However, the resourcefulness I had learnt in XIV Army came to my rescue. I persuaded the only ladies' hairdressing salon in the village to give me a quick 'back and sides' and, suitably tidied up, went off with renewed confidence for my meeting with General Roberts.

Needless to say, there was absolutely no reason for me to feel apprehensive. There is nothing stiff and formal about 'Pip' Roberts. He made me welcome and put me at ease with a drink. While we were waiting for his wife to return from the village we started to talk about Normandy. We hadn't got very far when Mrs. Roberts entered. I was introduced to her and was immediately captivated by her beauty and graciousness. She explained that she had been delayed while having her hair done and I hastened to assure her that I understood perfectly because I believed she and I shared the same hairdresser!

It was a delightful visit and during lunch, while talking about our mutual friend, Jean Brisset, I asked why *La Charge du Taureau* had never been translated into English. Surely there would be sufficient interest in such a book in England? "Yes, of course there would be," said the General, "why don't you do it!" Without thinking I found myself sitting to attention and accepting his 'order'. I realised then that, despite the passing of so many years, he had lost none of his powers of leadership and command!

So here is my translation of Jean Brisset's book. When you find mistakes in the story send them back to me for they are mine. Be tolerant of any gaucheries in the translation; I know it could have been done better. Remember the three people who inspired this book: 'Pip' Roberts, the young General who not only led 11th Armoured Division to victory but also embodied the spirit of the thousands who fought in it; Jean Brisset who, as a teenager, was seared by his experiences in occupied France and liberated Normandy and wrote his book 'to get it out of his system'; and Bill Holden, the Norfolk anti-tank gunner who later became a master printer and who, together with his son, Colin, printed this book.

Berkeley, California 1987   TOM BATES

INTRODUCTION

When I was just a young boy my father told me a lot about the first World War. He himself did not take part in it because he was the last-born of a family of seven boys but he told me how, one after the other, his six brothers had each been called to the Army and sent to the front to defend their country. I remember how he described the brave way in which his mother and father had hidden their anguish when twice, the first time in 1916 and the second time in 1918, the Mayor of their village had come to tell them that their sons, Arthur and Charles, had been killed in action. When their remains were returned to the family in 1921 my grandfather could not bear the sorrow. He died on the very same day the two coffins were received and the three of them were buried in one grave in our little churchyard, the father between his two sons.

I don't suppose that, as a child, I was as deeply moved by this sad story as I am to-day. If anything, I was probably rather proud of belonging to such a patriotic family. However, what I do remember is that it raised a great curiosity in me about everything that had to do with war. I asked questions of everyone: my teacher, the parish priest, my uncles, everybody. The more I learnt the more I wanted to know. I can even remember my boyhood feelings of regret that the Great War was to be *la derniere guerre!*

When the second World War started in 1939 I was 12 years old, too young to go into the Army but old enough to understand what was going on and to be a fascinated eye-witness to many of the battles fought by 11th British Armoured Division when, in 1944, they liberated my homeland, the Bocage region of Normandy. The French edition of my book, *La Charge du Taureau* was written for French readers, especially those who had been caught up in the fighting and who wanted to know the full story of just how their countryside was liberated.

I never expected that, one day, *La Charge du Taureau* would become *The Charge of the Bull!* In the Foreword to this edition Tom Bates has explained how this came about. Personally, I am delighted that the readership of my book has been so widely extended by this English translation because it gives me the chance to pay homage, in their own language, to all those who fought, suffered and died on the soil of Normandy for our liberation. I hope that the *Anciens Combattants* of 11th Armoured Division and their relatives and friends will find something of interest in this story of the exploits of their famous Division. In addition, I hope that the accounts of the actions and subterfuges of the French civilians and the French *Résistance* that paralleled their activities will also interest them. The accounts of the assistance given by the *Résistance* to 43rd British Infantry Division and to Flying Officer Norman Baker, an Australian Spitfire pilot shot down in our area, originally included in the body of the book, are now placed as Appendices at the end of this edition.

Finally, let me thank *les Anglais* who made this book possible: Tom Bates for the translation; General Roberts for re-fighting the battles of his Division on paper and making sure the accounts are accurate; Rose Coombs for her generous help while she was at the Imperial War Museum and Bill Holden for printing the book.

Flers, Normandy 1987 JEAN BRISSET

PREFACE

It is a great honour that a Frenchman, M. Jean Brisset, should write a book about a British Division. I am very grateful to Mr. Bates for translating the book into English and having it published.

It is good that all should know not only the courage of our soldiers, but also the trials, tribulations and courage of the indigenous population.

Mayfield, East Sussex, 5. 1. 89   G. P. B. R.

INTRODUCTION
(1st French edition)

Above all else, this book is dedicated to the memory of the soldiers who gave their lives so that we could regain our freedom. Although it is based on British military documents, it does not claim to throw a new light on the Normandy campaign. In paying homage to the soldiers of 11th Armoured Division it retraces the part played by that Division in the momentous operations in June and July 1944 that led to the break-through of the German front, the closing of the Falaise Pocket by the Allies and the destruction of the encircled enemy forces in August 1944. These last two operations are described in great detail because they took place in the Bocage, where I live, and led to its liberation.

The part played by the *Résistance* in these battles was very important. However, I have only described the activities of the *Robert Déan F. T. P.* group during the period in question, leaving the task of writing a complete history of the *Résistance* to a more competent person.

The founders of the *Francs-Tireurs Partisans* named this group after Robert Déan, a student at Caen University in 1941 when he was arrested by the Germans and sent to a concentration camp at Chateaubriant. As a reprisal for the killing of some Germans, or for some other act of sabotage, the Germans executed fifty of these young hostages. Robert Déan was among them. Also in this group was Guy Mocquet, aged 17, at that time the youngest hostage to be executed in France.

Although the *F. T. P.*'s were often under Communist domination not all their members were communists.

The *Robert Déan F. T. P.*, which was only one of many that worked directly under the orders of Allied Intelligence, is mentioned in many British military documents. (See *The 43rd Division at War* by H. G. Essame.)

The personal memoirs of various soldiers and civilians have been added to the reports of battles in order to alleviate any dryness or monotony of the writing.

While reading this book, the factors that determined the success of 11th Armoured Division will become apparent: the quality of the training it received in Great Britain for three years; the high degree of preparation that resulted in its skill in battle; the morale of its soldiers which was always very high despite heavy losses; the valour of its leaders and, in particular, the skill of General Roberts in exploiting any opportunities that presented themselves; and, finally, the mutual confidence at all levels of command that created a true *esprit de corps.*

All this was necessary so that the Division could live up to the reputation of its emblem, the Bull, which is always ready to charge an enemy and to pursue him until he is utterly destroyed.

Flers, Normandy 1975   JEAN BRISSET

PREFACE
(1st French edition)

All members of 11th Armoured Division are most honoured that their operations in Europe and particularly in France should have been recorded in French by a Frenchman. I say, 'particularly in France', because it was there that our fiercest battles were fought, it was there, in Normandy, that the task of freeing Europe from the Nazi yoke hung, for a moment, in the balance and it was there that the issue was decided.

As the triumphs and tragedies of 11th Armoured Division unfold in this book it will be seen that the morale of the Division was always very high regardless of the number of casualties. This was because we were not only fighting for a just and vital cause but were also coming to the rescue of friends who had themselves made great sacrifices for the same cause and had frequently paid the final price in the horrors of a concentration camp.

On behalf of the Division I wish to express our deepest thanks to M. Brisset for all the work and research he has put into this book. Not only has he produced an interesting and exciting story but he has also caught the spirit of the whole enterprise which played such a large part in its successful conclusion. I feel sure that anyone who reads this book will understand how grateful we are to the people of Flers for putting up such a fine, yet simple, memorial to 11th Armoured Division at Pont-de-Vère which will commemorate that spirit for many years to come.

Mallorca, 1975   G. P. B. ROBERTS

Major General
Commander 11th Armoured
Division
1943-1945

CHAPTER 1

BIRTH OF THE ARMOURED FORCES

11TH ARMOURED DIVISION

The Great War had gone on for almost two years before the first assault tanks appeared on the British front. At the beginning of 1915 it was realised that, because of the widespread use of automatic weapons, it was insane to expose men on the battlefield without protection. The infantry had buried themselves, digging lines of trenches protected by a tangle of barbed wire that ran, practically without interruption, from the North Sea to the Swiss frontier. Every attack launched against these defensive positions came up against enemy fire and the losses of the attacking forces were terrible and out of all proportion to the results achieved. Some prophets had foreseen this situation a long time before the war and H.G.Wells had even described a machine having strong resemblances to what would eventually be the tank. Now that the need had become a necessity many wild ideas were put forward but, actually, very few came to anything. However, among the high-ranking people who examined the concept of the tank and one of the first to order a study of it and to actually build one was the First Lord of the Admiralty, Winston Churchill. He did not hesitate to take advantage of his position to authorise the Navy to carry out the first experiments that were to have such a profound influence on the future. The badge of the Royal Tank Regiment shows, placed in the centre of a crown of laurels, the trapezoidal shape of the first specimens of what one would hardly now call a tank for it has so few points in common with the tank of to-day. It was shown to the British General Staff and to King George V on 29 January 1916. It is probable that the high-ranking dignitaries were very impressed with the capabilities of this new-fangled machine even though its speed was less than 5 miles per hour but few among them saw in it the means of revolutionising the art of war.

In 1916 the Germans brought such pressure to bear on the French at Verdun that the Allies planned a large English attack in order to draw off enough enemy forces from that part of the front so that the French army could recover. Accordingly, Sir Douglas Haig, the Commander-in-Chief of the British Expeditionary Force, assembled a large force on the Somme. Before launching his attack he asked if these new machines, about which the General Staff was beginning to talk, could be put at his disposal by 1 June. Production difficulties delayed the arrival of the first tanks until the beginning of September. Furthermore, the training and acclimatisation of the crews posed serious problems, so much so that even the instructors themselves did not know much more than their pupils. Prior to their use on the battlefield, the first of the 70 machines expected to go over to France demonstrated their capabilities in front of an assembly of officers. They decided to use them, not in a large block as had been suggested by a few far-sighted individuals, but in small groups of, at most, three at a time and in limited actions. The attacks started on 15 September. In all cases, the many mechanical break-downs and the difficulties of getting up to the front line meant that, out of two or three machines intended to work together, generally only one was capable of taking part in the local actions in which they were engaged.

The first of these actions took place on the outskirts of the forest of Delville. A tank commanded by Captain Mortimore moved forward at 0515 hours, followed, fifteen minutes later, by the infantry.

THE FIRST TANK IN FLERS

The second big attack that Sir Douglas Haig planned to launch on the Somme was supposed to advance on the right flank, on the northwest edge of the forest of Delville, but first it was necessary to eliminate certain enemy positions. This was Captain Mortimore's job. The task of the infantry was easy because the Germans fled before the spitting machine-guns of this fearsome monster. But their artillery soon found the range and the monster was quickly reduced to scrap. Such was the inauspicious start of a great career.

Having captured the first objectives, it was planned to open a gap in the enemy's defences that extended from the village of Flers (Somme) to as far as Courcelette. The main effort of the tanks was supposed to be in the Flers sector. Of the 49 tanks sent to do the job, only 38 were able to get up to the start line and go into action. Among them were many that were quickly put out of action by enemy artillery, or that sunk into shell-holes and trenches or that became entangled in barbed wire or blocked by rubble. The result was that nothing decisive or even significant was achieved. An impartial assessment of the results concluded that the tank attack was a failure. Nevertheless, a tank driven by Lt.Hasty did succeed in infiltrating right into the village of Flers and there they saw the Germans abandoning the ruins and retreating in disorder. The infantry were thus able to take the village with fewer casualties than usual.

Of course, there was still a lot to be done before they could obtain more positive results. For one thing, some means of communication had to be developed between the infantry and artillery and the driver of the tank, other than hand signals or thumps on the side of the tank. Also, the tank crews had to be specially trained because they were expected to know how to drive their machines, read maps, identify their targets, load, aim and fire their guns, and, at the same time, be alert to what was going on in the battle around them so that they could take advantage of any openings they created.

The lessons learnt from Lt.Hasty's success in the ruins of Flers, as well as from other isolated actions in which the rest of the tank force took part, continued to bear fruit even though, at the beginning, their only immediate effect was to restore confidence to the poor infantryman who now felt less vulnerable and better protected. From that first small triumph at Flers was born the bogey of the 'Tank Terror'. This alone was sufficient to ensure that the life of this new weapon was not snuffed out at birth by the accounts of its first setbacks. It was granted a high manufacturing priority and the production rate from British factories was maintained.

In 1944, after taking part in every major attempt by Montgomery to break out of the beach-head, the tanks of 11th British Armoured Division covered themselves with glory in the fighting in the Bocage. Flers, in Normandy, was the first major city to be liberated by the Division. Not to be overshadowed by its namesake on the Somme, it became the starting point of an amazing 'charge' that eventually carried the tanks wearing the emblem of the Bull to Amiens on 31 August and on to Antwerp on 4 September.

AFTER DUNKIRK

Few events in history have shaken the people of France, of Great Britain and of the rest of the free world as deeply as the German blitzkrieg into France and the Low Countries in May 1940. Of course, the quality of the German armies had been clearly demonstrated the previous September in Poland but Poland was far away and, in any case, it was not reckoned to be a 'Great Power'. So, although it had been hoped that Poland would hold out a little longer, when it took the armies of the Reich just one short month to make her capitulate the Allies were not unduly concerned or alarmed. It was not until the enemy, on his very first assault, overran the French defences and poured through the breach into the rear areas to disrupt the lines of communication, not until he shattered the numerically-powerful French army, not until he contemptuously chased the British Expeditionary Force ahead of him, not until the desperate evacuation at Dunkirk allowed them to escape by the skin of their teeth, not until Paris and then France fell, not until England was menaced by invasion — and all this in just three weeks' time! — it was not until all this happened that the eyes of the world and, in particular, the eyes of the British people, were opened to the reality of Nazi power and ruthlessness.

The effect on the morale and spirit of the British people produced by this prodigious but, none the less, disastrous evacuation and the desperate situation that resulted from it are too well known to need description. However, one of the lessons learnt does concern us. The Germans had mounted a 'blitzkrieg', a campaign led and won largely by tanks, one that, in speed, was like lightning when compared to the old methods of waging war. Now, at last, everyone in England understood that the aeroplane and the tank were the key elements in modern war.

During the months that followed Dunkirk, the words 'Panzer Division' took on an almost mystical significance. This was the force thought to be like a magic sword; it was the answer to a modern commander's prayer. Without armoured divisions no army could hope to be victorious. England owed it to herself to have these divisions for two reasons: firstly, to have the means of counter-attacking so that, if the Germans did try an invasion, they could be thrown back into the sea, just as they had done to the English, and, secondly, to enable them to return to the Continent when the time was ripe, to liberate France and Europe and, finally, to overrun Germany. This longed-for day was still far in the future but the necessary armoured divisions had to be formed without delay. In those days of short supplies and limited resources the armoured divisions were given priority in men and materials. They were to become the elite of the new army with which Great Britain would restore her desperate situation and would, once more, confidently re-enter the land battle against her enemy.

FORMATION OF 11TH ARMOURED DIVISION

11th Armoured Division was born of these grand resolutions. The Division began to take shape in December 1940, the time when most of its formations were created. Some of them were Territorial units specially selected for this new task, others were completely new. The 23rd Hussars, the 24th Lancers and the 8th Battalion Rifle Brigade all came on the scene at this time. Together with the 2nd Fife and Forfar, who arrived in July from Ireland, they formed 29th Armoured Brigade. The 22nd Dragoons, the 2nd Lothian and Border, the Westminster Dragoons and the 12th Battalion King's Royal Rifle Corps formed 13th Armoured Brigade. For more than a year, the 13th Regiment Royal Horse Artillery was the only unit of its kind in the Division. The 24th Lancers were the reconnaissance force, equipped with light armoured cars.

The organization of the new British armoured divisions was based on the idea of deploying the maximum number of tanks at the cost of other arms. The two Armoured Brigades, each comprising three Armoured Regiments, had about 350 tanks, whereas, in the whole Division, there were only 24 guns to support these units. As for the infantry, it too was reduced to the absolute minimum, three battalions in all. The choice of such an organization was inspired by the dominant role played by tanks in the German victories. The conclusions drawn from those victories were that an armoured division had only two roles to play: first, to find and destroy the enemy's armour, which did not need any infantry, and, second, to exploit any opening the tanks made. In this event, counter-attacks would only come from inferior, rear-eschelon, line-of-communication troops and to deal with these counter-attacks it was only necessary to have a small group of infantrymen, well armed and very mobile, so that they could follow the tanks closely and occupy and mop up the territory taken by the armoured advance. This was the origin of the motorised battalion in each brigade.

Strangely, other infantry units were placed in formations consisting mainly of artillery. In the case of 11th Armoured Division, this was the 11th Support Group which, in addition to the 13th

16

Royal Horse Artillery, also included the 75th Anti-Tank Regiment, the 58th Light Anti-Aircraft Regiment and the 8th Battalion Royal Ulster Rifles. All this was worked out in the spring of 1941. In the course of the summer the 8th Royal Ulster Rifles were replaced by the 12th Battalion Green Howards.

BIRTHDAY

Because of all these comings and goings it is very difficult to fix the exact date of birth of the Division; the date most often accepted is the period of March 1941 when Divisional Headquarters was formed and took command. The Division first saw the light of day in Yorkshire and it was there that her early days were spent. The Division learnt to walk and run on the moors of that county and it was there that she received her first tanks and was taken over by her first Commander.

EQUIPMENT

The tanks were Valentines, among the first of this type to be built in Great Britain. The Valentine was an excellent tank, reliable, not too clumsy and relatively easy to drive and maintain. On the other hand, it had certain defects: lack of speed, thinness of armour and too light a gun. This last-named deficiency was a common fault of British tanks of that period.

THE COMMANDER

The first Commander was Major-General P.C.S.Hobart (later Sir Percy Hobart). He had recently returned from the Middle East where he had formed and commanded 7th Armoured Division, the famous 'Desert Rats' who, with the rest of 8th Army, were eventually to drive Rommel out of Africa. Having commanded the first Armoured Brigade ever formed, he was well known for his great enthusiasm for tanks and his encyclopedic knowledge of them. His ability was immediately recognized and showed itself in his flair for training. All his energy and will-power were concentrated on this task, sometimes even to the point of ruthlessness. From the top to the bottom of the ladder of command, from the Brigadier to the private soldier, he gave no one any rest. However, they all respected his ability and his training methods.

General Hobart was a stern task-master and he left his stamp on the Division in many ways, not the least of which was its emblem, the Bull. He was particularly fond of this emblem.* A less obvious mark left by him on the Division was, quite simply, its battle-readiness; this was due, in large measure, to the lessons driven home by him.

In the spring of 1942 the results of the fighting in the Middle East showed what the ideal organization of an Armoured Division should be and what tasks it could be asked to perform. The Germans had reduced the number of tanks in their Panzer Divisions and had increased the infantry. A similar modification was made in the British Army. One of the two armoured brigades of 11th Armoured Division was dropped at that time and was replaced by a brigade of motorised infantry. This change made it possible for the Division to regain its momentum if it was slowed down or even stopped by enemy defences. It also made possible the establishment of bridgeheads and of close combat on ground that was difficult or unsuitable for tanks alone.

THE ARRIVAL OF THE WELSH INFANTRY

The replacement of an armoured brigade by an infantry brigade and the changes in tactics that resulted from this change also brought about the evolution of the 'Support Group'. This was

---

*General Hobart was particularly fond of the emblem of the Bull because it was part of his family's Coat of Arms. Later, when he was appointed to form and command 79th Armoured Division, the division of armoured 'funnies', he again chose the Bull as the divisional emblem though in a slightly different form.

broken up and became, essentially, the divisional artillery. The Green Howards then made way for the guns of the 151st Ayrshire Yeomanry.

159 Brigade, from 53rd Welsh Division, became the Infantry Brigade of the Division. It consisted of the 3rd Monmouthshire Regiment, the 4th King's Shropshire Light Infantry and the 1st Herefordshire Regiment.

The most intensive training took place from May to July 1942, ending in very extensive field manoeuvres that lasted for 14 days and were supervised by Montgomery himself. When this was over, the tempo of activity was increased still further by equipment changes. The Valentines were replaced by Crusaders, faster and much more comfortable. However, there was a lot to be done before they were judged suitable for action. The armour plating of the Crusader was thinner than the Valentine and, at first, it had the same weak armament. It was less reliable and required more maintenance. However, in August 1942, when the 47mm* guns started to appear in the turrets of the Crusaders and when the summer training had ended, the Division felt fully confident. It was well trained and ready for battle. Then came rumours of a possible posting overseas and to everyone that meant — North Africa.

OVERSEAS DESTINATION

General Hobart left the Division in September 1942 and was replaced by General Brocas Burrows who came to them from 9th Armoured Division.

During the first weeks of 1943 the Division was inspected, first, by the Duke of Gloucester and then by His Majesty, the King.

The decision not to send 11th Armoured Division to North Africa was made at the Casablanca Conference. In the days immediately preceding this Conference the military situation in Tunisia had altered so much that the need was no longer for tanks

*The Crusader Mark I was armed with a 2-pounder gun and the Mark II with a 6-pounder. (See *Great Battle Tanks* by Simon Dunstan)

but for infantry. The Commander-in-Chief of this theatre of operations personally made this request to the High Command gathered at Casablanca.

The advance party had already left for Africa when it was decided to cancel the move and new orders were issued. A large number of vehicles that had already been loaded on ships ready to leave from west coast ports had to be unloaded and driven back to their units, to the great surprise of their owners who had not expected to see them again until they caught up with them on the shores of the Mediterranean. All they could do was to resign themselves to staying in England and to undo all that had been done in preparation for the voyage. Gradually, training was resumed and field exercises, always supervised by numerous V.I.P.'s, were begun again. There were so many of these exercises that all members of the Division swear that the code names given to them are still deeply embedded in their brains and engraved on their hearts!

THE SHERMANS

It was just at this time that another change took place in the equipment of the Division; the Crusaders were replaced by Shermans. In North Africa, the Sherman had already proved to be the finest tank used by the Allies up to that time. Though slower than the Crusader, it was faster than the Valentine. It had thicker armour-plating and was armed with a 75mm gun. Its greatest advantage in comparison to the Crusader was the way its armour-plating stood up to high-explosive shells. This gave it a better chance against anti-tank guns or, more to the point, against enemy tanks. Moreover, being an American tank, it was produced in vast numbers and was so well built that the crews soon developed a feeling of real superiority—well, at least in numbers.

FURTHER CHANGES

While these changes were being made, there was a re-distribution of units among the various Army Corps. This resulted in the transfer of the Division from IX Corps to VIII Corps, under whose command it remained until 13 August 1944 when it was placed under command of XXX Corps.

Another important change was the loss by the Division of the light armoured vehicles of the 24th Lancers which were placed under Corps command. In their place the Division was given a unit called an 'armoured reconnaissance regiment'. The function of the newcomer was practically the same as its predecessor. Its incorporation into the Division was nothing more than a subterfuge to obtain a fourth armoured regiment but, at least, it did have an independent role. The new regiment posted to the Division was the 2nd Northamptonshire Yeomanry. They arrived in June equipped with the Centaur, a tank only good enough for training that they gladly gave up when the first British-made Cromwells were delivered.

Finally, there was a third important change, namely, the reinforcement of the infantry brigade by the addition of a back-up unit designed to support its battalions and augment their fire power. This was the 2nd Machine Gun Company of the Royal Northumberland Fusiliers who were equipped with Vickers machine-guns and heavy mortars. In addition, certain units were equipped, some at full strength, with self-propelled guns. The 13th Royal Horse Artillery received 105mm self-propelled guns, the 75th Anti-Tank Regiment, two batteries of M10 Tank Destroyers (a 76mm gun on the chassis of a Sherman) and a battery of 58th Light Anti-Aircraft Regiment, self-propelled Bofors. Finally, each troop of 3 tanks in the armoured regiments was given a Sherman equipped with an 80mm gun, the only gun capable of penetrating the armour-plating of the German tanks. These specially-equipped Shermans were known as 'Fireflies'.

TRAINING FOR DIVISIONAL OBJECTIVES

It has already been noted that at the end of the summer of 1942 the Division considered itself fully trained according to the standards of the time. Since then the danger of obsolescence of its equipment had been reduced and Great Britain now possessed the most powerful war machine that had ever existed on her soil. Only one thing remained to be done so that this machine could play the role that would be given to it when the time came for the invasion of the Continent: its training in Combined Operations.

For some time it had been rumoured, and the rumours were soon confirmed, that the Division would be employed, not in the assault, but for support and exploitation. With this in mind it was now necessary to carry out training exercises in order to learn how to disembark on a beach that had already been seized and how to get into action in the shortest time possible. This would mainly depend on the tank drivers. For the rest of the men, the training was epitomised in two words: 'water-proofing' and 'loading'. Numerous exercises, consisting of field manoeuvres, live firing, establishment of headquarters for the armour, the infantry and the artillery, took place from November 1943 until May 1944. The general satisfaction with the results was encouraging and heightened everyone's morale. There is no doubt that the realistic staging from start to finish of Operation EAGLE was due, in large measure, to the fact that the Division was now being led by men who had had wide and recent battle experience.

THE ARRIVAL OF 'PIP'

General Burrows was replaced in December by Major-General Roberts. All that was known of General Roberts was that he had taken part in the campaigns in Libya and Tunisia at various levels of command and that he had commanded two armoured brigades with great competence.

It is well known that all wars produce a crop of excellent officers who climb the ladder of military command more rapidly than their fellow officers simply by virtue of the outstanding feats of arms they accomplish as they advance in rank. It is very probable that, at that time, the new divisional commander held the record for World War II. When Germany invaded Poland he was a Captain in the 6th Battalion Royal Tank Regiment. Four years later, practically on his 37th birthday, he received the command of his first division.

It is not easy to describe General Roberts' remarkable qualities in simple terms. Brigadier Carver, himself a noteworthy *grimpeur d'echelons* * has recalled, in his *History of the 7th Armoured Division,* the debt that this famous formation owed to the person who commanded its 22 Armoured Brigade. He wrote: *The Division owed much to Brigadier Roberts...His outstanding leadership and almost uncanny skill won him the affection, admiration and confidence of every man in his Brigade.*

The appreciation of 22 Brigade was soon to be amply confirmed by the Division that now came under the command of General Roberts.

AN EXPERIENCED CHAIN OF COMMAND

Other officers came with the General from the Middle East, among them Brigadier Harvey, previously commander of 23rd Hussars; he took command of 29 Armoured Brigade. An entirely new regiment also arrived from the Middle East, the 3rd Battalion Royal Tank Regiment, in which General Roberts had first served as a subaltern and which had returned from the Mediterranean theatre in December 1943.

The Order of Battle of 11th British Armoured Division for most of the fighting in Normandy in given in Appendix A, page 240.

*Ladder climber.

CHAPTER 2

DISASTROUS 'SUPPORT' FROM THE ALLIED AIRFORCE

11th Armoured Division disembarked in France on 13 and 14 June 1944, landing between Bernières and Courseulles, just to the north of Bény-sur-Mer. For various reasons, small parties of vehicles and men belonging to the 2nd Northamptonshire Yeomanry and the 58th Light Anti-Aircraft Regiment were late in arriving. On the other hand, a Squadron of the Inns of Court Regiment, which was later to become the reconnaissance regiment of the Division, had landed on the soil of Normandy opposite Graye-sur-Mer, in the Canadian sector, just half an hour after the initial dawn assault on D-Day.

MISSION IMPOSSIBLE?

The task given to the Inns of Court was as bold as it was ambitious. They were to advance at top speed to the River Orne and to destroy all the bridges over it between Thury-Harcourt and Caen. There were six major road bridges over this stretch of the Orne: three were in the vicinity of Thury-Harcourt, one was south of the Forest of Grimbosq, one was to the east of Amayé-sur-Orne and the last was at Feuguerolles. In addition, there were two railway bridges. The plan was to prevent the build-up of German reinforcements to the west of the Orne. In particular, they were to stop reinforcements from reaching 21st Panzer Division which was thought to be in the Forest of Cinglais. (In fact, they were near Evreux). Before the bridges were blown, a force was supposed to leave from east of the river and reconnoitre towards the woods of Cinglais so as to make sure the panzers were actually there. After that, if it was still in a fit condition to do so, it was to continue east to watch enemy troop movements in that area. One group of this force was to branch off to take up observation posts in the Vimont area and there establish contact with advanced elements of 6th Airborne Division or lie low until the Airborne troops arrived. Another group was supposed to establish itself secretly in the vicinity of St. Pierre-sur-Dives where the main body of the English forces was supposed to arrive in a few days' time. If there was a delay they too were ordered to remain hidden until 6th Airborne arrived.

In the event that, somehow or other, the enemy succeeded in sending reinforcements west of the Orne, the four bridges on the River Odon, namely, those at Ragny, Le Locheur, Bougy and Gavrus, considered to be on their likely line of advance, were also to be destroyed.

REQUIREMENTS FOR SUCCESS

The success of this plan depended on three elements: swiftness of action, surprise and the determination of each group to carry out its task. There was no need to worry about the last of the three conditions because, although the Chiefs of Staff recognized that the plan was an ambitious one, once the briefing was over everyone was enthusiastic about his part in it and quite confident he could pull it off. The only requirement for success was that the two other elements, speed and surprise, must also work in their favour. Everything was based on the assumption that, after the initial Canadian assault had succeeded, all the troops and equipment of the Inns of Court would disembark without delay, cross the beaches, get up to the start lines, advance rapidly through the rear of the enemy and, following pre-set routes, reach all their objectives.

A BAD START

One of the two LCT's (Landing Craft, Tanks) carrying the Inns of Court Squadron first hit one mine and then another and eventually ran aground too far off shore to allow the tanks to disembark. Nevertheless, two half-tracks tried their luck but were immediately swamped by the waves. The second LCT succeeded in beaching without trouble and the first tanks immediately made for the two beach exits where one of them promptly ran over a mine!

The Canadians had met more resistance than expected. Because the amphibious tanks had not been able to support them in their assault, many beach stong-points had not been silenced. Still-active German 88mm guns destroyed some of the tanks; those that succeeded in by-passing the guns took a route blocked by German defenders who inflicted heavy losses on them. So much precious time was lost that, by night-fall, the most advanced elements had only reached the line of the Bayeux — Caen railway. So the results of the first day's fighting were rather disappointing: heavy losses and unattained objectives. But, worst of all, the element of surprise had been lost because of what had taken place during the disembarkation.

THE MASSACRE

Next morning, the survivors took the road to the Orne but now they had to deal with growing difficulties both from enemy tanks and from the Allied Airforces that, seeing them in enemy territory, mistook them for targets. At the crossroad at Jerusalem, Thunderbolts bombed them unmercifully. A direct hit smashed a half-track and set four tanks on fire. The crews were killed, burnt or wounded. Despite that, the survivors were not discouraged. They continued toward their objective, some of them getting as far as Tilly-sur-Seulles. However, as their numbers were being steadily reduced by the enemy, what remained of the Squadron was recalled for other tasks.

THE CANADIANS SUFFER.
A BLOODY SUNDAY AT ST.GEORGES

This sort of mistake, namely, Allied aircraft attacking their own troops, happened rather frequently, especially during the days immediately after the landings. The pilots were serving their apprenticeships and many of them were trigger-happy. Even though far inland, Canadian prisoners were not safe from such attacks.

The first Sunday after the start of the fighting in Normandy was 11 June. The day began as a day of prayer and meditation for the parishioners of St.Georges-des-Groseillers, near Flers. As with all the rural communities in that area, the residents had taken in their share of refugees and those who attended Mass had much to think about and to pray for. Flers had been partially destroyed. Hundreds of families were in mourning and many had lost everything. The worry about whether they would be able to survive once the fighting had passed through their region was added to the strain caused by the terrible events of the preceding week.

After taking the evening service and retiring into the presbytery at St.Georges, the Abbé Labutte was in the Curé's garden when a plane appeared and started machine-gunning not far from the village in the direction of the main road. A few minutes later someone rushed up to beg for priests and nuns to go to Le Mesleret right away to attend to the wounded and dying. When the Abbé Labutte arrived at the main road he could not suppress a shudder of horror on seeing the shattered, mutilated bodies. There were many of them lying on the road and in the ditches. The road surface was so covered with blood and human remains that he had the impression of being in a slaughter house. To the horror of what he saw were added the cries of the wounded, the groans of the dying and, over it all, the shouts of the Germans trying to control the Canadian prisoners they were guarding and to prevent any civilians from approaching them and giving them help.

THE SS COUNTER-ATTACKS

Because the German coastal defences were practically undamaged by the aerial bombardment, the Canadians had to overcome very stiff opposition. This held them up in their advance into the interior towards their D-Day objectives of which the most important was the capture of the airfield at Carpiquet. They spent a comparatively quiet night in the Villons-les-Buissons area and then set out at dawn on the 7th. During the night, the Germans, well aware of the menace to Carpiquet and to Caen, sent strong reinforcements to this sector of the front. 12th SS Panzer Division who, together with the Panzer Lehr and 21st Panzer Divisions, formed a formidable armoured force, rushed up from Evreux by forced marches. The heavy damage done to their lines of communication by the Allied airforces caused considerable delay. Practically all daytime movement was stopped. This meant that only advance elements of 12th SS Panzer could get into position in time to counter-attack the Canadians in the early morning while the rest of the Division had to take long detours in order to avoid the ruins of towns bombed on the evening of the 6th.

When day broke, Kurt Meyer, the commander of 12th SS Panzer, climbed up into one of the towers of the Abbey d'Ardenne from where he could see all the preparations of his opponents. He immediately decided to attack them without waiting for the rest of his Division to arrive. This decision gave him a quick success that morning but it also resulted in a check to the German thrust to the sea because it was carried out too weakly. The same thing happened to 21st Panzer on the left of the Allied line.

THE ENCIRCLEMENT

I was in command of 'A' Company of the North Nova Scotia Highlanders. We had led the assault of 9 Brigade of 3rd Canadian Infantry Division at dawn on 6 June near Bernières, wrote Major Rhodenizer. *Towards mid-day on the 7th we were fighting in the outskirts of Authie when we were surrounded by 12th and*

21st Panzer Divisions and overrun. Those who were not killed were taken prisoner. During the night we were taken to a school near Caen and, after spending the day of the 8th and the following night there, we were taken, on foot, to Rennes.

In spite of the German counter-attack, the right wing of the Canadians continued its advance and had some success, cutting the Caen — Bayeux road and taking Bretteville l'Orgueilleuse and Putot-en-Bessein. On the 8th, Kurt Meyer turned his efforts against 7 Canadian Brigade also. Violent fighting took place around Putot-en-Bessein which was held mainly by the Winnipeg Rifles who, in their turn, were cut off.

THE TACTICS OF THE SS

On that day, recalls Mr.Johnson, *we were subjected to a violent attack by units of 12th SS Panzer. The four Companies of my Battalion were sorely tried by this fighting that went on throughout the day. I was hit by shrapnel in the right leg. During the evening, the SS forced ten of our own men to march towards our positions while they sheltered behind them. Our men could not use their weapons against the enemy who, by this tactic, and in violation of the Rules of War, made us prisoners. After joining up with other companions in misfortune we were taken to a camp in Brittany. Among us were men of 9 Brigade, of 27 Armoured Brigade and several paratroopers from the 3rd Canadian Division front. We left Caen early on 9 June, passing strong German reinforcements along the way going up to the front. We had nothing to eat or drink and our guards had their work cut out to push away the French civilians who were trying to give us bread and water; those among us who were lucky sometimes managed to get some.*

ON THE WAY TO THE PRISONER-OF-WAR CAMPS

On the afternoon of 11 June, while the column followed the road that rises towards the hills that overlook Flers, four fighter-bombers,

American Lightnings, crossed a little in front of us, coming in from the west. I think I am right in saying that we all saw them, recalls Mr. Cook. *I remember thinking to myself as I watched them fly away that they were lucky to be free.*

THE MACHINE-GUNNING

Seated on the doorstep of a house near the crossroad at Aubusson, a woman was watching the prisoners pass while Camille Briard was trying to talk to them despite the guards. *No one was paying any more attention to the planes,* continues Mr. Cook, *when, by chance, someone turned around and, seeing the four planes dive towards the road, screamed for everyone to scatter. Like most of us, I waited a second or so to see what was happening before dashing from the road. I was too late. The first plane had already opened fire with its machine-guns and its 20mm canons and I was hit by the first hail of bullets.*

THE COURAGEOUS SERGEANT

Major Rhodenizer adds: *The first two planes opened fire on us. One of the prisoners, Sergeant Robert Higgins of the North Nova Scotia Regiment, courageously stood in the middle of the road and, under a hail of shells bursting all around him, made signs to the pilots by waving his jacket by the arms. Undoubtedly realizing their mistake, the last two planes swooped down but did not fire. Then all four of them flew off in the direction of the beaches.*

TOO BAD—HIS GOOSE IS COOKED!

Mr.Cook continues. *I was hit repeatedly and lost consciousness. The last thing I remember was one of my pals saying, 'It's too bad for Cookie, his goose is cooked'.*
Those among the wounded who seemed to have a chance of sur-

viving were taken, under escort, to the hospital at Flers while those beyond hope were left to die.

SERGEANT FOSTER'S AGONY

It was 'the longest night' for Father Labutte. *After I had prayed for the souls of those who were already dead I did my best to help those who were going to follow them. Soon only one remained. He was lying in an orchard near the road under an apple tree. His wounds were terrible; there was no doubt that they were mortal. I knelt down near this poor, unfortunate boy, barely 20 years old, who was taking so long to die and I prayed over him all that night. It was not till dawn that the Lord, taking pity on him for his suffering, agreed to receive back the soul that He did not wish to re-claim but that the mad murderers of men were forcing Him to accept.*

At the same time, at the other end of the world, in distant Canada, a mother prayed to the same God, as she did every night before going to sleep, to take care of her child.

Eleven Canadians were buried side by side in the cemetery at St. Georges-des-Groseillers. Three French civilians were also buried there and later a further three more soldiers of the thirty-six who were wounded also joined them. The survivors passed the night in a barn on the Lesellier farm where some civilians managed to bring them food secretly.

The next day, two officers, Lieutenants Campbell and Smith, escaped with the help of some civilians. They were re-captured ten days later while trying to cross into the American lines. The first now lives in New Brunswick while the second has become a Member of Parliament in Ottawa.

DID OUR FELLOWS DO THAT?

Father Labutte recalls: *I will always see this haggard officer supporting himself with one arm in a corner of the house into which we had taken some of the more seriously wounded men, muttering to himself, 'Surely it's not possible! Did our fellows really do that?'*

CHAPTER 3

THE FIRST BATTLE

THE SITUATION AND OBJECTIVES

After an uneventful crossing, the main body of 11th Armoured Division was ready for action by the middle of June. It started to organize itself on the outskirts of the little villages of Cully and Lantheuil, both smothered by the dust of incessant convoys, and to get ready for its turn to go into battle.

The Atlantic Wall had not been sufficiently strong to prevent the Invasion. In spite of formidable obstacles, the battle of the beaches had been won. The Germans, following Rommel's plan that put great faith in mines and concrete blockhouses to impede the invasion, now had to quickly organize a defence in depth. Field-Marshal Von Rundstedt, who was Chief of the German Armies on the western front, tried to correct the mistakes of his subordinate by forming a mobile armoured strike-force in reserve. However, because of the constant pressure maintained by the Allies on the entire front and because of his lack of infantry, the enemy was forced to use his armour in defensive roles. In the meanwhile, his 15th Army, all ready for action, was waiting for the 'real' invasion to take place across the *Pas de Calais*.

Montgomery's plan was to draw most of the German armoured forces on to the British sector. Rommel fell in with this plan and concentrated his forces there in order to prevent the capture of Caen and the enlargement of the beach-head to the east. It was crucial for him to prevent the advance of the Allies in the direction of the lower reaches of the Seine for various reasons: the river was the last natural obstacle defending the launching ramps of the V1 and V2 rockets and it lay across the vital lines of communication along which reinforcements could be sent to Normandy. Furthermore, an Allied break-out in the direction of Paris would cut off forces in the west and endanger the naval base at Le Havre. This base was indispensable to those German naval forces still operating against the English ports, lines of communication and embarkation points. Finally, the last reason was to prevent an eventual link-up between the forces already established in Normandy and those that the Germans expected would soon be coming across the *Pas de Calais*.

For these reasons, the enemy committed all his available armour and a large part of his infantry to the battle of attrition that Montgomery was determined to wage around Caen. Admittedly, this decision prevented the Allies from breaking out in the direction of Falaise, into country more suitable for tanks and airfields, but it allowed them to make progress at the other end of the line and to seize the Cotentin peninsula. By 17 June the peninsula was cut off by the American 9th Infantry Division when it reached the west coast near Barneville. St. Sauveur-le-Vicomte had been taken the evening before by the paratroops of 82nd Airborne Division. On the 19th Montebourg fell and on the 20th it was the turn of Valognes. Cherbourg itself was attacked on the 22nd and, after three days of a fierce but hopeless resistance, Von Schlieben and Admiral Hennecke surrendered to the Americans.

OPERATION EPSOM

In the meanwhile, German resistance was growing in the south of the Cotentin, particularly around St. Lo. Now that he had sufficient forces at his disposal, Montgomery decided to launch his first big attack to the west of Caen. On 25 June, VIII Corps of 2nd British Army, consisting of 15th Scottish Infantry Division and 11th Armoured Division, assembled to the north of the Caen—

Bayeux road with the intention of attacking in full strength towards the Odon river. The attack was supposed to start with an assault by the Scottish infantry in the direction of St. Manvieu and Cheux, following behind a tremendous barrage. Once these two villages had been taken, 11th Armoured was supposed to pass through and advance to the Odon, making it possible for 15th Scottish to establish a bridgehead there. Then, after crossing the stream and taking Hill 112, 11th Armoured were supposed to make for the river Orne where the 15th Scottish were to establish another bridgehead — and so on and on. On paper, it seemed like a very simple way of by-passing Caen to the south-west and thus debouching into the Falaise plain. Eight German panzer divisions were going to be used to frustrate this plan because the loss of Hill 112, the pivot of the defence in this sector, would inevitably have brought about the fall of Caen.

The Odon is a small, peaceful stream that winds itself between the valley of the Orne and the Caen — Avranches road. Its name was practically unknown before 1944 but now thousands of soldiers from both sides remember this insignificant little brook with horror. On some days, its flow was dammed by the bodies lying in its bed and its waters ran red with blood. At times, its bridges and fords were more desperately fought over than Hill 112 itself.

THE ATTACK

At 0730 hours on 26 June, behind an impressive barrage, 15th Scottish went into the attack and captured St. Manvieu and Cheux. At 1230 hours, 11th Armoured took over the attack with the tanks of its 29 Armoured Brigade undergoing their baptism of fire. They crossed the Caen — Caumont road to the south of St. Manvieu and the right wing, consisting of the 2nd Northamptonshire Regiment, was ordered to thrust immediately towards the Odon behind an artillery barrage. The rubble in the village of Cheux was so great that 'A' Squadron of this regiment had to spend a lot of time clearing a passage for themselves. Furthermore, before they could leave this scene of devastation, they had to mop up snipers and

German infantrymen armed with *panzerfausts* who lay in wait for them everywhere, in the orchards, in the ruins, behind poultry sheds and in the embanked hedgerows. Many of the enemy were also killed while trying to get close to our tanks in order to stick explosive charges or magnetic mines on to them. Some succeeded and blew themselves up with the tanks and tank crews.

Because of the delay in fighting their way through the village, the artillery barrage had to be laid on a second time but the opposition of 12th SS Panzer Division, fanatical to the last man, was still very strong. Time and time again, rather than surrender or retreat, they chose death. Furthermore, the enemy positions were held in depth rather than all being concentrated in the front lines; this minimized the effects of the artillery barrage. Before 29 Armoured Brigade could continue towards the Odon, the Scottish infantry had to be brought in to mop up and consolidate the positions won on the right flank. In fact, from the high ground at Rauray, the uncaptured objective allocated to 4 Armoured Brigade, the Germans made the positions held by 11th Armoured at Haut du Bosq very uncomfortable. Those commanding heights were left in the enemy's hands and this so influenced the coming battle that it is fair to say that this was one of the reasons for the eventual failure of Operation EPSOM.

THE INFANTRY'S TURN

While the tanks of 11th Armoured Division were trying to clear a path for themselves up to the Odon, the infantry battalions of 159 Brigade were preparing to go into battle in their turn. After having changed their positions several times in the course of the afternoon because of the fluidity of the fighting, the men of the 3rd Monmouthshires, 4th Shropshires, 1st Herefordshires and 8th Rifle Brigade went into action in the narrow corridor that had been carved through the German defences. When night fell and the noise of battle diminished, the sky was lit up by rockets and seared by flashing tracer bullets. At midnight, on the left, the Welsh of the 3rd Monmouths set off in the direction of the sector they were supposed to occupy, namely, the area to the north-east of the Odon. The night was very dark. They had to stop frequently to study maps that seemed so inaccurate. It was soon realized that the Battalion had wandered off its line. Towards three o'clock in the morning, when they arrived at a completely deserted little village, the C.O. decided that it would be best for them to pass the rest of the night there. Just before daybreak, some men of 'D' Company heard voices speaking in French. The voices seemed to come from a clump of trees not far from them. They investigated and found a farmer who, with his family, had taken refuge in a shelter to pass the night. The civilians seemed very surprised to see *les Tommies* in the same area where the Germans had been the night before. The farmer told them that they were at Mouen. It was obvious that the Battalion had pushed a little too far to the left but it was also obvious that the enemy, who had evacuated the village just some hours before, would not be slow in attempting to recapture it when day broke. While 'C' Company were left in the village to protect their rear, the rest of the Battalion made for Colleville. From there they went on to capture Mondrainville so that, for their next move, they could attack the objectives that had originally been given to them, namely, the heights just to the north of the Odon. They arrived there at 0730 hours.

Shortly after the departure of the Battalion, 'C' Company, in its turn, prepared to leave the village. Just then it was attacked and encircled by a strong group of German tanks and infantry. A fight to the death ensued and it soon became obvious to the Company Commander, Major Richards, that their position was hopeless. He succeeded in breaking out with a handful of unwounded men. Only 14 of them rejoined the Battalion. Of those who did not make it back, 21 were killed and all the others were wounded and taken prisoner. For them, it was their first and last battle. Two days later Major Richards was killed by a shell.

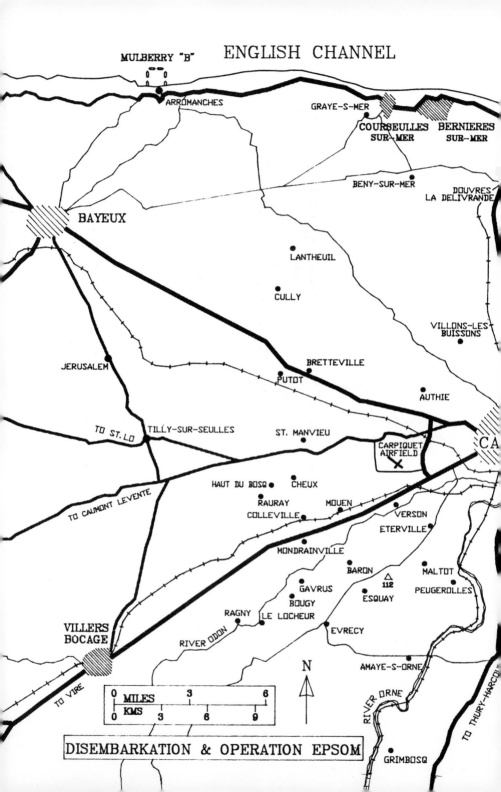

ENGLISH CHANNEL

MULBERRY "B"

ARROMANCHES

GRAYE-S-MER

COURSEULLES
SUR-MER

BERNIERES
SUR-MER

BENY-SUR-MER

DOUVRES
LA DELIVRANDE

BAYEUX

LANTHEUIL

CULLY

VILLONS-LES
BUISSONS

JERUSALEM

BRETTEVILLE

PUTOT

AUTHIE

TO ST.LO

TILLY-SUR-SEULLES

ST. MANVIEU

CARPIQUET
AIRFIELD

CA

TO CAUMONT LEVENTE

HAUT DU BOSQ

CHEUX

RAURAY

MOUEN

COLLEVILLE

VERSON

ETERVILLE

MONDRAINVILLE

BARON

△ 112

MALTOT

PEUGEROLLES

GAVRUS

ESQUAY

BOUGY

RAGNY

LE LOCHEUR

EVRECY

VILLERS
BOCAGE

RIVER ODON

N

AMAYE-S-ORNE

TO VIRE

RIVER ORNE

TO THURY-HARCOU

| 0 | MILES | 3 | 6 |
| 0 | KMS | 3 | 6 | 9 |

GRIMBOSQ

DISEMBARKATION & OPERATION EPSOM

THE CROSSING OF THE ODON

After this disastrous night, the attack was resumed on the whole front of 11th Armoured Division; everywhere they met the same fierce resistance. It was only in the afternoon that the first tanks managed to get up to the river where they took the bridge, intact. Two Squadrons of tanks of the 23rd Hussars, followed by the infantry of 'H' Company of the 8th Rifle Brigade, crossed over and started to climb towards Baron and Hill 112. Towards midnight the main body of 159 Brigade was established in the bridgehead and secured the following positions on the general line from Baron to Gavrus: on the left and to the north of the Odon, the 3rd Monmouths; to the south of the river, the 4th Shropshires; in the centre and midway up the hill, the 23rd Hussars together with the 8th Rifle Brigade; to the right, the 1st Herefords.

THE ASSAULT ON HILL 112

The next day, 28 June, while 159 Infantry Brigade was consolidating its positions, 29 Armoured Brigade re-took the high ground behind which was the village of Esquay. This was carried out by two Squadrons of the 23rd Hussars and a Company of the 8th Rifle Brigade. The whole morning a furious battle was waged and often the tanks had to destroy the fanatical enemy defenders by crushing them to death with their tracks while they sheltered in their slit trenches. The leading tanks of 11th Armoured reached the crest and chased the last of the enemy from it. However, behind the summit, the German tanks, well camouflaged and making good use of the ground, made things tough for their assailants and gave them no chance to re-group themselves for further attacks.

At nightfall, the 3rd Royal Tanks took over from the 23rd Hussars while on the right the 2nd Northamptonshires were charged with supporting the infantry who were in a precarious position on the summit. Because the orders were given out so late and because of the delay at the start line caused by a heavy barrage of mortars and rifle fire, the last-named were unable to set off before nightfall.

The terrain was very rough; even in daylight it would have been difficult for them to follow the designated route. Furthermore, the Northamptonshires had recently been equipped with Cromwell tanks whose silhouettes were not yet familiar to the British army. Consequently, they were often mistaken for Panthers or even Tigers and treated as such by their own artillery. In the darkness, those who could make it arrived but 'A' Squadron got lost. Seven of their tanks wandered around all night. By a miracle, they did not bump into the enemy and were able to rejoin their unit the next day. The others were unable to make contact with the infantry they were supposed to support. They went past their objective without realizing it and pushed on to attack the German positions. But, standing firm, the German defenders met them with a fusillade of destruction as, one by one, the tanks, very obligingly, offered themselves as targets.

Next day 52 men did not answer the roll call.

ON THE CREST

At that time Hill 112 was the heart of the German defensive system on that part of the front. From its summit the British could see the airfield at Carpiquet with its hangars and concrete runways; they were still in the hands of the Germans and regarded by them as one of the vital strategic positions for the defence of Caen. The enormous chimneys of the steel mill at Colombelles could also be seen over the rooftops, standing erect like sentinels guarding the bastion protecting the eastern flank. To the south they could see the plain crossed by the Caen — Falaise road. They knew that the Germans would not be slow to react.

Though supported by the tanks of the 3rd Royal Tank Regiment, the 23rd Hussars and the 2nd Fife and Forfar Yeomanry, the Rifle Brigade infantrymen were soon put to a severe test. While they overlooked the enemy positions, they themselves were under direct observation by the enemy. They were under fire from three sides simultaneously: from Carpiquet in the north came salvoes of shells from the German artillery; from the south came the 88mm shells of Tiger tanks buried hull down like so many fortresses; from the woods of Rauray to the northwest other tanks had them under fire. To all this was added the infernal and demoralizing noise of *Nebelwerfers* * that 11th Armoured Division was experiencing for the first time.

Despite the efforts of two additional infantry divisions, the 49th on the right and the 43rd on the left, (later in the story we will again find these Divisions at the side of 11th Armoured Division) the enemy maintained pressure on both flanks of the salient created by the thrust up Hill 112. The Luftwaffe also joined in the party. In the afternoon of the 30th it became clear that the enemy was getting ready to counter-attack. He brought in the 1st, 2nd, 9th and 10th SS Panzer Divisions and massed them round the English positions in addition to the Panzer Lehr and 12th SS Panzer Divisions that had been fighting there since the beginning of the offensive. These forces represented the total strength of I and II Panzer Corps.

THE PANZERS COUNTER-ATTACK

In the morning, a reconnaissance aircraft signalled that large armoured forces, coming from Villers-Bocage, were heading in a north-east direction on each side of the Odon and the Caen — Villers-Bocage road. The Typhoons of 2nd Tactical Air Force were soon on the scene in force and dive-bombed the enemy, coming in one at a time in single file, while, at the same time, the little artillery spotter planes radioed back the targets one after the other to the guns of three Army Corps. The whole front burst into flames. The German counter-attack was planned for seven o'clock in the morning but it could not get under way until six o'clock in the evening. As soon as they set out they were hit by a veritable tor-

---

*German multi-barrelled mortars with from 5 to 10 barrells, capable of firing 150mm calibre projectiles weighing 75 lbs. to a distance of 7,300 yards; 210mm projectiles, 248 lbs., 8,600 yards; 300mm projectiles, 277 lbs., 5,000 yards. Most of the *nebelwerfers* on the British front were 6-barrelled; the troops called them 'Moaning Minnies'.

nado of fire from the British Corps artillery as well as from the guns of 15th Scottish and 11th Armoured Divisions. Only 6 tanks managed to reach Cheux where they were stopped by anti-tank guns. The German attack was halted everywhere except at Gavrus where the bridge was lost. On the other side of the salient a group of 40 tanks was discovered near Carpiquet and destroyed by Typhoons. Well before nightfall it was obvious that the panzers had shot their bolt and the battle developed into a series of minor, local skirmishes

In the meanwhile, Lieutenant-General Dempsey commanding 2nd British Army was uneasy because only seven of the eight enemy armoured divisions reported to be available had put in an appearance on his front. He also expected another counter-attack the next day. In order to carry out Montgomery's master plan he could not allow himself to suffer any serious reversal so he ordered 11th Armoured Division to pull back from Hill 112 during the night and to get ready to face another counter-attack the next day. One brigade of 43rd Infantry Division relieved 11th Armoured in the bridgehead south of the Odon.

29 ARMOURED BRIGADE EVACUATES HILL 112

Night had fallen on the crest when number 3 Section of 'C' Company of the 8th Rifle Brigade signalled that 8 Tiger tanks, accompanied by about 150 infantrymen, were approaching the Company positions from the west. Star shells burst into the sky and machine-guns chattered into action. The long-awaited counter-attack was finally taking place to the relief of the high-strung nerves of the expectant British soldiers. The artillery immediately came to their aid and had a devastating effect on the ranks of the attackers. At the end of a quarter of an hour, the tanks, their infantry support wiped out, called off the attack.

For the rest of the night everyone stayed on the alert while 10 and 12 Platoons, which occupied the most forward positions facing south towards Esquay, peered anxiously into the darkness. About 100 metres in front of them was a barbed-wire enclosure held up by posts planted every 10 metres. Staring into the night, it occasionally seemed to them that the posts took on human form, wearing helmets and carrying rifles!

Just an hour before dawn the order was given to withdraw. Some time before, most of the transport had been sent to the rear so there was now an ungodly rush for places in the remaining vehicles by the retreating men. 29 Armoured Brigade was very glad to relinquish its place of honour on the summit to someone else. In the meanwhile, 159 Infantry Brigade continued to hold the bridgehead that it had captured so valiantly, until, at last, it was relieved in its turn on 6 July.

While this was going on, the second German counter-attack that General Dempsey was expecting did not materialize. This was probably due to the fact that during the night following the first counter-attack, Bomber Command released 1000 tons of bombs, some with delayed-action fuses, on Villers-Bocage; the Allied High Command thought the next counter-attack would come from there. That night, Villers-Bocage was wiped off the map!

LESSONS OF THE FIRST BATTLE

On the whole, 11th Armoured Division could draw satisfaction from the results of its first taste of battle. Those who did not understand Montgomery's plan thought that the operation's objectives had not been taken and they looked around for a scapegoat to blame for the 'defeat' but the general feeling was that, despite its heavy losses in men and equipment, the Division had acquitted itself well. It had penetrated deeply into the territory of a powerful enemy and it had repulsed all the counter-attacks on its flanks. Its troops had received their baptism of fire and had proved themselves in combat. The morale of the Division soared to new heights.

29 Armoured Brigade had penetrated the enemy's positions, taken some territory from them and held on to it for two days in spite of the repeated attacks of their best troops.

159 Infantry Brigade had established and held a bridgehead in

a wooded and hilly region that was difficult to defend and had been under constant artillery and mortar fire. With the assistance of their own artillery, they had been able to smash several counter-attacks. Furthermore, in the person of Lt.Colonel Churcher, Commanding Officer of the 1st Herefordshires, who was promoted to replace Brigadier Sandie on the second day of the battle, the Brigade found just the leader it needed.

After this first battle in which all the soldiers and units of 11th Armoured Division had taken part, the men developed a feeling of self-confidence that they would never lose and that was undoubtedly the reason for their future success. The lessons they learnt from the battle of the Odon served them well in their next, much tougher battle: Operation GOODWOOD.

CHAPTER 4

BATTLES ON THE CAEN PLAIN

MONTGOMERY'S BATTLE PLANS

While 11th Armoured Division enjoyed a well-earned rest during which it re-organized its forces after the fierce battles of the Odon, Montgomery kept up the pressure on the British-Canadian front with a view to pinning down most of the enemy forces there. At the other end of the front, the Americans made strong attacks to the south in order to secure the base from which to launch the break-out towards the Brittany ports that eventually took place at the end of July. In order to make it easier for them, Montgomery decided to step up his efforts on the eastern end of the front with his primary objective being the capture of Caen. This was to be followed by an attack on each side of the River Orne and then an attack in the Caumont sector.

It was clear that the Germans attached the greatest importance to the defence of Caen since 700 of the 900 tanks they had were in this sector. They were placed under the command of Panzer Group West and held the front between the rivers Drome and Orne. From 4 to 6 July, Montgomery, therefore, planned to push 12 SS Panzer Division out of the airfield at Carpiquet. This operation was a natural follow-up to the establishment of the Odon bridgehead and had to precede any frontal attack on Caen. This tough task was given to the 3rd Canadian Infantry Division who lost more men there in two days than they had lost on D-Day.

Two days later Montgomery unleashed a massive attack to capture Caen. The attack was preceded by an aerial bombardment of the northern part of the city by 500 heavy bombers. H.M.S. *Rodney, Roberts* and *Belfast* joined in together with all the Army artillery. The result was that the advance of our troops into the city was delayed by the extensive ruins, while the enemy remained in possession of Faubourg de Vaucelles from where they fiercely resisted any attempt to establish a new bridgehead over the Orne.

The entrance into Caen was followed by a new attack designed to enlarge the Odon salient. The capture of Maltot on 10 July threatened the encirclement of the enemy forces trapped in the triangle formed by the Orne and the Odon. This brought a quick reaction from the Germans that had the effect of re-kindling the fighting around Hill 112. Once again, the enemy was compelled to throw the two armoured divisions into the battle that he had planned to pull out and replace with infantry divisions so that he could form an armoured reserve. A few days later, two more panzer divisions were brought into this sector but a new attack by the British on 16 and 17 July, this time on Evrecy, forced the Germans to retreat hurriedly to meet this new danger. The only armoured division the Germans had in reserve on 18 July was 12th SS Panzer Division. Despite the fact that they were seriously weakened by the continual fighting around Caen in which they had been engaged since 6 June, they were thrown into the battle again. Thus, every time the Germans tried to replace an armoured division with an infantry division, Montgomery, following his plan, attacked in another sector bringing on an attrition that, little by little, weakened 7th German Army and Panzer Group West.

THE RIVAL FORCES

By mid-July, the German forces consisted, at least on paper, of more or less 27 divisions of which 8 were armoured. However, of the 540,000 men thrown into the battle, 160,000 had already been lost and 30% of their tanks had been destroyed. The 6 divisions in Brittany were stripped of part of their strength in order to reinforce Normandy, while, of the 12 full-strength divisions in the south of France, no more than 7 or 8 could be spared because the rest were pinned down by the *Maquis*. Meanwhile, the 15th German Army, that could have been very useful to Rommel, waited expectantly for the 'real' invasion to take place across the *Pas de Calais*, the Straits of Dover. The Germans were more convinced than ever that this threat would materialize because on 12 June they had started launching their flying bombs from the Pas-de-Calais area.

On the other hand, the Allies had enlarged the beach-head enough to ensure breathing room for the forces needed for a large-scale break-out. These forces consisted of 12 U.S. divisions, of which 3 were armoured and 15 British and Canadian divisions, of which 4 were armoured.

OPERATION GOODWOOD

In a personal memorandum to General Dempsey, Montgomery stated. "Object of this operation: to engage the German armour in battle and 'write it down' to such an extent that it is of no further value to the Germans as a basis of the battle. To gain a good bridgehead over the Orne through Caen and thus to improve our positions on the eastern flank. Generally to destroy German equipment and personnel." He then went on to stress that the eastern part of the front must continue to be held at all costs as a bastion so that the major American offensive, Operation COBRA, could be launched in the west a few days later.

THE PLANS

Operation GOODWOOD was the most powerful attack launched by the British during the course of the battle for Normandy. Nearly half of 2nd British Army took part in it under VIII Corps commanded by Lieutenant-General Sir Richard O'Connor.

The number of heavy bombers that was used in preparation for the attack and during it was greater than in any other operation in support of ground forces.

Even though, in detail, the plans for GOODWOOD were very complicated, the broad outline was relatively simple. Three Armoured Divisions, the 11th, the Guards and the 7th, had to make their way into the narrow sector to the east of the River Orne that had been held continuously since 6 June by 6th Airborne and 51st Highland Divisions. The 750 tanks of the three Armoured Divisions were ordered to break through the German defences and then attack the rear of Caen. Once the enemy lines had been pierced the tanks could debouch into the Falaise plain. In order to widen the axis of the attack, two Infantry Divisions, the 3rd and the 51st, were detailed to protect the flanks of the break-through and were to be helped in their tasks by 350 more tanks. A formidable aerial bombardment was to smash the German positions on the axis of advance of the armoured columns. More than 2000 planes were to participate. And 750 guns were to put down a barrage, reinforced by Navy ships anchored off shore.

THE DIFFICULTIES

Mounting and carrying out this plan presented many difficulties. Two days earlier, Montgomery had launched an attack in the sector between Evrecy and Esquay. To maintain the element of surprise for the attack he planned for 18 July, the armoured divisions had to be kept to the west of the Orne until the last minute. Then the three divisions had to cross the river, one after the other, through the bottlenecks created by the bridges before they could follow each other into action.

The 750 guns which were to put down the initial barrage from the west bank of the Orne were at the limit of their range. To stay in the battle they then had to be moved and re-positioned on the other side of the river but only after the last of the tanks had crossed.

The attack had to take place in a sector where the Germans had their strongest positions and where conditions were most favourable for the defence. Because Rommel was sure that one day he would be attacked in this sector, he had concentrated all his available resources to defend this vital part of his front. He had laid out his defence in five mutually-supporting lines to a depth of 15 kilometres. Their dispersal would also enable them to escape the worst effects of any bombardment. With nearly 300 *nebelwerfers,* more than 100 88mm anti-aircraft guns positioned as anti-tank guns, a bare 100 tanks, 200 pieces of artillery and thousands of infantrymen entrenched in the many small villages that they had transformed into so many fortresses among the wheat and beetroot fields, the Germans were ready to meet the attack.

THE BOMBARDMENT

At dawn on 18 July the clear sky and lack of wind announced a beautiful summer day. It was so calm that the men waiting to cross the bridges could hear the sound of the Channel surf in the distance. Suddenly, at 0530 hours, the sky was filled with the droning of hundreds of aircraft engines. Flak opened up on the first wave, breaking the charm of the sunny morning. Oblivious of the guns, the bombers flew majestically right on to their targets, released their bombs, half-turned and made for home. Their wings reflected the rays of the rising sun as they banked away. The soldiers left their tanks and vehicles in order to watch the awesome spectacle that lasted 45 minutes. Almost immediately, the medium bombers of the U.S. Airforce followed the heavies and started to saturate the German front lines with fragmentation bombs. Unfortunately, their targets were hidden by the smoke and dust created by the previous waves and the enemy defences were not completely neutralized. Next came the artillery shells to which were added the salvoes from H.M.S. *Roberts, Mauritius* and *Enterprise* anchored off the coast of Normandy.

That day 7,000 tons of bombs and 1,250,000 shells battered the enemy positions.

11TH ARMOURED DIVISION ATTACKS

11th Armoured Division set off at 0730 hours, following as closely as possible behind the creeping barrage, with 3rd Canadian Division making for Colombelles on the right and 3rd British Division advancing on Sannerville and Banneville-la-Campagne on the left. 29 Armoured Brigade was in the van, led by the 3rd Royal Tank Regiment and 'G' Company of the 8th Rifle Brigade who carefully followed the narrow lanes marked through the mine fields laid by 51st Highland Division. At 0940 hours they reached the Caen — Troarn railway line and the barrage let up for five minutes to allow them to negotiate the steep embankment there. On the right flank, 159 Infantry Brigade, consisting of the 3rd Monmouthshires, 4th Shropshires and 1st Herefordshires, supported by the tanks of the 2nd Northamptonshires, advanced to clear the villages of Cuverville and Demouville. The first was taken at 1015 hours and the second at 1430 hours. During this time the tanks of the 3rd Royal Tank Regiment and the 2nd Fife and Forfar Yeomanry kept going until they reached the second railway line, covering nearly 10 kilometres in less than two hours.

THE TRAFFIC JAM IN THE REAR

All was going well up to that time. However, an enormous traffic jam had developed in the rear. The Guards Armoured Division had made its way through the mine fields with great difficulty and was behind schedule thus leaving the left flank of 11th Armoured dangerously exposed. Behind them, 7th Armoured Division, whose advance elements should have followed close behind the two leading divisions, was held up by Canadian troops who had not managed to overcome the German resistance at Colombelles. When 7th Armoured Division was finally able to get going, it was only to be held up again by the Guards Armoured Division which blocked all the roads.

THE CONSEQUENCES

Deprived of support on its flanks, the situation of 11th Armoured Division was giving some cause for concern despite the fact that it had attained all its objectives by noon. Nevertheless, it not only continued to advance towards Bourguébus Ridge but it also stayed in contact with the enemy all along its front. But the enemy had now recovered from the shock of the early-morning bombardment. Just as the spearhead of the attack reached Hubert-Folie, 88mm anti-tank guns started to open fire on the tanks of the 3rd Royal Tank Regiment and on the infantry of the 8th Rifle Brigade who accompanied them. The armour-piercing shells crashed in from all sides and it was impossible to pin point where they were coming from. The leading tanks were soon hit. Then Panthers appeared on the left and, to avoid being massacred, the 3rd Royal Tank Regiment had to pull back behind the railway embankment. From the cover of the embankment they were able to duel with the Panthers on better terms.

MARTYRDOM OF THE 2ND NORTHAMPTONSHIRES ...

The 2nd Northamptonshire Yeomanry, whose tanks had supported the 3rd Monmouthshires in the capture of Cuverville and Demouville, were ordered to go to the aid of the 3rd Royal Tank Regiment. Many of their tanks were destroyed by anti-tank guns firing from the high ground occupied by the factories at Cormelles. As they approached Bras and Hubert-Folie, where they were supposed to link up with the 3rd Royal Tank Regiment, enemy opposition and their losses increased. All they found of the 3rd Royal Tank Regiment were burnt and abandoned tanks and they were unable to make contact with the survivors. Furthermore, their squadrons were now completely exposed on open ground that rose gently towards the heights of Bourguébus. They too were stopped by the 88mm guns and were obliged to take shelter behind the embankment and abandon the tanks that had been put out of action and set on fire.

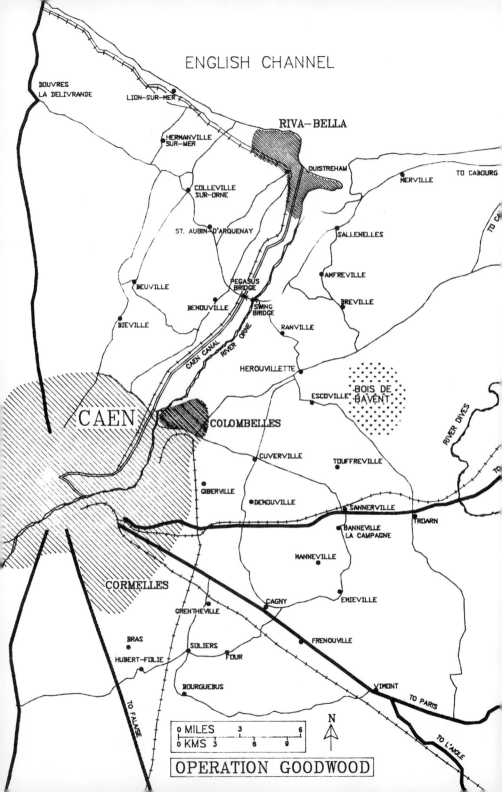

OPERATION GOODWOOD

... AND OF THE 2ND FIFE AND FORFARS

On the left flank of 11th Armoured Division the 2nd Fife and Forfar Yeomanry had also crossed the railway line. They then made for Soliers and Four with their tanks advancing in drill order behind the artillery barrage, just as if they were on training manoeuvres. By the time they reached the two villages they were out of range of the British guns sited on the other side of the River Orne and, because of the immense traffic jam in the rear, those guns could not be brought any closer. The guns had to stop firing just when 29 Armoured Brigade needed them most!

Although the early-morning aerial bombardment and the artillery barrage had obliterated the forward German positions, the major part of their deep defensive system had escaped practically untouched because it was outside the bombardment target zone and beyond the reach of the British guns. Furthermore, General Eberbach, the Commander of the German armour*, alert to the danger of a break-through in this sector, had re-grouped the tanks of 1st and 21st Panzer Divisions so that they could counter-attack from the south and south-east and thus destroy the tanks of 11th Armoured Division and re-gain the ground lost up to the Caen — Troarn road.

The Panthers surprised a group of tanks of the Fife and Forfar in the area between Four and Frénouville, catching them still in their parade-ground formation as they moved in close order over the open ground. The Fife and Forfar tanks were caught in the cross-fire of the Panthers and more of them would have been destroyed if the Germans had been able to re-load their 75mm guns more quickly for rapid fire. Both the Colonel of the Regiment and his second-in-command were hit and the Squadrons, bereft of leadership, were cut off from the rest of 29 Armoured Brigade.

*Panzer Group West. It was re-named 5th Panzer Army on 1 August 1944.

NEXT THE TURN OF THE 23RD HUSSARS

Realizing that something was wrong on the Fife and Forfar front, the Brigadier sent the tanks of the 23rd Hussars to their aid from his reserve. Not knowing what was going on, after they had crossed the Caen—Troarn road, the Hussars sent their 'B' Squadron on ahead to reconnoitre. They worked their way in among their unfortunate brothers-in-arms to see what was going on only to be hit and set on fire themselves. The Panthers had opened fire on the newcomers also. In a few seconds, four of their tanks were hit and started to burn. Captain Blackman and Sergeant Bateman each destroyed a Panther but immediately after they themselves were knocked out. The others withdrew, firing with everything they had. They took shelter behind the nearest hedge which gave poor protection as they learnt when, every so often, the air was torn by the shrill whistle of a shell followed by the dry crack it made in hitting and penetrating the armour-plating. There would be a spray of sparks and then tongues of flame would envelop the Sherman. The next instant, the survivors, blackened and burnt by the explosion, would get out of their tank and run away from it as fast as possible while at the same time trying to extinguish their flaming clothes. Occasionally, one of them would re-mount his tank to try and help a wounded comrade get out before it was too late while one could hear the crackling of the flames as they devoured the interior of the tank and disgorged clouds of black smoke. Then, as the ammunition starts to explode in the great heat, the stricken tank shudders in its death convulsions.

'B' Squadron landed hit for hit. It was assisted by 'A' Squadron which had come up on the right while 'C' Squadron, taking advantage of a dip in the ground on the left, managed to sneak up to within 300 metres of Four. Seeing some Panthers in the direction of Cagny, they opened fire and destroyed two of them but paid the price because by doing so they revealed their positions to the defenders of Four who fired into their midst at point-blank range. In less than a minute 16 Shermans were hit without having a chance to shoot back or to find a good position from which to carry on the battle. The wounded and the burnt dragged themselves towards shelter while the armour-piercing shells continued to rain on the stricken tanks, soon reducing them to mere carcasses and, finally, to coffins of steel.

115 TANKS DESTROYED

At dawn on 18 July they had hoped for a break-through. When twilight fell, 11th Armoured Division had lost 115 of its tanks, almost half its total strength! Darkness brought an end to the fighting. Then the long processions of stretcher-bearers appeared, searching all over the battlefield for those of the wounded who had not been able to get back to the shelter of the embankment. Ambulances went back and forth all night, swamping the first aid stations with their pitiable loads.

SERGEANT JIM CASWELL'S STORY

What happened that day and night on the battlefield can best be described from the accounts of two veterans of 3rd Royal Tank Regiment. Sergeant Jim Caswell recounts: *The bombers arrived at dawn. It was a sight I will never forget. An hour and a half later we were given the order to advance. Our objective was about 7 kilometres ahead and once we had captured it, the other regiments of our Division, following the corridor we had marked out for them, had to make a dash across the plain in the direction of Falaise. The aerial bombardment and the artillery barrage had completely demoralized the enemy and our advance was easy. Hundreds of German soldiers surrendered and many tanks and guns were destroyed. However, the most serious obstacle was the Caen— Troarn railway line and crossing a very deep ditch at this place proved to be difficult for our tanks. This obstacle delayed our attack and gave those German tanks that had not been destroyed the chance to withdraw and fall back on to some very good defensive positions. As soon as we had negotiated the line of the railway track we re-assembled in attack formation. Until then our losses had been light. From the tank's wireless we learnt that 11th Armoured's infantry was in the process of clearing the villages we had by-passed.*

Because of the delay in crossing the ditch at the railway line, the artillery barrage was now too far ahead of us. It proved to be very difficult to re-direct its fire and this reduced its effectiveness considerably. However, we continued to advance towards our first objective. It was at this moment that the right flank of my Squadron was threatened by 3 camouflaged Tigers concealed in a wood to our left on Bourguébus Ridge. Most of our 20 tanks were hit in a matter of minutes. We were on the right of our regiment so I ordered the driver to make a left turn so that we could get into a good position from which to fire back. Just at that moment I spotted an 88mm gun pointing at me. I saw the terrible flash of its muzzle and heard the shell whistle by. As our armour-plating could not stand up to it I ordered my driver to go into reverse. He did so, very promptly, but we had hardly gone a few yards when another shell hit us. There were 3 of us in the turret; the navigator was killed outright and my wireless operator, seriously wounded, collapsed into the rear of the tank. In a Sherman it is impossible to see what is happening in the driver's compartment so, using the intercom, I asked the driver and the machine-gunner if they had been hit. I did not receive a reply.

All the while, the tank continued going in reverse. As I had no control over it, I left the turret and climbed on the front in order to try to open the trap-doors for the driver and machine-gunner. The doors were bolted on the inside and I could not open them. I hammered from above with all my strength but no one answered me so I concluded that both had been killed. I realized then that it was impossible for me to regain control of my tank. It was still going backwards and was steering itself towards the enemy's right flank. I took the only possible decision; I abandoned the tank. I climbed into the turret again, untangled my wounded wireless operator from his wires, and tipped him over the side into a field of wheat. I went back once more to the front of the tank to try to free my two unlucky comrades. I had no more success than I did the first time. After a last look at my navigator, who lay dead at the bottom of the turret, I finally abandoned the tank.

I had to run back at least 100 yards to the place where I had left my wireless operator. I followed the tank tracks. I found him in the wheat field. While I was putting a dressing on the most serious of his wounds he asked me if I had brought his cigarettes! In my troop he was the only one who smoked and he always had a bag full of tobacco on him in case he had to abandon the tank. He was badly wounded and I had to tell him that the bag I had with me only contained grenades. They would be more useful to us than tobacco in trying to make our way back past enemy patrols. Saying this, I took him over my shoulder and headed for our lines. I had to crawl and walk for 2 miles before finding a first aid station. After handing over my comrade to the doctor I collapsed and it took me several weeks to recover my nerve.

A few years ago I visited the graves of my two comrades. They are buried side by side in the cemetery at Banneville-la-Campagne. But it was not till 1969 that I had the chance to meet my wireless operator again. Naturally, we exchanged memories and he explained the mystery of how the tank continued in reverse after the driver sat dead in his seat. My driver, who had fought with me in the desert, had, without my knowledge, made a gadget that kept up the engine revs without it being necessary for him to accelerate it himself. What's more, he always went into reverse drive when getting ready to fire and this explains why, even though he was mortally wounded, the tank continued on its own way.

It was only a few years ago that I read in a book written by a veteran of 3rd Royal Tank Regiment that during the night of 18/19 July, together with some companions, he had sneaked into the midst of the disabled tanks to see if they could rescue any of the wounded. While there they had heard the characteristic noise of a Sherman skidding in reverse drive as it was blocked by some obstacle.

THE ADVENTURES OF 'BUCK' KITE
AND PETER ELSTOB

The adventures of another troop of the same regiment are worth recounting. The Sherman of Sergeant 'Buck' Kite and his wireless operator, Peter Elstob, had had a hard day. As night fell, its engines began to give signs of overheating and it was necessary to stop more and more often to allow them to cool down. Normally, Sergeant Kite would have dropped out to save his engines but his Squadron had urgent need of all its tanks so, showing once again the courage and determination that had already earned him a decoration in North Africa, he continued to fight alongside his comrades.

Just when they found themselves face to face with a German anti-tank gun the engines stalled and the tank came to a halt. It could not have happened at a worse time. 'Buck' Kite found himself a witness at the execution of two nearby tanks without being able to do a thing about it but perhaps his forced immobility saved his life. Night fell. After a while, the driver managed to get the tank moving on only three engines. The Sergeant decided to get out of this precarious situation before they were destroyed by a deluge of shells and mortar bombs. At that very moment, just when they thought they were out of trouble, two German star shells lit up the tank as if it was broad daylight and caught them as they were climbing up over the railway embankment. Shells hit them on the rear. The explosions probably starved the engines momentarily of air and, already straining heavily to get up over the obstacle, they stalled again, leaving the tank tettering helplessly on the embankment, its nose in the air. The driver tried to get the engines to start but without success while the Germans, taking advantage of the tank's predicament so brightly illuminated by the star shells, continued to spray the tank and everything around it with fire.

The sergeant gave the order to abandon the tank at the worst possible moment because just then the maelstrom of a barrage engulfed them. They got out of their useless tank as quickly as they could, poured petrol inside it and threw in a match and then, stomachs to the ground, crawled for cover on the other side of the embankment. After the tank commander had made sure that they

were all 'present and correct' the five men made their way back
to their own lines. On the way, they saw the silhouette of a Sherman profiled some distance away near a thicket. Thinking it was
one of theirs, Corporal Elstob left his group to have a look at it.
There was not far to go but it proved to be extremely difficult and
tedious to crawl from one shell hole to another but when he eventually got there he saw that the Sherman was irrecoverable.

By the time Elstob returned, the other members of his crew had
disappeared. Later he learnt that they had been rescued by the
tanks of another regiment while they waited for him to return.
It was only then that he realized how much time his reconnaissance
had taken. To add to the confusion, enemy planes, that would
only dare fly at night, started to bomb the embankment. Elstob
had to take shelter in a shell hole and could not move for fully
half an hour. He spent the time reflecting on his situation and
reviewing the events of the day. The more he thought about it the
more he wondered whether his tank had actually caught fire
because he did not remember seeing any flames when they abandoned it. To clear his conscience, he crawled back again to where
the tank had been left. He saw a dark mass between two burning
tanks and, as he approached it he saw that, sure enough, it was
his Sherman, its nose still pointing at the sky. Although the ground
all around was plastered with bomb and shell craters the tank
appeared to be unhit. He first took the wise precaution of making
sure that there were none of the enemy prowling around and then
he crawled into the tank. The interior smelled of petrol but he
saw that, by a miracle, it had not caught fire.

Elstob adjusted his wireless set and sent out a call to which his
C.O. soon replied. He gave the C.O. his report, told him where
he was and asked him if he should destroy the tank or try to re-
start it and bring it back. In no uncertain terms his Colonel told
him to try to re-start the engines and bring the tank back. He also
told Elstob that there was another tank not far from him with a
wounded man on board whom he should bring back if he was able
to start the engines. The wireless operator of the second tank had
stayed near it because its wireless set still worked. Corporal Elstob
made contact with him and told him that if he could re-start his

engines he would head towards him as silently as possible so as not to attract the attention of the enemy who laid down a storm of fire at every noise and movement on the battlefield.

Elstob was less than 400 yards from the enemy and was between two burning tanks that lit up the countryside with their flames. But the first problem was to get the tank moving. The corporal saw, with relief, that the shell that had hit them in the rear had only shaken the engines and after some coaxing two of them agreed to start. This was just enough to get the Sherman moving. As it would have been too dangerous to turn the tank around to face in the direction he wanted to go, Elstob, feeling rather like a Sioux Indian on the prowl, put the tank into reverse and backed out as silently as possible. After retreating blindly in this way for a few minutes, Elstob thought he could not be far from his goal when suddenly he heard a cry, "Stop! Stop! I'm English." Although he was rather suspicious he did stop, got down from his tank and found himself face to face with an English corporal who was shaken and speechless. The man's outstretched arm was pointing at something. Elstob looked in the direction he was pointing and saw why the man was terrified. The rear of his tank had stopped just on the edge of a disused quarry. At the bottom of the quarry was the other corporal's tank in which the crew was sleeping! What a narrow escape!

Elstob immediately remounted his tank and put some distance between himself and the edge of the precipice. He picked up the corporal and a man from the crew and the three of them headed for the place where the wireless operator was waiting for them with the wounded man. His wounds were very serious. Both his legs were crushed below the knee. Elstob dressed them as best he could and between them they managed to slide the wounded man into the tank without inflicting too much pain on him as they made him as comfortable as possible. Although he had been in terrible pain for a long time, the man was still conscious, still showed great courage and a determination to live and was even able to thank his rescuers for all they were doing for him.

The corporal from the other tank and his driver got into Elstob's tank and while Elstob, who had received directions on how to get back, went ahead on foot, the unusual procession made its way past the burning wrecks. The flames were dying down and the bombardment had stopped. Elstob guided the tank with a flashlight. He never could understand why he was not picked off by a sniper because, although he had covered the light as well as possible, it could still be seen from some distance away.

They finally arrived back at their headquarters just before dawn and found the Medical Officer waiting there for the wounded man. Later, in their turn, the exhausted engines of the Sherman received attention from their doctors, the mechanics.

THE LUFTWAFFE PUTS IN AN APPEARANCE

So, on this day, 18 July, 29 Armoured Brigade lost a lot of equipment. However, in a number of cases, some of its units were able to pull out without too much damage and withdraw to the rear under cover of darkness. The loss in men would undoubtedly have been much greater if the Germans had thought to use anti-personnel or incendiary shells on the men as they abandoned their disabled tanks but because there were so many tanks used in the battle the enemy gunners had no lack of targets for their armour-piercing shells and used them only.

Alarmed at the magnitude of the attack, the Germans decided to call on their last aerial resources. They reasoned that, although the losses inflicted on the British had been very heavy they were replacable whereas their losses were not. It was therefore vital for them, at almost any price, to disorganize and destroy as many as possible of the British reserves waiting to resume the attack at dawn. Now was their best chance to wipe them out.

A little before mid-night the German bombers appeared over the British sector to the east of the River Orne and started by dropping flares. 11th Armoured Division's historian maintains that this was absolutely unnecessary because, even if the bombs had been dropped completely haphazardly they were bound to hit something, such was the congestion in that area. He recalls that the flares were dropped almost exclusively on the right flank where they lit up

11th Armoured Division Headquarters, the reserve armour and reinforcements for the next day's battle together with those who had survived the massacre of the day just over, the divisional transport and auxiliary services. After the flares came the bombs. They hit a large number of vehicles and set them on fire and they caused many fatal casualties. The Fife and Forfar who had already suffered heavily on the previous day lost 40 of their reinforcements in this one raid.

SECOND DAY OF THE BATTLE

At dawn on the 19 July, when the losses were more exactly known, General O'Connor, the Commander of VIII Corps, had no further hopes for a quick break-through in the direction of Falaise because he knew that the enemy would have called up all his available reserves and deployed them opposite him. However, because the Guards Armoured Division was still practically untouched, 7th Armoured Division had not yet been in action and 11th Armoured still held the ground they had won, he decided to resume the battle without delay in order to nail down the enemy and destroy him completely. In the light of the experience gained in the previous day's fighting and after verifying that the Germans' in-depth defensive system had survived the aerial bombardment, he reverted to a more orthodox plan for the battle. He decided to use larger numbers of infantry in support of the tanks. Accordingly, in the early hours of the morning, the infantry of 3rd British Division, supported by tanks, attacked enemy positions in the direction of Emieville. Four times they attacked and four times they were repulsed. A little to the south the Guards Armoured Division resumed its attack on Cagny and Four while 7th Armoured got into action at last and attacked in the direction of Soliers and Bourguébus.

THE ATTACKS ON BRAS ...

Aligned side by side, the two Brigades of 11th Armoured were assigned to the area of Bras and Hubert-Folie. The 2nd Northamptonshires made an unsuccessful attack on the first village and the 3rd Royal Tank Regiment had to go to their rescue. With the support of the infantry of the 8th Rifle Brigade they penetrated into the maze of houses in spite of very strong opposition from anti-tank guns and *panzerfausts* of the 1st SS Adolf Hitler Division. At 1730 hours the 3rd Monmouthshires relieved the Rifle Brigade who then made for Hubert-Folie, their second objective for the day. Fighting went on for a long time in the ruins and the Welshmen had to clear the village wall by wall and garden by garden. Every yard of ground was defended to the death by the SS troops of 1st Panzer Division. In addition, the German artillery did not hesitate to shell the hamlet heavily even before their own troops had been pushed out of it.

... AND ON HUBERT-FOLIE

While this was going on, 'G' Company of the 8th Rifle Brigade, supported by tanks of the Fife and Forfar, carried out an assault on Hubert-Folie behind a smoke screen which hid them from the German artillery. Cut off from reinforcements, the defenders who were attacked at 2000 hours were overcome by 2115 hours. In the confusion some Germans captured a damaged Sherman tank and managed to get it running. This trick was soon discovered by the British infantry who then had the rare chance of finding out how easy it was to destroy one of their own tanks!

The village was then handed over to their colleagues of the 4th Shropshires. They were immediately counter-attacked, probably by reinforcements who arrived just at that moment and who were chased away. It was 10 o'clock in the evening before the Germans acknowledged defeat and even then they renewed their assault at dawn the next day but without success.

THE RELIEF

On 20 July, 11th Armoured Division was first pulled back from the front line and then withdrawn from the battle itself so that it could re-organize and re-equip itself. Its place was taken by 7th Armoured Division and by the infantry of 3rd Canadian Division who had succeeded in pushing the Germans out of the south of Caen and from its suburbs. 3rd British Infantry Division, which had been guarding the left flank of Guards Armoured Division, continued to make slow progress towards Troarn.

THE RESULTS OF GOODWOOD

GOODWOOD was severely criticized because of the high price that had to be paid for such meagre results. The two main points of criticism were: the aerial bombardment which had not been able to destroy the in-depth German defences, and the bottle-neck at the bridges over the Orne that had prevented the Guards and 7th Armoured Divisions from closely following 11th Armoured and protecting its flanks while it spear-headed the attack.

On the other hand, the German losses had been very heavy. Their 16th G.A.F. Division had been wiped out and 21st Panzer Division had been reduced to the strength of a single battalion. Convinced that the British would renew their attack in the same sector as soon as they had reinforced themselves, Eberbach continued to pull in his armour from the other sectors in order to concentrate it around Caen. The result was that on 25 July 645 German tanks opposed the British on the Caen front while only 190 were left to oppose the Americans who were about to launch their heaviest attack, Operation COBRA.

CHAPTER 5

BREAK-OUT IN THE BOCAGE

OPERATION BLUECOAT

At a meeting in London on 7 April, 1944, Montgomery had revealed his overall plan to his Army Commanders. The plan was as follows: once they were ashore and firmly established, he would threaten to break through the enemy front in the east, in the Caen area; this would draw the enemy's armour to that sector; the British and Canadian armies would make them fight and would wear them down by repeated attacks; when the German reserves had been drawn to the east and exhausted there, the real break-out would take place in the west. That task was given to General Bradley's American troops. Once the break-out had been achieved, the whole front would then pivot on Caen as the hinge.

After the immense and costly efforts of the British and Canadians on the Caen plain, the ball was now in the Americans' court. Initially planned to be launched on the 19th, the American attack could not get under way until 25 July because of bad weather that prevented the air forces from carrying out the massive bombardment that was to precede Operation COBRA.

At the same time, VIII and XXX British Corps were getting ready for Operation BLUECOAT.

REORGANIZATION AND REINFORCEMENTS

By 22 July the whole of 11th Armoured Division was pulled back into reserve between Caen and Bayeux. The losses suffered during the preceding battles were made up by the arrival of reinforcements of men, vehicles, tanks and materiel. At the same time, the two Brigades making up the Division were reorganized. The experience gained in the recent battles showed the absolute necessity of closer cooperation between tanks and infantry. Because of the nature and configuration of the ground over which the Division had to fight, tanks could not advance without the protection of infantry and, depending on the circumstances, the infantry had to be ready at a moment's notice to either go ahead of them or follow them.

With the reorganization, each of the two Brigades of 11th Armoured Division had 2 armoured regiments and 2 infantry battalions. 29 Brigade consisted of the tanks of the 23rd Hussars and the 3rd Royal Tank Regiment and the infantry of the 8th Rifle Brigade and the 3rd Monmouthsires. 159 Brigade consisted of the tanks of the 2nd Fife and Forfar and the 2nd Northamptonshires and the infantry of the 4th Shropshires and the 1st Herefordshires.

FIGHTING IN THE BOCAGE

The Bocage extends to the south of Bayeux. It is close country, very beautiful, heavily wooded, with hills that stretch beyond the horizon and are cut up by valleys that sometimes form narrow passes. Many streams cross and water this region. The roads meander between heavily wooded heights, climbing and descending the hills, following the serpentine bends of the rivers and crossing over the numerous water courses. The fields are small, surrounded by thick hedges and cut up by many sunken lanes. The only battles that had ever taken place in this region were back in the Middle Ages and at the time of the *Chouans*, local partisans who opposed the Republic armies after the French Revolution of 1789. (They were so named after the distinctive *cri de la chouette* or ululation they used as a recognition signal). No, the Bocage makes a very unsuitable battlefield for the attacker. Nevertheless, it was there that the German 7th Army was defeated and there that the break-out, fought for so fiercely by the British, was eventually made.

ASSIGNMENT OF TASKS

While the Americans were breaking through the German front to the west of St. Lo, at the other end of the line the 1st Canadian Army, commanded by General Crerar, having become operational on 23 July, maintained its pressure in the direction of Falaise. The American 3rd Army captured Lassay and Periers on the 27th, Coutances on the 28th and then, crossing the river Sienne, headed towards Avranches and Granville. On 28 July the American 1st Army, in its turn, took the offensive in the direction of Vire and Mortain. Montgomery decided to attack to the south of Caumont-l'Eventé in the direction of Vire and Mont Pincon in conjunction with the American attack. The tasks given to VIII and XXX Corps of 2nd British Army were to protect the left flank of the Americans during their advance into Brittany and to deny the enemy the use of Vire and Mont Pincon, respectively, as pivots on which to organize their retreat.

XXX British Corps, composed of 43rd and 50th Infantry Divisions and 7th Armoured Division, was given the following objectives: Amayé-sur-Seules, Villers-Bocage, Aunay-sur-Odon, Mont Pincon, Saint-Jean-le-Blanc and Condé-sur-Noireau.

VIII British Corps, composed of 15th Scottish Division, the Guards Armoured Division and 11th Armoured Division was to launch its attack to the south of Caumont, in the direction of Sept-Vents, with the Scotsmen leading the way. They had to clear the way for a strong push by the Guards Armoured Division who were given Vassy as their first objective after which they had to cut the important Vire—Condé road and then take Mont de Cerisy. In accordance with this plan, the entire Guards Division would push towards Cathéolles through Saint-Martin-des-Besaces and Le

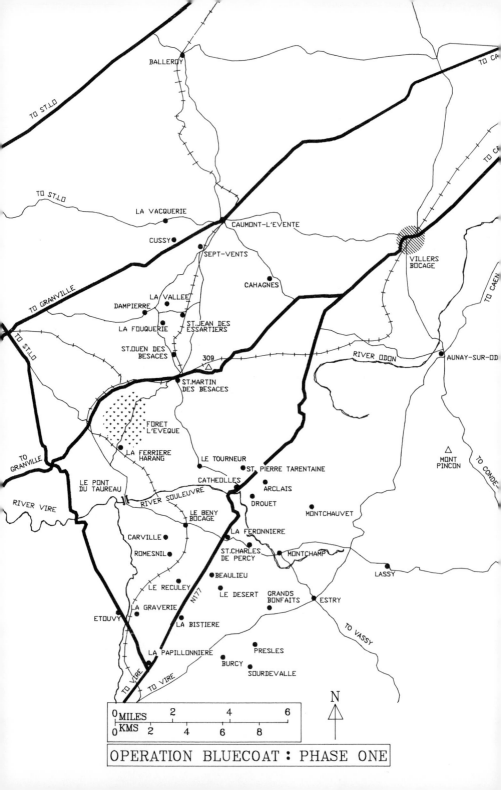

Tourneur. After that, they were to form two columns that would converge on Vassy, the one on the left, made up of the Grenadier Group, going for Montchauvet and La Chapelle-au-Cornu, and the other, consisting of the Irish and Coldstream Guards, heading towards La Ferronnière, Saint-Charles-de-Percy, Montchamp and Estry. This audacious thrust of the Guards Armoured Division was to be flanked on the left by 43rd Infantry Division and XXX Corps advancing towards Condé-sur-Noireau and on the right by 11th Armoured Division. On paper, the latter's role was only to cover the right flank of the Guards and to maintain contact with their cousins in 1st American Army. In the event, however, 'Pip' Roberts' men were going to have good reason to remember, very vividly, the *blitzkrieg* they launched that would force VIII Corps to change its plans. As the Divisional historian wrote: *The part played by 11th Armoured in this operation was considerable. Compared to many other successes it was not spectacular. No great tank battle was fought, no important city was taken, no records were broken for numbers of prisoners captured and kilometres covered. However, in the space of three weeks, the enemy defences were overwhelmed, their efforts at resistance crushed and their troops driven towards their destruction.*

GETTING INTO POSITION FOR THE ASSAULT

11th Armoured Division started its move towards the extreme western end of the British front during the night of 28/29 July. After passing through Bayeux it reached the forming-up area near Balleroy and Caumont. The drivers who made that night journey will always remember it as a nightmare. The roads were crammed with vehicles and tanks all going the same way. The enormous mass of six divisions all pushing in the same direction and all apparently in complete confusion provided 2nd British Army with the overwhelming force that would soon break the back of the enemy.

'BLACK SUNDAY' FOR THE HEREFORDS

At dawn on 30 July, after the usual aerial bombardment by the four-engined heavy bombers of the Royal Air Force and the medium bombers of the United States Air Force, the guns of the Ayrshire Yeomanry opened fire to cover the Herefords who led the advance of 159 Brigade on the right as they made for the villages of Cussy and La Vacquerie and the nearby woods. The start-line for the infantry was an apple orchard that contained a mine field that had been laid by the Americans. (It should be noted in passing that the Americans had occupied this sector since 20 June and that the battle-lines in this area had remained fairly static). Two fields had been profusely sown with mines but Divisional Headquarters could not obtain accurate maps of the mine-field from their American neighbours.

On the eve of the attack, the Royal Engineers had cleared a few lanes during the night but some mines, buried more deeply than usual, were not found. The first victims were a transport truck and its passengers and also several tanks of the Fife and Forfar Yeomanry. The mine-clearing had to start all over again and many hours passed before it was possible to mark out a safe path along which they could extricate themselves from the mine-strewn orchard.

Needless to say, all this activity was observed by the enemy and he rained shells and mortar bombs down on them. The ground was so hard the Herefords could not dig slit trenches but had to lie out in the open under the downpour until the mine-clearing troops had finished their work. Finally, the advance got under way and the battle started for the capture of Cussy. The enemy resisted fiercely, bringing down heavy machine-gun fire from nests well concealed in the hedges and woods. By 1800 hours, the objective had been taken and the Shropshires, taking over as relief, made progress in the direction of La Fouquerie, supported by the tanks of the Fife and Forfar.

The Herefords' losses for this first day's fighting were heavy: 22 men were killed, one of them a Captain, and 104 men were wounded, among them two officers. The day would go down in the annals of the Regiment as 'Black Sunday'.

TROUBLE ALSO ON THE LEFT

The left column, formed by 29 Brigade and consisting of 3rd Royal Tank Regiment and 8th Rifle Brigade, advanced parallel to 15th Scottish Division on a road out of La Vallée to the south-west of Caumont, advancing on Saint-Martin-des-Besaces after by-passing Dampierre and Sept-Vents. Although opposition was not as strong as on the right, they still had many mines to contend with and clearing them in the woods on both sides of the road made progress slow and difficult. That night the column stopped between Dampierre and Saint-Martin-des-Besaces. The 3rd Monmouths followed behind them. They were surprised by a German force armed with machine-guns that had been 'overlooked' in an orchard near Sept-Vents; the Germans were wiped out in less than 20 minutes. The tanks of the 23rd Hussars, who had had their troubles with mine-fields, arrived just in time to help the Monmouths take Saint-Ouen-des-Besaces. But first, before occupying the village, they had to overcome the resistance put up by nests of machine-guns and anti-tank guns. German guns then shelled the village and set some houses on fire. Eventually all was quiet and everyone settled down for the night.

A DARING NIGHT ATTACK

While this was going on, the Scotsmen, supported by the 6th Guards Tank Brigade, had seized Hill 309 that dominates Saint-Martin but the town itself remained in enemy hands. Because 11th Armoured Division was in a good position to do so, it was ordered to seize the village and to cut the Vire—Villers-Bocage road to the west of Saint-Martin. The first task was given to 29 Brigade, the second to 159 Brigade. Both, therefore, were going to have to carry out a night attack.

Despite fierce enemy resistance, 8th Rifle Brigade carried out its nocturnal advance along both sides of the Caumont — Saint-Martin road and, by dawn, was in position along the railway line, ready to attack.

SEE YOU AT BREAKFAST!

The Shropshires, who had taken La Fouquerie after relieving the Herefordshires, were just settling into their slit-trenches for the night when they were ordered to cut the road to the west of Saint-Martin. Because the men were exhausted their officers were rather dubious about having to lead them in the dark, into enemy territory, to attack positions about which they knew little or nothing. Warned about this, General Roberts got in touch with General O'Connor, the Commander of VIII Corps, and had the order confirmed that they had to cross the eight kilometres that separated them from the road in question that night so that they could be in position there by dawn of the 31st. Major Robinson weighed up the problems he faced: how were they to find their way in the dark?; how were they to keep control of such a group of men?; what should they do if they ran into the enemy?; should they go across country or should they follow the road?; should they ask for tank support or should they rely on artillery alone?; or should they make their way in silence so as to escape detection?

While he was searching for an answer to these questions his senior commanders began to get impatient. Twice Brigade Headquarters called to ask if he was going to get cracking or not! Eventually, they set off at 3 o'clock in the morning, guided by Captain Clayton into a night as black as ink with Lieutenant Bourdillon leading a section of the Shropshires armed with Sten guns as they plunged into the unknown. "See you at breakfast — I hope!" said Major Robinson to Captain Clayton before he disappeared into the darkness.

THE CAPTAIN'S GOOSE

The Companies crept along a narrow path, one after the other in silent, Indian file as they moved across country from farm to farm and from hamlet to hamlet. The night march went without incident except for a frightening experience that happened to Captain Clayton.

We had just crossed the brook that runs to the south of La Fouquerie and had started to climb the hill when we sensed rather than saw that we were in a village. As we were turning to the right at the corner of a house we suddenly heard a noise coming from a doorway. Four of my 'gangsters' immediately sprang into action and, all together in one burst, fired through the door. After waiting a while and not hearing anything they lit their flash-lights—and took their fingers off the triggers. Captain Clayton was sure it was a goose but Dick Mullock swore it was a turkey. Whatever it was, with the contents of four Sten guns in its body, the poor bird had no further use in the kitchen unless it was to serve as a strainer!

THE ATTACK ON SAINT-MARTIN-DES-BESACES

By daybreak on 31 July the Shropshires were in position on the Saint-Martin—St. Lo road at a point about 1500 metres from Saint-Martin. They soon received orders to attack Saint-Martin from the west while the Rifle Brigade attacked it from the north. 'B' and 'C' Companies of the Shropshires, covering each other, made their way along each side of the road and, supported by the Fife and Forfar tanks, captured the village in spite of enemy anti-tank guns that hit one of the tanks. The Rifle Brigade was less fortunate because the railway line from whence they attacked prevented the tanks of 3rd Royal Tank Regiment from supporting them. They were soon pinned down by enemy machine-guns that inflicted some losses on them. At 1100 hours the Shropshires handed over Saint-Martin to the Scotsmen; but first they lined up their prisoners in threes and marched them back to the rear.

THE BRIDGE THAT CHANGED EVERYTHING

Just at this moment a report was handed in to 11th Armoured Division of a remarkable discovery by a troop of reconnaisance armoured cars of the Household Cavalry. Taking advantage of the night advance of the Shropshires to the Saint-Martin—St. Lo road, they had patrolled far ahead of the front held by 159 Brigade. In the Forêt-Levêque they found a path that appeared to be undefended. They made a dash through the forest at full speed and continued on down to the Souleuvre river. There, to their utter astonishment, they discovered that the bridge was neither guarded nor prepared for demolition despite the fact that it was on the main St. Lo—Bény-Bocage road.

'PIP' ROBERTS ACTS

When the message was received at Division Headquarters, General Roberts immediately saw how to exploit this stroke of luck. His actions changed the course of the battle and had a profound effect on the campaign. Whereas previously the Guards Armoured Division had been ordered to advance up to and beyond Vassy, the capture of the Souleuvre bridge now made it possible for 11th Armoured Division to play the principal role by getting to the Vire—Vassy road before anyone else. With the swiftness of decision that characterizes all great commanders and without any hesitation, Roberts gave the order to his Division to cross the bridge and make for Bény-Bocage, realizing full well that the move would cut the German 7th Army in two and deny it its main escape route to the east.

But first things first; the most urgent need was to send reinforcements to the Household Cavalry armoured cars in position near the bridge. The tanks of the 2nd Northamptonshire Yeomanry were best placed to do this because, at that moment, they were not in action. Since the previous day their role had been to watch the right flank of 159 Brigade and, if possible, make contact with the Americans. They were on their way to do this and were near

The badge of the Royal Tank Regiment shows the trapezoidal shape of the first
tanks built in Great Britain. It was a tank of this type that was demonstrated
to King George V and the British General Staff on 29 January 1916. (cf p.11)

The insignia of 11th Armoured Division was a black bull on a gold field. It was emblazoned on all the vehicles of the Division and was worn as a shoulder flash by those who served in it. It was originally chosen by Major-General P. C. S. Hobart, the first Commander of the Division. A bull passant was the crest of his family's Coat of Arms.(cf p.18)

Major-General G. P. B. (Pip) Roberts, a Captain in the 6th Royal Tank Regiment at the outbreak of the war in September 1939, took command of 11th Armoured Division in December 1943 on the eve of his 37th birthday. He was then the youngest Major-General in the British Army and had a reputation for being a 'thruster' who led from the front. Here he is seen in his White scout car with his driver, Corporal Saggers of the 8th Rifle Brigade. (cf p.22)

I.W.M. #B9183

Sherman tanks of the 23rd Hussars on the way to Cheux for the attack towards
the River Odon and Hill 112 during Operation EPSOM. (cf p.39)

Tanks of 11th Armoured Division making their way across the Caen plain in the direction of Bourguébus and Hubert-Folie during operation GOODWOOD, the attack launched on 18 July, 1944 to the east of Caen. (cf p.47 et seq.)

I.W.M. #B7524

Under the protection of tanks of the 23rd Hussars, the motorised infantry of the 8th Rifle Brigade cross the road from Villers-Bocage to Villedieu at St. Martin-des-Besaces on their way to La Ferrière-Harang. (cf p.75 et seq.)

Men of the 2nd Independent Machine Gun Company, Royal Northumberland Fusiliers, waiting for the approaches to the Souleuvre bridge to be cleared before continuing on to Le Bény-Bocage during Operation BLUECOAT. (cf p.65 et seq.)
I.W.M.#B8490

The guns of 151st Field Regiment (Ayrshire Yeomanry) advancing towards Vire after crossing the Souleuvre bridge during Operation BLUECOAT. (cf p.65 et seq.)
I.W.M.#B8478

The guns and tanks of 11th Armoured Division getting ready to cross the Souleuvre river during Operation BLUECOAT. (cf p.65 et seq.)

I.W.M. #B8489

Another bridge over the Souleuvre was captured by 11th Armoured Division at Cathéolles. This enabled the Guards Armoured Division and the 6th Guards Tank Brigade, coming from Saint-Pierre-Tarentaine, to continue the advance in the direction of Montchauvet. (cf p.80)

I.W.M. #B8599

Infantrymen of the 3rd Monmouthshire Regiment. This Battalion suffered the heaviest casualties of all the units in 11th Armoured Division. (cf p.238)

The Story of the 23rd Hussars

Every day the infantrymen are in battle against the enemy. They march and fight, march and fight.... Now, watched over by the tanks, they sleep before their

The men of the 4th King's Shropshire Light Infantry take advantage of a lull in the fighting to snatch a brief nap after having made a night march of 8 kilometres so that they could seize positions near St. Martin-des-Besaces at dawn. (cf p.72 et seq.)

Sergeant Sear of the 23rd Hussars enjoys the victor's rewards after destroying a German tank in Le Bény-Bocage. (cf p.78)

I.W.M. #B8339

The jeeps of Lieutenant Evans and Captain Blackman, 23rd Hussars, go through Le Bény-Bocage during Operation BLUECOAT. (cf p.76)

Before continuing the fight in the direction of the Vire—Vassy road, men of the 23rd Hussars pose for a photograph at Le Bény-Bocage. (cf p.77 et seq.)

I.W.M. #B8343

Corporal Ken Ball, 2nd Northamptonshire Yeomanry, the 'Tiger' hunter. (cf p.92)

Author's collection

Bren-gun carriers of the 8th Rifle Brigade entering Presles during Operation
BLUECOAT. (cf p.87)

'B' and 'D' Companies of the 4th King's Shropshire Light Infantry, supported by Bren-gun carriers of 'S' Company, are the first to enter Vassy. (cf p.135)

the Shropshires who were in position just to the west of Saint-Martin when the order came through. They managed to get a few tanks across the railway line while 'C' Squadron was held up by an anti-tank gun that covered the railway line and destroyed one of their tanks. The group of tanks that got across, commanded by Lieutenant Dyson and Sergeant Taylor, was ordered to head as fast as possible for the bridge and to establish themselves there while waiting for reinforcements. They did this after crossing the La Ferrière-Harang road in a dash, spraying the Germans still there with a hail of machine-gun bullets. A little later, after taking up positions around the bridge, they captured a despatch-rider from 21st Panzer Division who was carrying a code for decyphering wireless messages. When 2nd Army's monitoring service subsequently intercepted and decoded various messages they learnt why this breach had been left open in the German defences. The messages were between the commanders of the German 3rd Parachute and 326th Infantry Divisions. Each asserted that the road in question that marked the boundary between them was the responsibility of the other.

Be that as it may, what mattered to the British was that the front had been breached and that it should stay breached.

DIRECTION: ETOUVY

Once he was assured that the bridge was firmly held by his men and well aware of the vital role it could play in the battle, General Roberts next turned to make his peace with his superiors. The historian of 11th Armoured Division writes: *The capture of the bridge and the advance southward which it made possible was unquestionably a turning-point in the campaign in France. The battle beyond Caen had obstructed the collection of a counter-attack force sufficient to halt the American drive further west. This advance prevented the immediate reinforcement of that force. In order that the stroke might be exploited, the army plan was changed and its most westerly troops became recognized as the main striking component. The commanding heights around Le Bény-Bocage,*

originally the objective not even of 15th Scottish but of XXX Corps
on their left, now lay within our grasp and we were ordered after
securing them to push on with all speed to Etouvy. *

A DAY OF WINE AND ROSES

The tanks of the 23rd Hussars carrying the men of the 3rd Monmouths arrived at the bridge a few hours after their colleagues of
the Northamptonshires. They had passed through the Forêt-
l'Evêque without incident. It was a joy and a tonic for all to be
able, at last, to advance on French soil without having to fight
for every inch of the way as they had had to do up to then. What's
more, in addition to that, the first village they went through at
the edge of the forest, La Ferrière-Harang, gave them the kind
of delirious welcome that was to become commonplace but that,
up to then, they had not experienced. All the inhabitants crowded
into the road to greet them. The girls of the village offered them
flowers. Cider, liqueur and calvados flowed in torrents! The
welcome was so warm, the cider so refreshing and the population
so friendly that it became more and more difficult to persuade
the valiant liberators to continue their advance. It was at that
moment that Captain Blackman at the head of a column of tanks
opened fire on some German 105mm guns and machine-guns that
had turned up to spoil the party. The cannon fire had the effect
of dispersing the villagers who ran for cover thus allowing the column to continue on its way to the Souleuvre.

*TAURUS PURSUANT—A History of 11th Armoured Division by E. W. I.
Palamountain, British Army of the Rhine, 1945.

ON TO BÉNY-BOCAGE? ... NOT THAT NIGHT!

Just as the leading tanks were cautiously crossing the bridge an explosion occured and two men of the Monmouths, seriously wounded, tumbled from the tank on which they had been riding. Thinking that an enemy anti-tank gun had fired at them, 'B' Squadron of the 23rd Hussars laid down smoke and, behind that screen, worked their way very carefully into the woods to try and locate the enemy. While this was going on, the Welshmen continued to make progress through the woods on both sides of the road to Bény-Bocage. As they came out of the woods they were pinned down by well-camouflaged machine-gun nests. There was not enough room for them to deploy all their Companies so they called up 'C' Squadron of the Hussars who came to their rescue and cleared the road. When the Hussars were about 50 metres from the top of the hill, just as they came up to support the infantry, the lead tank ran on to a series of mines that knocked it across the road, blocking the way for those following. This decided them to halt the advance for that day and the Monmouths took up defensive positions for the night.

In the meanwhile, 'B' Squadron, zig-zagging through the trees deep in the wood, found a path that led to the crest. The tank men found nothing there that could have fired on them from above and caused the explosion that had alarmed them after they had crossed the bridge. The mystery was later solved when they noticed that the wounds of the two men had been caused by a *PIAT** carried by one of the men; the heat of the engine of the tank on which they were riding had caused it to explode.

While clearing the woods on the crest, the tanks ran up against a self-propelled gun that scored several direct hits on the leading tanks before it was destroyed. After that the two Squadrons withdrew back to the bridge to pass the night there in greater safety.

*Projectile Infantry Anti Tank, the British hand-held anti-tank weapon.

THE RECEPTION AT LE BÉNY-BOCAGE

At dawn on 1 August, after the sappers had removed the mines, 'B' and 'C' Squadrons of the Hussars renewed their attempt to enter Le Bény-Bocage by following the same road they had taken the day before. Just then they were ordered to stop and leave the way clear for their colleagues of the 3rd Royal Tank Regiment. However, Sergeant Sear, who was about to enter the town, turned a deaf ear and, with his comrades, arrived at the town centre where he turned his gun on a *Mark IV* a few yards away and set it on fire.

While 'C' Company of the Monmouths cleared several farms around the town, surprising a section of German infantry about 10 men strong who, on the appearance of the Monmouths, fled across the fields to be chased and shot like rabbits, the tanks of the 3rd Royal Tank Regiment and the men of the Shropshires made their entrance into the city. The soldiers had their first experience of what happens when a town is liberated. All the bells rang at full peal, the civilians lined the road on both sides and cheered the troops, the vehicles were covered with flowers and the drivers and soldiers were kissed by the country girls. Le Bény-Bocage had hardly suffered from the war and it was liberated practically without any fighting but it gave them a fantastic welcome. Rifleman Kingsmill described what happened very well in a letter he sent his family that evening.

We had a marvellous experience this morning. Will you believe me when I tell you we assisted in liberating a small town. Really, I have never seen people so crazy with joy. Everyone screamed, waved their arms, cheered, applauded, kissed his neighbour or sung the Marseillaise—all at the same time! I wonder if I can paint the picture for you. The marketplace is about 80 yards by 20 yards. At one end there is a burnt and blackened German tank, still smouldering. At the other end, where I am, there is a group of soldiers in a hotel. One can see them through window frames empty of glass. The moment any soldier manages to free himself from the embraces of one girl he is 'captured' by another.

I have to stay in the truck because of the ear-phones hanging round my neck but the rear is open and so, by standing up, I can see what is going on. A villager comes towards me with a great big smile—and a glass of champagne! It is really good, fresh and sparkling. The glass is hardly empty when an old woman, at least 80 years old, shakes my hand like a mad person while crying, "Merci M'sieur, merci beaucoup." She almost weeps with joy. All this gives me a lump in the throat. A policeman at the lower end of the square hangs up an enormous tricolour flag. There are flags everywhere, even in the telephone booths and on the sides of the fountain. Brand new 'Cross of Lorraine' armbands appear on the sleeves of the young people and they seem very proud to show that they are French again. Another glass is offered, and accepted, and many others follow. Everyone throws flowers and all the vehicles are decorated with them. Then, not from pity but really because it delights us to do so, it is our turn to give them candy, chocolates, biscuits and cigarettes. Everyone smokes; even a schoolboy tries it. All the while a young, five-year-old girl leaps around like a lamb in springtime. The people mill around, kissing each other again and again, the mother her daughter, the husband his wife, the soldiers the girls. 'Drunkeness'. 'Delirium'. It is difficult to find the right word. It is an extraordinary sight that I will never forget. A Frenchman tells me he hid a machine-gun in his house since 1940. This morning, the morning for which he had waited so long, he killed 9 boches with it! The little girl with black eyes and curly hair returns. She waits for me to shake her hand, taking her turn with all the others. The whole village is crazy, crazy with joy. It is wonderful!

BUT THE WAR GOES ON ...

Of course, the entire Division could not take part in the rejoicing. 'A' Squadron of the 3rd Royal Tank Regiment, accompanied by two companies of the 4th Kings Shropshire Light Infantry, attacked the heights that overlook and dominate the whole area to the north-west of Bény-Bocage. After brushing aside the enemy without too much trouble, the Commanding Officers of the two regiments installed themselves up there. The two other companies of the

Shropshires, still supported by the Royal Tank Regiment, were next sent in the direction of the Souleuvre river to capture the very important bridge on the Caen—Vire road. Situated in a deep valley, overlooked on all sides by wooded heights, the place, so easy to defend, was difficult to get to. Colonel Silvertop of the 3rd Royal Tank Regiment and Major Robinson of the 4th Shropshires even had to leave their vehicles behind and thus lost contact with their headquarters. After a stiff fight the bridge fell into their hands. One of the companies guarded it while the other advanced up to the village of Cathéolle which they occupied for the night. For some hours after the capture of the bridge, enemy vehicles, ignorant of the fact that it had fallen into the hands of the British, continued to approach it from the directions of Villers-Bocage and Montchauvet. They received a warm reception and soon the two roads were strewn with destroyed and burning trucks while their occupants, about 80 or so, were made prisoners.

It was in the course of this fighting that Captain Clayton was the victim of an unfortunate incident that nearly cost him his life. Commanding 'B' Company of the Shropshires and slightly wounded during the capture of the bridge, he was evacuated in a German staff car that had just been captured. As it passed through the British lines it was seen as a suitable target and was fired on. The Captain was hit again, this time much more seriously. However, he had a robust constitution because he not only survived both the enemy and the friendly fire but also the stiff dose of morphine given to him to kill the pain.

In May 1970, after attending the first memorial ceremony held in Flers in honour of 11th Armoured Division, Captain Clayton returned to the vicinity of Bény-Bocage to try to find the French civilians to whose house he had been taken after being wounded and who were the first to attend to him. He remembered that the man of the house had a wooden leg. Having found the house, he knocked on the door and an old woman answered it. Opening his dictionary, he tried to explain the purpose of his visit. The lady did not understand because Captain Clayton really got himself tangled up in his translation. Mistaking the French word, *timbre*, which means a postage stamp, for the English word 'timber', he was talking about a *jambe de timbre*, a 'postage-stamp leg', instead of a *jambe de bois,* a 'wooden leg'. No wonder the lady was puzzled. Finally, he managed to make his meaning clear by gestures. The dear old soul told him she remembered everything very well and that her husband, whose leg had been amputated after the 1914 war, had been dead for two years.

LA FERRONNIÈRE ...
OR IS IT SAINT-CHARLES-DE-PERCY?

After enjoying a short rest at Bény-Bocage, the 8th Rifle Brigade took to their carriers and, in company with another squadron of the 3rd Royal Tank Regiment which had been very active that day, headed towards the important intersection at La Ferronnière. Because the cartographic service of the British Army had mis-read the French maps, they had marked this place on their maps as *Saint-Charles-de-Percy* while the real name of the crossroad did not appear. Wherever they were, the houses lining the road at this intersection were cleared of Germans without serious resistance. This was now the second place at which the Vire — Caen road had been cut by 11th Armoured Division. As at Cathéolles, the enemy was surprised to find himself facing another unexpected road-block. In anticipation of the reaction this would produce on the enemy when he realized that one of his main escape routes had been cut, the Rifle Brigade asked for reinforcements. Already one German tank had come from the direction of Villers-Bocage to test the strength of the road-block and other disturbing movements of armour were spotted coming from the direction of Vire. Some anti-tank and self-propelled guns were, therefore, sent to the Rifle Brigade so that they could hold off a possible counter-attack but the rest of the day and the following night passed without anything happening.

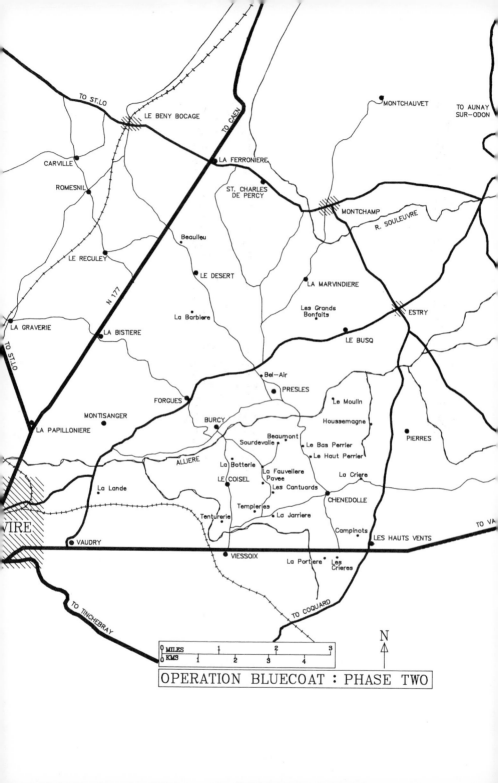

OPERATION BLUECOAT : PHASE TWO

11TH ARMOURED DIVISION SURGES FORWARD

It was obvious that, up to this time, the advance of 11th Armoured Division had completely disorganized the enemy because his reactions were uncharacteristically slow. Short of troops, he was forced to deal with not only the Americans on the right as they pushed south but also the Guards Armoured Division on the left. The Americans were slowed down in their drive towards Vire while, from 1 August, the Guards were subjected to a series of brutal counter-attacks by 21st Panzer Division who had established themselves on the heights of Montchauvet and Arclais.

On 2 August it looked as if the Division could continue its advance not only towards Etouvy but also generally in a south-westerly direction towards Vire, the centre of a network of roads that run to the east and northeast.

FIRST INTO VIRE

Accordingly, in the morning, patrols of the 2nd Northamptonshires were sent to find out what enemy forces were in this part of the Bocage. They thus became the right-flank guard of the Division. Two Squadrons, 'A' and 'B', headed for Vire by route N177 while 'C' Squadron probed on their right. They did not run into opposition until, taking the road from Bény-Bocage, they arrived at Etouvy. They judged that Etouvy was held too strongly so they slanted to the left in order to return to the highway at La Bistière where they hoped to join up with 'A' Squadron. From there they planned to make a dash for Vire because some civilians had told them that Vire had been evacuated by the Germans. The report was certainly true that morning and it is too bad that the British were unable to send in a force of infantry immediately so as to occupy this important communication centre so vital to the enemy.*

---

*General Roberts comments: 'The fact was that we had strict instructions from Monty, through Corps, that we were not — repeat NOT — to go into Vire. That was the American objective. I must add that we had already 'had words' with the Americans earlier on in the battle as we had been accused by them of utilising **their** road.'

The tanks at the head of 'C' Squadron destroyed an anti-tank gun at the crossroad at La Papillonnière and also some trucks loaded with ammunition and German infantrymen which, unsuspectingly, arrived on the scene. Two groups of tanks commanded by Lieutenants Saxby and Grimstone got as far as the suburbs of Vire but were shelled by artillery situated to the west of the city. Having almost run out of ammunition and with no supporting infantry with which to hold the city, they went back to La Bistière where they replenished their ammunition before returning to La Papillonnière.

All the while, the rest of the Division kept penetrating further and further south with the Vire — Vassy road as their objective.

FROM LE BÉNY-BOCAGE TO CHÊNEDOLLÉ

Two columns were formed. The one on the left, led by the tanks of the 23rd Hussars and the infantry of 8th Rifle Brigade, followed, in reserve, by the 3rd Royal Tank Regiment and the Shropshires, advanced from Bény-Bocage towards Beaulieu, Le Desert and Presles. Their progress was rather slow because the lead units were continually engaged in a series of fights against self-propelled guns or the armour of 9th SS Panzer Division which now made its first appearance on the Division's front. The opposition was particularly strong at the Vire — Estry intersection. Nevertheless, the head of the column continued its advance towards Presles which was reached without incident while some tanks stayed in position around Hill 218. Just at this moment a mix-up occured that could have been disastrous. As enemy armour was prowling around on all sides, artillery support was often requested. The gunners' Forward Observation Officer who accompanied them saw a column of tanks on the right, climbing the heights to the south of Burcy, in the direction of the villages of Pavée and Sourdevalle. Thinking that they were the enemy, he was just about to call down a heavy barrage on them when Major Blacker recognized the tanks as belonging to the Fife and Forfar Yeomanry and, just in time, stopped the over-zealous gunner. However, just then, the troops holding the intersection were attacked by a Panther that was well hidden by the high banks. It caused them a lot of trouble before it was knocked out. The few German infantrymen who accompanied it then decided to withdraw.

THE BASTION OF GRANDS-BONFAITS

Because of the danger that threatened the left flank of the column, the 4th Shropshires, supported by the 3rd Royal Tank Regiment, were ordered to seize the little village of Grands-Bonfaits and to dig themselves in there. This little hamlet comprises just two or three farms and a few orchards. Situated about 2 kilometres from the intersection, it was the 'bastion' that ensured the security of the left flank. But the bastion was not held without loss because other enemy tanks attacked the tanks of the 3rd Royal Tank Regiment and destroyed three of them. Wisely, the remainder made a detour to the left where they were within a hair's breadth of being lost. 'D' Company commander of the Shropshires, who had taken his men right across the front of the enemy tanks, managed to bring them back in good order thanks to their wireless set. As Major Thornburn wrote later: *I am sure it was the only time I can remember when a Number 38 wireless set worked properly without fading and that saved our necks.*

The Royal Tank Regiment, taking a narrow, sunken path, managed to rejoin the infantrymen whom they were supposed to be protecting. As they came in one by one, the tanks lined up along the hedges, taking shelter behind the banks wherever they could find cover and yet be ready for any enemy attack.

At about this time, the forces that had been guarding the intersection were able to resume their advance towards Presles. From there, always very aware of the danger on their left, 'A' Squadron was sent out alone along a road parallel to the highway to Chênedollé in the direction of Le Moulin and Houssemagne while the remainder climbed the heights of Perrier by the direct route, accompanied by the infantry of the Rifle Brigade.

THE GERMANS REACT

'A' Squadron of the 23rd Hussars had just passed the village of Le Moulin when it was attacked. It got out of the narrow lane and made for a field in order to disperse its tanks. Seeing that they did not have any supporting infantry, the Germans sprang a trap for them. As soon as the British tanks entered the field the well-camouflaged enemy tanks opened fire on them from all sides, all together and at point-blank range. The effect was devastating. In less than a minute all 'A' Squadron's tanks, except four, were hit and set on fire. The crews of the four surviving tanks first drove their tanks to cover and then went back to the aid of the wounded. They showed great courage and determination in getting the wounded to safety despite the storm of shellfire that swept over them continuously. Captain Taylor re-organized what remained of the Squadron and, with the help of some reconnaissance tanks that came to their rescue, led them back down the path to Presles and to Perrier, taking their wounded with them. On the way they had to fight fiercely to smash a way through the *panzergrenadiers* who were lying in wait for them. Once all the wounded had been evacuated, Captain Taylor led the four survivors from the disaster across the fields and rejoined the rest of the 23rd Hussars in Bas-Perrier.

CHÊNEDOLLÉ TAKEN—AND LOST!

From Bas Perrier, 'B' Squadron of the 23rd Hussars, together with the Rifle Brigade infantrymen, set out for Chênedollé and then on to the Vire—Vassy road, their main objective. The villagers knew that German tanks were prowling all around the area and they were nervous at the sight of the first British tanks. They probably had a presentiment of the horror that was going to engulf them during the next seven days. In fact, it was not long before the first Panther appeared and destroyed Sergeant Allsop's tank. Luckily, none of his crew was wounded. *The tank commander walked calmly back past the rest of the Regiment with his crew* *looking rather irritated, like someone whose car has broken down at a tiresome moment.* *

The infantry of the Rifle Brigade left their carriers and, with the support of four tanks, began to clear the village. They had hardly gone a few yards when the Panther re-appeared in the middle of the village and sprang on them. Two direct hits on the turret stopped it. The crew should have been reduced to porridge but, to the amazement of the anti-tank gunner who put on this display of markmanship, the Panther simply went into reverse and disappeared behind some houses.

The opposition they ran into around the village of Le Moulin, not far from Chênedollé, showed that the enemy had concentrated his forces on the left and that the main danger threatened from the east from whence the enemy was in an ideal position to counter-attack. It was therefore decided to withdraw from Chênedollé to a strong position on the Bas Perrier heights and to pass the night there.

FROM LE BÉNY-BOCAGE TO BURCY AND PAVÉE

The right-hand column that comprised the tanks of the Fife and Forfar Yeomanry and the Welsh infantry of the 3rd Monmouthshire Regiment also left the Bény-Bocage sector at dawn in order to make for the Vire — Vassy road via Carville, Le Reculey and Burcy. They reached the little village of Burcy early in the day and found it nestled in the hollow of a pretty valley. The villagers showed *les Anglais* how delighted they were to be liberated at last and the bells rang at full peal. Towards the end of the afternoon the column, making use of a path and sometimes going across the fields, climbed the hill that overlooks the Vire — Vassy road. It took up a defensive position around the hamlet of Pavée and passed the night there. Battalion headquarters of the 3rd Monmouths was installed at the farm of M. Robert Taflet. Two Companies were deployed in front of the village and the other two in the rear.

*The Story of the 23rd Hussars (p. 94).

THE VIRE—VASSY ROAD IS CUT

While this was going on, a troop of tanks commanded by Lieutenant Brownlie reached the Vire—Vassy road. He tells the story. *I approached the highway by a sunken lane too narrow for the tank. With one track on the bank and the other in the rut of the lane it was difficult to steer. Disaster struck! The second tank tipped over, blocking the way for the others. I was forced to go on alone towards the highway. I stopped and, donning a German helmet, crawled up the bank to spy out the land. From there I watched the dead-straight road for more than three miles on each side. It was deserted. While the others were still jammed in the lane I returned to my tank, drove it across the highway and, backing in, placed myself in a lane from which I could see without being seen. After about ten minutes a solitary motorcyclist appeared in the distance, coming from Vassy and climbing the hill at full speed. When he was about 20 yards away he saw us. Wondering who we were, he slowed down and started to weave across the road. My corporal and I opened fire simultaneously, he with a pistol and I with a German rifle I had picked up. With a bullet in each leg, the motorcyclist was left in no doubt as to our identity.*

Some moments later the other Fife and Forfar tanks arrived having finally managed to extricate themselves from the sunken lane. They, too, positioned themselves on the road and it was not long before they spotted some Panthers in the direction of Chênedollé. They opened fire at long range but it was obvious that at that range the 75mm guns of the Shermans were ineffectual. They then put out a call over the wireless for Typhoons and in no more than 20 minutes the fighter-bombers were overhead.

THE CALVADOS KNOCK-OUT!

I will always remember that hot August day on which we arrived at the Vire-Vassy road, writes Colonel (former Lieutenant) Brownlie. *While the shells fell around us from the direction of Chênedollé, a farmer, completely disregarding the danger, came up to us with a bottle and some glasses on a tray. He went from tank to tank, offering the thirsty crews a refreshing drink. When my turn came, thinking that it was white wine, I swallowed the entire contents of the glass in one gulp—and nearly choked to death! I could hardly breathe! It was calvados! It knocked me out but I survived. Since then I have learnt the correct way to drink this delicious liqueur.*

The Typhoons soon appeared overhead. The artillery used smoke-shells to mark where the Panthers were and the Typhoons dive-bombed them with their terrible, deadly rockets. The German tanks quickly dispersed but some stayed behind, smashed to pieces. This perfect cooperation between the R.A.F., the artillery and the tanks ensured that the road would remain cut until the end of the afternoon.

The Squadron withdrew towards the village of Pavée, not wishing to remain on the highway during the night while Lieutenant Brownlie's troop had to contend not only with the German tanks and grenadiers but also with a swarm of American Thunderbolts. These planes attacked them repeatedly despite the recognition signals such as the orange phosphorescent panels displayed on top of the tanks and the yellow smoke emitted by special smoke generators. By a miracle, no one was hurt except the German prisoner who had been shot on his motor-bike and a wireless operator who cut his hand on an empty rations box when he jumped into a slit trench!

THE SALIENT HELD

That evening the Vire—Vassy highway remained cut and firmly under the control of two strong groups of British forces in positions on the heights that dominated the road from the north. These two forces, the 23rd Hussars with the 8th Rifle Brigade on the left, to the east, and the Fife and Forfar Yeomanry with the 3rd Monmouths on the right, to the west, were both in strong positions each with a village in the valley behind them, Presles to the east and Burcy to the west, with a path running between the villages and forming their line of inter-communication. In his fine book, *The Proud Trooper,* Colonel Brownlie wrote: *For the third time in six weeks 11th Armoured Division found itself at the point of a narrow salient. On the right the Americans were still more than 16 kilometres behind us while on the left the Guards Armoured Division was at about the same level. Further to the east, XXX Corps was slogging along in the direction of Mont Pincon. It was decided, therefore, to stop 11th Armoured's advance so that they could hold the salient against increasing pressure from the Germans who were preparing to launch a major attack in the west, thrusting in the direction of Avranches so as to cut off the Americans who had penetrated deep into France.*

11TH ARMOURED DIVISION TANKS RE-ENTER VIRE

While the advance of 11th Armoured was stopped along the Vire—Vassy road, the 2nd Northamptonshires, who were guarding its right flank to the northeast of Vire, had a very busy day. At dawn on 3 August one of its squadrons headed towards Etouvy, a second went towards Vire by Highway 177 and a third, passing by Montisanger, reached the Paris—Granville railway line without meeting any opposition. 'B' Squadron got into Vire and made contact with a representative of the F.F.I. who confirmed that the city still seemed to be empty of Germans while 'C' Squadron finally made contact with the Americans who were making progress to the north of Etouvy. All seemed to be going well for the Northamptonshires. They had advanced more than 30 kilometres in three days, had run into little opposition and had suffered only a few casualties. Their morale was very high; they felt they were on top of the world!

HARD TIMES FOR THE NORTHAMPTONSHIRES

However, after 1400 hours everything changed for the worse. 'B' Squadron, returning from Vire, reported that Tiger tanks, accompanied by infantry, were advancing in their direction. Immediately, the F.O.O. with them gave the enemy positions to the gunners but at the last moment the guns were ordered to wait because Typhoons were on their way to attack the enemy. An air O.P. went up to direct them but was promptly shot down by the enemy so that the Typhoons never found their target.* Because of this the enemy tanks were able to get in among the Northamptonshire tanks without a single shot having been fired at them. It was now too late to order the British artillery to intervene because the damage would have been inflicted on both sides. A tank battle started but the Tigers, their sides protected by the slope and thickness of their armour, had no fear of the 75mm's and immediately took the initiative. Three British tanks were destroyed and the others were hit while retreating to form a new defensive square a little to the north of the highway. While they battened down they were mauled by other Tigers situated on the high ground to the west of Burcy. These same tanks also threatened to cut off the squadron that had reached the Paris — Granville railway line near La Lande. That squadron was ordered to retreat. At the same time another enemy detachment attacked Headquarters Squadron in position at La Bistière. Soon the three squadrons began to lose one tank after another without being able to do anything to the Tigers. When night fell, it was the turn of the *panzergrenadiers* to infiltrate into the positions held by the Northamptonshires and they found new victims with their *panzerfausts*. At daybreak, 31 men did not answer the roll call and many tanks had been destroyed.

*The Regimental History of the 1st and 2nd Northamptonshire Yeomanry; page 126.

THE TIGER HUNT

On this hectic afternoon the 2nd Northamptonshires had to call upon their auxiliary services to save as many of their tanks as possible because the Divisional infantry were at Grands-Bonfaits, Bas-Perrier and Pavée. From mechanic to cook, they all took up weapons and assisted in the defence of their tanks. Ken Ball, who took charge of a group of maintenance mechanics, describes what was, for him, his supreme moment. *One very hot and sunny day we were put on alert towards noon. 5 Tigers had managed to slip past our front lines and were probably heading towards us in order to attack our transport and supply vehicles. We were ordered to arm ourselves with PIAT's in case the Tigers came in our direction.*

I remember I took a young driver with me as assistant. We positioned ourselves on a very steep hill that looked down on a Y intersection about 40 yards away. In front of us there was another hill similar to ours from which we were in plain view. 'I only hope the enemy doesn't come from that direction,' I said to myself.

We started to dig a slit trench but the ground was so hard and rocky that, instead, we lay down in a ditch protected by a hedge barely a foot high. Because of the slope of the ground we had an excellent view from on top down to the intersection way below us but we certainly would not have been able to do anything about a threat coming from the hill opposite. Because the emergency was so sudden we did not have time to prepare a better camouflaged or more elaborate position; good heavens, I clearly remember how exposed we felt, my young companion and I. (I was an 'old' man, a corporal 24 years old!).

Holding on to our PIAT we asked ourselves if it was not rather like trying to stop a tank with a pea shooter to attack it with a projectile from this length of sawn-off tubing.

We were there about half an hour, spread out on the ground, when we suddenly heard the sound of tracks, the noise reverberating in the hard ground and chilling me to the bone. I stopped breathing so that I could more clearly see which direction the tank was coming from. To my great relief it came along the road but, all the same, if my first shot missed I would certainly be dead before I

could get off a second. The rumbling of the tracks biting into the
gravel became louder and louder. Our fears grew as the sounds
came nearer and nearer. I wondered what was going to happen
in the next few minutes. All of a sudden, there, at the bottom of
the road, a tank appeared. I had it nicely in my sights and let it
approach as near as possible so as not to miss it. I would press the
trigger at 50 yards. A few yards closer...and then I suddenly made
out the familiar outline of one of our Shermans!
Half an hour later the alert was called of.

9TH SS PANZER PREPARES TO ATTACK BAS-PERRIER

The tanks of the 23rd Hussars and the infantry of the 8th Rifle
Brigade who had had such a warm reception from the *panzers* the
previous day at Chênedollé and Le Moulin were withdrawn from
the heights of Bas-Perrier during the night of the 2/3 August. The
Germans, who were determined to use the Vire — Vassy road for
their projected counter-attack on the American bottleneck, had
brought round two SS Panzer Division, the 9th and 10th. The German tanks were divided into two independent battle groups; the
first, re-assembled at Pierres, headed for Presles in order to cut
the British forces off from their reinforcements and to attack them
from the rear, and the other group, massed on the heights near
La Crière, attacked them in front of Bas-Perrier itself. The German artillery was stationed on both sides of the road from
Chênedollé to La Portière, Les Hauts-Vents and Campinots.

The ground that 11th Armoured Division's two Brigades occupied between Chênedollé and Presles was made up of fields
bordered by banks and high hedges crowned with numerous trees.
Sunken lanes criss-crossed in every direction. Here and there were
farms surrounded by apple orchards. To the east one could see
the bell tower of Estry. This town was going to be the strong-point
of the German defence, the pivot on which the enemy was determined to hold the line Mont Pincon — Vire and which, in spite of
the repeated attacks by two armoured divisions, would not
capitulate until the whole German army was in headlong retreat

and trapped in the Falaise pocket. To the south, their positions were dominated by a wooded height, Le Haut Perrier, which hid Chênedollé from them. The dense woods acted as an anti-tank obstacle for the British because the enemy armour could only move through them with great difficulty. On the other hand, the nearest clumps of trees stopped only 200 metres from their positions and provided ideal cover for any enemy infantry force preparing to launch an attack.

PRESLES IN THE HANDS OF THE SS AGAIN

Towards 10 o'clock in the morning, while everything appeared to be calm again in this sector, a sentry suddenly signalled that half-tracks sent to salvage some damaged tanks of the Hussars, accompanied by an ambulance, had been taken prisoners by the Germans near the village of Presles. Through field-glasses, the officers were able to confirm that Presles was full of German soldiers who were taking up positions in and around the houses in the village. In addition, some Panthers were seen and engaged but at that extreme range the Sherman 75mm's could do no more than force them to take cover behind the houses. They noticed that two Germans had installed themselves in the bell-tower of the church, using it as an observation post; a few well-directed shells sent them scurrying away like rabbits.

BAS-PERRIER IS CUT OFF FROM THE REAR

The guns of 13th Royal Horse Artillery, installed at Le Desert, started to pound the village. Unfortunately, there were not sufficient troops available and so it was a question of abandoning the positions at Bas Perrier in order to launch a counter-attack on Presles. The next thing that happened was that their only supply route was cut. The enemy could now attack them from the south and the north at the same time. The German tanks, not very numerous but very skillfully handled, took full advantage of the terrain, making the Hussars and the Rifle Brigade, already edgy by what had happened the previous day, most uncomfortable. For one thing, they found themselves on a forward slope, practically without cover, overlooked by a hill and hemmed in at the rear by a very deep valley that the enemy was sure to use for his attack. Secondly, the 75mm's of the Shermans could not hold their own in a long-range duel with the 88mm's of the Tigers. Thirdly, the 75mm's gave their positions away when they fired because they emitted a large flame and some smoke whereas the Germans used a smoke-less and flame-less powder. It was impossible to locate a German tank when it fired unless one happened to see the track made by the shell in the air. Generally, you did not know of the presence of an enemy tank until its shells hit you.

THE SS ATTACK

Three companies of the Rifle Brigade together with 'B' and Headquarters Squadrons of the Hussars were in position on the right-hand side of the road from Presles to Chênedollé. Because of the configuration of the ground, if an attack came from the direction of Pierres or La Crière they were much more exposed than 'A' Squadron (or what was left of them) or than 'C' Squadron who were on their left. The Germans, taking advantage of their superiority at long range, decided to exert pressure on 'B' Squadron who were the most visible and the most vulnerable. Little by little, the enemy found the range and shells fell closer and closer. First one tank was hit, then a second and then some more. The British tanks answered shot for shot but their 75's were hopelessly ineffective at that distance.

Next came the turn of Headquarters Squadron who had, up to then, escaped notice because they were hidden behind a hedge. Major Wigan first had his tank hit. He went to another which suffered the same fate a few minutes later. However, his third choice got through the ordeal unscathed.

Following their usual tactics, after having destroyed or damaged as many of their opponent's tanks as possible, the Germans began to deluge the area with high-explosive and smoke shells. More and more of the tank crews were wounded, as were the infantry of the Rifle Brigade who had to endure the massacre without being able to do anything about it. A First Aid Post was improvised in a sunken lane. In spite of the plainly-visible Red Cross, an American fighter-bomber discharged all its rockets at the ambulances and other vehicles in the area. Fortunately, only the trucks were hit. The situation of the wounded was desperate. Because the enemy occupied Presles, evacuation was impossible; nor could urgently-needed medical supplies get through.

And so the day was spent in repulsing the enemy's counter-attacks and retaliating by inflicting heavy losses on him. In spite of the fierce siege fighting, two patrols of the Rifle Brigade managed to get into Chênedollé but could only bring back unimportant scraps of information.

When night fell the intensity of the battle died down. Then the besieged received some heartening news; 3rd British Infantry Division was getting ready to attack Presles in order to re-open their lines of communication to the rear.

A DAY OF WAITING AT PAVÉE

On this particular day, 3 August, the Fife and Forfar Yeomanry and the 3rd Monmouths, dug in around the village of Pavée, seemed to have a quieter time of it than their hard-pressed neighbours to the east, the Hussars and the Rifle Brigade. However, that morning, the force that had cut the Vire—Vassy road the previous day was compelled by strong enemy pressure to abandon its advanced positions and to rejoin the rest of the widely-scattered forces to their rear. No doubt encouraged by this withdrawal the Germans constantly harassed the formations holding Pavée.

While this was going on the guns of 151st Ayrshire Yeomanry took up positions just to the rear of Pavée.

The marauding German groups were generally made up of one or two tanks supported by a platoon of infantry belonging to 9th SS Panzer Division. One of their men was captured and found to have in his possession a map on which was drawn, with astonishing precision, the exact positions of all the units of 11th Armoured Division. This showed how thoroughly the enemy had carried out his reconnaissance and confirmed that he was about to launch a serious attack.

GRANDS-BONFAITS WAITS TOO

At the other end of the line held by 11th Armoured Division, the village of Grands-Bonfaits, occupied by the Royal Tank Regiment and the Shropshires, was a thorn in the flesh of the Germans because it was so close to their strong-point at Estry. On that same day, 3 August, these two units had to endure a ferocious attack, not only from the Germans who held Estry, but also from *panzers* that were heading towards the southeast. These *panzers* were on their way to attack and cut off the British in the Presles — Burcy sector so that they could re-open the Vire — Estry and Vire — Vassy roads to their supply convoys.

PRESLES RE-TAKEN
COMMUNICATIONS RE-OPENED
THE RELIEF STARTS

During the night of 3/4 August, the 2nd Warwicks of 3rd British Infantry Division attacked Presles and re-took it without great difficulty. Towards noon, the road was re-opened, priority being given to ambulances which arrived from Bas-Perrier full of wounded and left Presles without losing any time. At 1500 hours, just as the relief of the Warwicks by the Rifle Brigade was under way, shells came whistling in from all directions. Everyone took cover and the next ten minutes were very unpleasant. Then the characteristic chatter of a *spandau** announced that the enemy's counter-attack from Chênedollé was coming through the woods.

*German light machine-gun

GOOD WORK BY THE ARTILLERY

The tanks of the Hussars fired into the tree-tops while the Divisional artillery rained hundreds of shells on Chênedollé, thought to be where the enemy were assembling and forming up for the attack. In addition, all available mortars were used to lob over their bombs so as to burst in the trees immediately in front of the positions held by the infantry. These measures stopped the counter-attack in its tracks but it was fortunate that, due to the nature of the ground, the *panzers* could not intervene.

The relief was carried out without incident, the Rifle Brigade taking over the responsibility of holding Presles which, after two days' fighting, was unrecognizable from what it was like just forty-eight hours before. In the evening, another bombardment announced another counter-attack. This was stopped in the same way as before and the ensuing night passed without further incident.

ALL IS STILL CALM AT BURCY

Very little was happening in the Pavée sector. The troops who were there took advantage of the calm to improve their defences and to send out numerous patrols. Each time they all returned with the same story: the enemy was preparing a massive assault. This was also corroborated by the statements of the civilians who came to take refuge in what was, for a time, a quiet zone. But the wait was becoming intolerable and the nerves of the men were stretched to breaking point.

DEATH COMES AT FULL SPEED

The 'bastion' at Grands-Bonfaits met and repulsed one attack after another. The men who held it realized that the safety of the left flank of their Division depended on them. At last, some tanks of the Guards Armoured Division succeeded in getting as far as the neighbouring village of La Marvindière; this was no mean feat.

Among the men of the Royal Tank Regiment who had to repulse the enemy attacks was Sergeant 'Buck' Kite who, his adventures to the east of Caen behind him, now occupied a positon with his tank in a field near Grands-Bonfaits. He recalls: *It was the morning of a beautiful, sunny day. I was just cleaning up a bit after breakfast when, suddenly, the field was torn by shell and mortar explosions. I dived into my tank with my crew and immediately went into action against an enemy tank that had sneaked up on us by creeping up, unseen, behind a hedge. It was less than 100 yards from us. I think we hit it because it did not continue to come on at us. The Shropshires, who were under our protection, held their ground.*

Then the silhouettes of two more Panthers appeared in the wheat field next to us. The wheat, almost ready for harvesting, was high and each time the enemy fired at us the shells slashed a narrow furrow through the stalks. One of the two tanks was destroyed. Suddenly, I saw the cannon of the other tank that was still in action swing round in our direction. There was nothing I could do but watch the glint of the approaching shell. I can still see the wheat stalks parted by the passage of the shell. In a split second it will hit us. Death is coming at me at full speed!

'Buck' Kite was seriously wounded but for his outstanding conduct in this action he was given a second bar to the Military Medal he had been awarded in the Western Desert, the first bar having been won during GOODWOOD.

THE MARTYRDOM OF CHÊNEDOLLÉ

All day long on 5 August the Germans launched a series of attacks and counter-attacks on Bas-Perrier. The same methods that had been used the previous day were used again and again to repulse them. Soon there were no leaves left on the trees and their slashed branches raised their arms to the sky imploring that this massacre of men and nature should stop. But Chênedollé and all around it had to continue to endure the terrible martyrdom inflicted on it by the British artillery.

THE SUPPLY PROBLEM

It took great courage to drive the supply convoys between Presles and Le Bas-Perrier. The route was infested with snipers who constantly set ambushes. The trucks often had to be escorted by tanks to open the way and protect them on the road. At one very critical moment, just when Presles had been re-taken by the Germans, a supply convoy, laden with gasoline and ammunition, lost its way and took a wrong turn. As luck would have it, it arrived safely at Le Bas-Perrier just when things were becoming desperate for the defenders.

THE TANKS NEED A REST TOO

The German attacks slackened on the evening of 5 August. It appeared that 9th SS Panzer Division had exhausted itself by launching all those repeated attacks that gained no ground but caused such heavy casualties.

That evening, it was decided to bring back the tanks of 'A' and 'B' Squadrons to La Barbière for a rest. The little village of Bas-Perrier was left in the hands of the Warwicks who were better equipped for this kind of fighting. As they withdrew, the tank crews were aghast at the desolation of the countryside and the devastation that had overwhelmed it. The small fields, so peaceful before the battle, were strewn with the carcasses of tanks, cratered by shell-holes and gashed by caterpillar tracks. Many blackened, burnt trucks littered the ground near the hedges. Near them, crosses made of two twigs with a helmet on top marked the place where one of their dead comrades had been buried. Those who were withdrawn that evening for a rest had hardly spent more than half an hour outside their tanks in 48 hours. Those who stayed were going to be there for two days more.

THE STORM MOVES TO PAVÉE AND BURCY

New refugees arrived at Pavée at dawn on 5 August hoping to find shelter there. They reported what the Germans were doing, told of the vast preparations they were making and begged to be evacuated to the rear as soon as possible. The Monmouths, therefore, sent out patrols to find out what was going on. Among those patrols was one that went back in the direction of La Botterie and did not return. For their part, enemy patrols became more and more aggressive and examination of their dead showed that they belonged to 9th SS Panzer Division. By late morning, enemy tanks and infantry had re-occupied Burcy thus cutting off the 11th Armoured Division forces holding Pavée.

Just after noon, a veritable tornado of shells and *nebelwerfer* bombs swept over the Monmouths and the tanks of the Fife and Forfar. The attack presaged by this intense 'stonk' materialized at 1600 hours. German tanks and infantry advanced behind the inexorable, never-ending barrage. The Divisional Artillery, installed back at Le Desert, immediately came to the rescue. However, under such strong pressure from the enemy, the Fife and Forfar tanks, which had been holding positions in front of the infantry, were withdrawn to avoid being overwhelmed by the assault waves. While retreating they continued to fire, inflicting very heavy losses on the attackers. When they reached the crest of the ridge held by the Monmouths they stood their ground; to have retreated any further would have meant abandoning the infantry to certain massacre.

THE INFERNO

The fighting raged for 20 minutes. The German infantry advanced in short rushes. Hiding behind newly-bound sheaves of wheat, they succeeded in infiltrating the positions of 'C' and 'D' Companies in the fields in front of the Taflet farm. Some of the SS even got as far as the farm house where Battalion Headquarters was. They were despatched with cold steel. At first, some positions were lost but then the situation was restored as the defenders fought back valiantly and inflicted heavy losses on the enemy. At 1700 hours, the SS, who had had no more success than at Bas-Perrier, abandoned the attack.

For their part, the Fife and Forfar and the Monmouths had also suffered heavy losses and many transport vehicles scattered round the Taflet farm were on fire. The silence that fell at the end of the attack was broken by the sound of cartridges and grenades exploding in the heat and, from time to time, by the deafening roar when a shell or a mine went up. Columns of smoke rose above the burning trucks.

Although the attack had been repulsed the Welshmen were in a sorry state. They had been under constant attack for a week. Many of the platoons had been reduced to less than half strength. They had had to march and fight all day without rest and then mount guards at night and remain in a constant state of alert. In addition, they had to patrol ceaselessly and fight all the time to keep their supply line open because the Germans repeatedly returned to Burcy to harass them and to cut their vital link to the rear. Tension and fatigue began to take their toll as, more and more, the men realized what a perilous position they were in. There they were, at the very tip of a deep salient and neither the Americans on their right nor the Guards Armoured Division on their left could do anything to help them.

THE GERMANS GET READY

On 6 August the Germans were on the eve of launching a massive counter-attack against the Americans between Vire and Mortain. They had finally taken the decision to withdraw some troops from the Pas-de-Calais and send them to the Caen sector. This allowed them to pull out their armour and re-assemble it into a strong force to the south of Vire. Their plan was to smash through and capture a key hill on the outskirts of Avranches and thus cut the American 3rd Army off from its supply base. This was the first time since the Invasion that the enemy had been able to assemble such a formidable mass of tanks. (The only other time he was able to do the same thing was later in December for the Battle of the Bulge in the Ardennes). This armoured group consisted of 1st and 2nd SS and 2nd and 116th Panzer Divisions, both reinforced with additional infantry, and 17th Panzer Division with its complement of infantry. The importance attached by the enemy to the success of this operation is shown by the fact that even the bombers that were normally used to lay mines in the Channel each night along the length of the invasion beaches were diverted to support this armoured ground offensive.

While this attack against the Americans was being prepared other units of 7th German Army vigorously resisted 2nd British Army in its push towards Vire, Estry and Mont Pincon. 11th Armoured Division had thrust a deep salient into the German defences. It had cut the roads leading from Vire to Villers-Bocage and Estry and the Vire — Vassy highway was under its control. For several days, 9th SS Panzer had ceaselessly tried to wipe out 11th Armoured's salient on the ridge south of Burcy and Presles but without success.

10TH SS PANZER ATTACKS

On 6 August another SS Panzer Division, the 10th, was brought round to protect the right flank of the Mortain counter-attack and it resumed the attacks on the ridge at Bas-Perrier and Pavée. This was part of the overall effort made by the other Panzer Divisions to maintain, at all costs, the defensive line Mont Pincon — Estry — Vire.

On that same day, 6 August, only two of the four squadrons of the 23rd Hussars remained at Bas-Perrier to give support to the 2nd Warwicks of 3rd British Division. The previous night had been calm but at noon everyone was brought up with a jerk at the unmistakable sound of an 88mm shell. Some Tiger tanks had escaped the surveillance of the patrols and, taking advantage of the night and early-morning mist, had managed to sneak into the woods on the very top of Bas-Perrier. Some newly-arrived tanks and trucks of the Hussars were destroyed by German infantry who also managed to occupy the farm buildings on M. Bertrand's farm while, at the same time, the Warwicks occupied the farm house. After a brief pause the German attack resumed at about 1600 hours. A very heavy concentration of *nebelwerfer* bombs poured down on Battalion Headquarters of the Warwicks causing many casualties and completely disorganizing it just when firm leadership was most needed to deal with the next assault wave. This time several Tigers took part. The Divisional artillery broke up the attack with a most-welcome rain of shells. German guns answered the British, shell for shell. The tanks of the Hussars spat anti-personnel shells into the tree tops above the enemy, trying to stop the advance of the SS who had already forced Headquarter Company of the Warwicks to withdraw and who now came dangerously close to overwhelming 'C' Squadron. Soon, many of the recently-arrived tanks of the Hussars were hit.

THE SITUATION GETS WORSE...

In the village itself, an entire company of the Warwicks was surrounded and heavily bombarded. Only one of the four tanks sent to their aid, the one commanded by Sergeant Smith, reached them and when he arrived there he found himself face to face with a Panther! Less than 30 yards apart, the two monsters played cat and mouse with one another around a house. Neither dared to make the first move in case it put itself at the mercy of the other. Finally, under cover of a barrage of shells and mortar bombs, the Panther withdrew. As he no longer had anyone to fight, the gallant Sergeant did the same thing. On the way back he rescued the crew of a disabled tank that had been 'captured' by the SS but which had refused an invitation to surrender. Amid a hail of bullets the tank was taken in tow and dragged back to safety.

...THEN GETS BETTER

The battle raged with undiminished fury all afternoon. Despite the efforts of the Hussars and the Warwicks and the artillery, whose gun barrels glowed red hot, the enemy ended the day by infiltrating on the left flank and, in the evening, even succeeded in reaching the top of the hill above Bas-Perrier where they took on the Hussar tanks with *panzerfausts*. Luckily, some of the tanks, better camouflaged and better placed to deal with the intruders, were able to stabilize the situation. The intruders were discouraged and the Warwicks took heart. When night fell, the Warwicks and the Hussars formed a 'box' in readiness for a night attack but the assailants withdrew and the positions lost during the day were re-occupied before dawn.

RELIEF FOR THE MONMOUTHS

At last, on 6 August, 10th SS Panzer Division put in an attack in the Pavée—Sourdevalle sector, trying to eliminate the 'festering abscess' of the 3rd Monmouths and the Fife and Forfar Yeomanry. The night had been comparatively calm after the battle waged by 9th SS Panzer Division the previous day but at first light the German artillery started a methodical 'stonk' of all the British positions, one after the other. However, some good news did arrive that morning. The Americans were getting close to Vire and the Guards Armoured Division had fought their way up to Estry and were preparing to attack it. In addition, the 1st Norfolks of 3rd British Infantry Division were on their way to relieve the Monmouths in the afternoon.

YET ANOTHER ATTACK BY THE SS

After having had a very rough time coming through Burcy, the 1st Norfolks started to take over the positions of the 3rd Monmouths at about 1700 hours in preparation for the relief. The enemy must have seen this activity because he resumed the bombardment of this sector with even greater ferocity. It was clear to the C.O.'s of the two Battalions that a new attack was imminent. Orders were issued that the troops who had been relieved had to return to their old positions and Lt.Colonel Orr of the Monmouths took overall command of this mixed force, now called the NorMons. At 1745 hours, the two companies deployed on each side of the road that runs up the ridge from the Taflet farm watched the advance of a large force of German infantry supported by Tiger tanks. Their main effort was directed along the path that separated the two companies. Their advance was stopped, thanks to an energetic counter-attack launched by troops held in reserve. The enemy next shifted his efforts to the west. At 1930 hours the situation was critical and communications with Battalion Headquarters were cut.

THE DESPAIR—AND JOY—OF THE GUNNERS

Every available gun was called on to stop the enemy advance on the right. Even the American artillery took part. But the gunners of 151st (Ayrshire) Field Regiment, who had been attached to the Division ever since it arrived in this sector, had a moment of despair. They were running out of ammunition! By 9 o'clock in the evening they only had a few rounds left. The situation was desperate because there was no other artillery unit nearby that could give support. Just then a miracle occured. A convoy of 30 ammunition trucks came chugging up the hill towards them, having somehow got through Burcy. All was saved! The guns kept firing in support of the defenders of Pavée and Sourdevalle.

HAND-TO-HAND FIGHTING

In spite of this the enemy pressure did not slacken. His troops came on again and again and came to within less than 200 yards of Battalion Headquarters. Hand-to-hand fighting took place along the hedges surrounding the Taflet farm. While the tanks of the two adversaries waged a fight to the death, the enemy artillery continued to shell the once-lovely apple orchards that now sheltered both the trucks that had brought the Norfolks up and those that were waiting to take the Monmouths away. The trucks and the buildings soon went up in flames and the air was choked with suffocating fumes. It was only the approach of darkness that persuaded the fanatical SS that their efforts were useless and slowly, little by little they began to withdraw from the fight. As the German infantry faded away, counter-attacks won back the ground lost in the afternoon and three newly-arrived German tanks were destroyed. The shelling from their artillery slackened and finally stopped. When night fell the battle was over.

THE HIGH PRICE OF 'GOOD LUCK'

In retrospect, although one can say that it was a stroke of bad luck that the SS attack came in at just the moment when the Monmouths were being relieved by the Norfolks for, undoubtedly, there was some confusion while the handing-over was taking place, yet it was good luck that there were two battalions in place at the time because a single battalion could never have withstood the fury of 10th SS Panzer Division in attack. But the price was high. Of approximately 550 men who took part in this particular fight, 160 were killed and wounded. On the other hand, despite the fact that some positions were overrun, not a single man was taken prisoner.

About 80 British soldiers, Norfolks and Monmouths, who were killed in and around the village of Pavée from 5 to 12 August, were temporarily buried in a field opposite the Taflet farm house. The bodies have long since been removed but to this day the field is known as *Le Champ des Morts,* The Field of the Dead.

THE SS ARE EXHAUSTED

On 7 August, 10th SS Panzer Division was too exhausted to renew the attacks it had launched the previous day on the entire front held by 11th Armoured Division. Nevertheless, it was ordered, once more, to seize, at any cost, the heights occupied for the past week by the redoubtable troops wearing the emblem of the Bull. A few Tigers made a strong attempt to sally out from the woods around Chênedollé but the artillery, and particularly the fighter-bombers were watching and either destroyed them or chased them back into the woods.*

The lull in the fighting allowed the relief of 11th Armoured Division by 3rd British Infantry Division who were well versed in the kind of fighting that would now take place along this part of the front. The Guards Armoured Division relieved the 4th King's Shropshire Light Infantry and the 3rd Royal Tank Regiment who, together with the 2nd Northamptonshire Yeomanry, their ranks seriously depleted since their adventures at La Bistière, still held Grands-Bonfaits.

*General Roberts comments: *If it had not been for the Corps artillery I doubt if we would have held the Germans. The Divisional artillery 'keep the heads of the enemy down' but don't do much killing but the medium artillery really do some killing. From personal experience I knew this only too well and so made quite sure that I kept in direct touch with CCRA (Commander Corps Royal Artillery) and when things got really bad I could always get him to direct all his guns (three Regiments of 4.5 or 5.5 guns) on to our front. I am told that in the Germans' final attack, when every Corps gun was brought on to them, the fields in front of us were strewn with German dead. We certainly owed a lot to 'Hammer' Mathew (Brigadier A. G. Mathew), the CCRA (Commander Corps Royal Artillery) and, of course, to our own Divisional CRA (Commander Royal Artillery), Brigadier B. J. Fowler.*

CHAPTER 6

REMEMBRANCE OF THINGS PAST

OLD SOLDIERS RETURN

The survivors of 11th Armoured Division, and the survivors of the units which relieved them, vividly remember the battles that raged around the villages of Burcy, Presles and Chênedollé and in the hamlets of Pavée, Bas-Perrier, Le Moulin and Grands-Bonfaits. Major Davey who, in 1944, was the Adjutant of the 3rd Monmouthshire Regiment, returned in 1971 accompanied by Major Ruffell who had also been at the Monmouths' headquarters in 1944. Without any hesitation and despite the many changes in the appearance of the countryside after so many years, Major Davey found the exact place under an apple tree on M. Robert Taflet's farm where the slit trench had been dug that sheltered him and his Colonel's Command Post. M. Taflet had been told that Major Davey was coming and was there to meet him. He and the Major exchanged many reminiscences and re-lived the terrible time they had both been through in the early days of August 1944. Both men clearly remembered where the vehicles and ambulances and lorries had been parked, where the destroyed buildings had been situated and where the dead had been buried.

Having first searched the farm for mementoes, Major Davey followed the road up to the crest of the hill to the place where, at a sharp bend, a narrow path, bordered with tall trees, branches off. He recalls: *It was right here that I was nearly killed. I*

*had left the Command Post in order to guide some officers of the
Norfolks up to where the front line positions were. They had just
arrived to relieve us. We came up to the position without showing
ourselves. However, the crew of a Tiger hidden in an orchard on
the other side of the road must have seen the glint of the anten-
nae of my portable wireless set. The Tiger, not being able to fire
directly at us through the trees, signalled where we were to the*
nebelwerfer *battery back in the Viessoix area. A few seconds later
the characteristic sound of 'Moaning Minnies' announced the arrival of the first salvo of mortar bombs. They landed a few yards
in front of the sunken lane that sheltered us. I was covered with
dirt. Pieces of rock flew all around us. A second volley arrived and
this time it exploded in the tops of the large trees right above our
heads. The shrapnel crackled as it buried itself in the trunks of
the trees and in the soil of the lane. I disappeared under a heap
of shattered branches and torn leaves. I waited for the third volley
but happily it never arrived.*

With typical under-statement, Major Ruffell grimly remembered
that coming down the hill from Forgues into Burcy was like
descending into Hades but he took satisfaction in remembering
that he had, nevertheless, managed to bring his munitions convoy through the storm of shellfire and deliver its precious cargo,
intact, to the defenders at Pavée.

A CIVILIAN REMEMBERS

On the morning of 2 August M. Bertrand fled from his farm in
the village of Perrier near Chênedollé.

*Someone said that the English were close by but I did not ex-
pect to see them that very day. For the past two or three days the
noise of gun-fire had been growing louder and louder and had
been coming nearer and nearer but the movements of the German troops in our area were much the same as usual and did not
indicate to us that the front was very near. So, when I heard the
sound of a motor car behind me and turned round, I immediately
realized that it was not a German vehicle and that the men on board*

wore the typical 'Tommy' helmets. It was a jeep full of English soldiers. They did not give me a chance to show my delight but asked me, "Are any Germans here?" I replied that I had not seen any that morning but that the previous day there were some at Chênedollé. As if to confirm my words, just then a German motorcyclist came into view. Noticing our group, he slowed down, hesitated and, seeing all the weapons pointing at him, got off his motorcycle and hurriedly surrendered. I helped the English search and disarm their prisoner who, after being briefly questioned, was quickly escorted to the rear. The information they gleaned did not alarm the English soldiers and they kept going in the direction of the village. I then returned to my farm where I told my family the good news. Delighted to have been liberated, we spent the rest of the day offering glasses of the wine we had hidden all through the Occupation to every British soldier who came by.

According to the information given to us by some of the soldiers who spoke a little French, their orders were to establish a roadblock on the Vire—Vassy highway and, if possible, maintain it. Gradually, as the day wore on, the battle seemed to grow louder. We had the distinct impression that tank battles were taking place in two directions, towards the village of Chênedollé and towards the village of Le Moulin situated about midway between Presles and Pierres. We were left in no doubt that the Germans had regained control. Their artillery began to alarm us. Towards the end of the evening, the tanks that we had seen heading southwards came back along the road in the opposite direction and got ready to pass the night under the protection of the infantry who accompanied them.

We spent the night in the trench we had dug just behind the farmhouse. We found it difficult to get to sleep after all the excitement of that day. The discomfort kept us awake and we worried about what would happen the next day if the front was established in our area.

When day came we had to face reality; we were right in the front line! All that day the battle raged in every direction and we felt we were encircled. But what could we do to get away from there? The English seemed more and more unwilling to allow us to go back and forth between the lines. Furthermore, the shells that fell

111

all around us hardly gave us a chance to leave our shelter. Some of the farm buildings were hit and English trucks and tanks lay wrecked everywhere. Disregarding the machine-gun fire, stretcher-bearers were constantly busy evacuating the wounded to the First Aid Post that had been established in one of the sunken lanes.

The second night was even more noisy than the first. There was a terrible barrage in the direction of Presles and all night long we heard the rattle of automatic weapons, like hail stones. The following morning, seeing that ambulances were carrying the wounded back towards the valley, we thought that the road must now be open. We decided to take advantage of the first opportunity that presented itself to distance ourselves from the fighting in which we had been trapped for the past two days. The livestock was also suffering. Our beautiful mare had been hit by shrapnel and had deep wounds on her neck and under the shoulder. So we decided to make for the rear on foot.

Carrying a small pack in which we put our most precious possessions, even though they were not necessarily the most useful, and pushing my 1-year-old daughter's pram, our little group, accompanied by our dog, first headed for Presles. Then, making our way along the valley, we arrived at Burcy and started to climb in the direction of Forgues. When we arrived there we could go no further because German troops, supported by tanks, were counterattacking from Estry in the direction of Vire. Since it had become impossible to leave the battle-zone we decided to return to Burcy where, we thought, the valley would give us the best shelter. But we soon had to change our minds because the situation there was no better than anywhere else. Some Germans had been taken prisoner in the morning and, while waiting to be sent to the rear, were under guard in the village. A little later the enemy returned. They freed their men and took as their prisoners those who just before had been their gaolers. Someone told us that the English had established themselves in strength in the hamlet of Pavée and that the civilians from there would be evacuated by trucks that same day. We arrived at Robert Taflet's farm just as the last truckload of civilians left! Those who were unable to find a place on the trucks or who did not want to leave made room for us in a

*farm building. We thought we would be able to shelter there un-
til the end of the fighting and made ourselves as comfortable as
possible. Until then, the hamlet did not seem to have suffered
much. The English were there in strength with tanks, artillery and
infantry. For the moment we felt safe. The night was calm.*

*The next morning, 5 August, it seemed to us that the activity
grew from hour to hour. Small patrol groups left and returned.
Knowing that I spoke and understood German, an Englishman
named Gilbert asked me to follow him in order to interrogate some
prisoners. I thus had the satisfaction of transmitting information
about the enemy positions to the English. I told them that German artillery was installed on the top of the hill at Viessoix while*
nebelwerfers *were situated in the village of Templeries. I don't know
if this information was any use to them but towards noon a terrible artillery barrage started that must have gone on for several
hours. Shells and mortar bombs fell all around us. A munitions
truck, hit by a shell, started to explode. A torrent of English shells
swept over our heads before crashing down just a few hundred
metres in front of us. When the building that sheltered us was hit
our situation became critical. Suddenly we smelt smoke mingled
with the smell of dust and gunpowder. The roof was on fire! If
we did not want to be roasted alive we would have to move again.
I thought for a moment or two and then decided that our best
chance of survival was to return to Beaumonts. There we could
use the cellar as a shelter and, if we had to die, it was better to
die at home. Holding my youngest daughter in my arms and leaving the now useless pram in charge of our dog (he would not let
anyone come near it and was eventually killed at his post), we made
off across the fields. We arrived at the farm in the evening and
lost no time in taking shelter. The night was terrible. Shells fell
all around us. The frightening and insufferable screaming of the*
nebelwerfers *was added to the noise of the exploding and whistling bombs. The flashes of the explosions lit us up as if it was broad
daylight and through the opening framed by the entrance to the
cellar we could see the bent silhouettes of soldiers rushing to and
fro, throwing themselves flat on the ground and getting up again
in synchronization with the arrival of the shells. Looking back on*

it, I remember the scene as a stage-setting backdropped by the line of the Perrier heights and lit up by an enormous and hellish fireworks display.

Because of the artificial brightness we did not realize that day had arrived. A fog, mixed with dust and smoke and smelling of gunpowder, filled the valley and covered the high ground in an immense shroud. Visibility gradually improved as the gloom dissipated. The guns were silent. We were finally able to leave the shelter that had almost become our tomb. Several cubic metres of earth, thrown up by the shells, had covered the roof of our shelter. The men who had fought all night rested. The wounded were evacuated and the dead buried. Reinforcements took their places in the trenches dug in the vegetable garden and the only way they could get in and out of the farmhouse was by a window in the rear. This was because the Germans occupied the buildings opposite the farmhouse and were in positions behind the hedge surrounding the orchard.

We knew that the quiet was only because of the poor visibility so we had very little desire to stay there much longer. When we were offered an escort to take us to the rear we did not hesitate to accept. As we went along the road we passed a slit trench in which a number of German prisoners slept under the eye of a sentry. Not one of them stirred but, just the same, our escort urged us to hurry along, nervously cocking his rifle and glancing back every few paces.

We exchanged escorts a little further on. Then they made us climb on top of a tank and we bumped across the fields, shaken as if we were in a carriage pulled by bolting horses, until we finally arrived at a place that seemed to us like paradise compared to the hell we had just left.

We were so badly thrown around during the tank ride that our belongings, tied up by my wife in a smock knotted at the four corners, were scattered all along the road. And so we lost the few things we had been able to save! The following Sunday we attended Mass at La Graverie, still covered with dust and in our dirty, torn clothes. The service was conducted by an English priest and many soldiers attended it. At the end of the service, having learnt that I lived not far from Chênedollé, the priest sought me out and put the holy vessels into my safe keeping. I don't know how he had saved them from being vandalized. "Take them back to your church when all this is over," *he said and added,* "I hope it will still be standing."

After the middle of August the gunfire seemed to fade in the distance and we were allowed to return to the house. When we arrived at Bel-Air we were appalled at the sight that greeted us on the slope of the hill opposite us. All the way from the village of Presles the hillside seemed to have been smashed down, ravaged and ripped up. The hedges no longer existed and the trees, stripped bare of their leaves, held their denuded branches up to the sky. Here and there the fire-blackened carcasses of tanks lay around together with wrecked trucks; all kinds of equipment lay scattered all over the place. One could now see the burnt remains of many farms that normally were hidden from view behind the trees and copses. Stunned, we gazed at a countryside that had been turned into a battlefield.

As we walked down the road towards the village of Presles prior to climbing up Perrier Ridge we knew that we would find nothing standing at our farm. Small mounds of freshly-heaped earth, some alone, some in groups, showed us where men had been buried. They lay in road-side ditches, at the bottom of hedges, in fields and at the entrance of a sunken lane. As we approached our farm the stench of decomposing bodies of dead cattle was insufferable. Definitely, our first task was going to be to get rid of them. Our farm was in ruins. All the buildings were burnt down but at least we were safe and sound. Now we had to face life or what was left of it as best we could. I went across the fields to the village of Sourdevalle and returned back to Perrier. I saw only desolation and ruins—not a living soul. The bodies of dead animals littered the place together with the bodies of dead Germans whom their comrades had not been able to bury before leaving. Some of them had been lying in the open for nearly a fortnight and were so decomposed that they could not be properly buried. Unfortunately, many of those bodies had to be dealt with in the same way that we dealt with the remains of the dead animals. It is not surprising that many a German family which returned after the war to look for the body of a brother or a father, knowing for certain that he had fought his last battle in this area, was unable to find a trace of him.

As far as the harvest was concerned, it was a dead loss. The wheat and the second cut of hay were so thoroughly burnt and flattened that even when one stood in the middle of a field it was impossible to say what had been planted there. It was only when one drew near to the hedges that one might be able to see, here some wheat, there some hay and so on. That year we did not even harvest potatoes. They had either been dug up or cut up by the shells or mashed into the ground by the caterpillar tracks of the tanks. And the apples? Just look at the poor trees!

While crossing the last meadow that separated me from the farm, I came across the body of my poor mare. She must have lived quite a long time despite her wounds because she was not in a state of advanced decomposition compared to the other animals ...

Ammunition lay all over the place but, thank God, there were no mines. Some places in the area were literally stuffed with them. La Jarrière and a dozen hectacres around it remained a waste land for a long time because of the danger from mines. Despite warnings and, sometimes, because of carelessness, many accidents happened. M. Fleury was seriously wounded in this way and when Madame Lecomte and Madame Motard rushed to help him one was killed and the other was wounded. The four men carrying the victims on a ladder improvised as a stretcher also, in their turn, trod on a mine that, fortunately, only smoked without going off and claiming yet another victim. Another inhabitant of the village who returned to his home with his children escaped death by a miracle. An anti-personnel 'S-mine' jumped out of the ground and hit him on his belt. His tobacco pouch saved his life because it deadened the impact and probably interferred with the action of the fuse.

KEN THORPE'S MEMORIES

This account is taken from a letter to the author from ex-private
Ken Thorpe, formerly of the 2nd Battalion The Royal Warwickshire Regiment. The 2nd Warwicks were in 185 Brigade of
3rd British Infantry Division. For the Battle of Perrier Ridge, the
three battalions of 185 Brigade were placed under command of
159 Brigade of 11th Armoured Division. In 1970 Mr. Thorpe
returned to visit the battlefield situated exactly on M. Bertrand's
farm. His letter gives a simple account of what one infantryman
went through.

*There are experiences in life, some good, some bad, that memory
imprints ineffacably in a man's mind ...*

*Although none of my comrades nor myself had anything to do
with Satan's Empire, on 6 and 7 August we found ourselves right
in the middle of Hell! After getting through all the fighting in Normandy up to that time I came within inches of death at Bas-Perrier.
More or less by a miracle, I am, as far as I know, the only survivor
of a platoon which, on 7 August 1944, was ordered to attack and
occupy the house situated on the left side of the road that leads
to the top of the hill. The others? They were all killed along the
hedge that separates the fields from the house and its garden or
while trying to reach the house.*

*The Bertrand farm and the fields that surround it were in the
middle of a furious battle that has been recorded and registered
in history as the Battle of Bas-Perrier Hill. There were some other
farms near the Bertrand farm but they were less difficult to capture and less costly in lives. The two houses at the top of the hill,
one on each side of the road, had been turned into strongpoints
by the Germans of 10th SS Panzer Division. They did not have
many soldiers but they did have a Tiger tank, murderous beast
that it was, and several machine-gun nests in and around the two
houses. The camouflaged Tiger was on the road just over the hill
and from there was able to watch all our movements. Our mortars and tanks were on the Presles side of the hill.*

*I was an infantryman in the 2nd Battalion The Royal War-
wickshire Regiment. We had come from the Caen area in order*

to relieve troops of 11th Armoured Division. We had had a week's well-earned rest after having landed at dawn on D-Day at Lion sur Mer and being in action without respite for 6 weeks after that.

Our first objective under 11th Armoured Division was a house in the village of Presles. We had attacked this house at midnight on 5 August and found there, not Germans as expected, but two old people. Before the attack we were told that the village was held by the Germans and that we had to capture it at any cost in order to re-establish contact with the English troops cut off on the heights of Bas-Perrier. So that night's work ended well and everyone, including the old couple, was vastly relieved.

We dug slit trenches around the house and settled down for the rest of the night. Following the usual procedure, each of us took his turn on guard; we wondered what the next day would bring.

There are very few dull moments at the front. To our disgust, we had to get back on the road at high noon and climb up towards the summit from where we were just able to see the Bertrand farm, faintly, below the crest. High up on the road, on the right-hand side, there is a little field almost hidden by the surrounding trees. I seem to remember that there were more trees there in 1944 and that the hedges were thicker. We placed four of our mortars in the middle of this field. Tanks, some still active, others abandoned, lined the hedges. We were ordered to take up positions along the hedge in the trenches dug by the men we had just relieved. Perhaps you will find it puzzling that other British troops were already entrenched here while the preceding night our unit was sheltering in Presles. Well, this was typical of the Normandy fighting because of the orchards and farms and the general lay-out of the land. The 'front' of an army does not really exist except on paper. It is often hard to find, it is not a straight line and it is ill-defined. One thing the army does not supply you with is an extra pair of eyes; you just have to watch out for yourself.

We were mercilessly bombarded in this small field. I believe it was the worst bombardment we were ever subjected to by the notorious 'Moaning Minnies', so called because each projectile whistled and screamed while it was on its way to you. They came over in groups of six and did great damage, both physically and *mentally.*

It was there that, again, I had a lucky escape. I was eating an apple when it was shot out of my hand by a bullet or by a piece of shrapnel. I must confess, I had stolen that apple the previous night from an orchard in Presles but even so I was not happy to have it snatched away from me in that way. I had no desire to emulate William Tell! In any case, the apple was sour!

The next and last phase of the battle then started. We were ordered to occupy the Bertrand farmhouse and the two buildings at the top of the road. As far as the house was concerned, this was easy because it was empty. On the other hand, the farm buildings posed another problem. They were defended by some young Germans, very fanatical, as I later discovered. With regard to the tank's crew, they seemed much younger than I and I was only 19 years old. First of all, we tried to attack on the right where there were some stables but we could only get as far as the orchard. We lost some men there. A Tiger's 88mm gun was very accurate but our mortar shells rained down on the enemy with incredible accuracy. And so, while the officers decided on the next move, we waited and stood to for several hours. Finally, it was decided to wait until the next day and they ordered us to dig in. Fortunately, in most of Normandy the ground was not too hard and we were always eager to burrow down into it.

Our section received orders to take up positions near the Bertrand farmhouse and garden. I remember that, running along the path that led to M. Bertrand's sister's house that, at that time was sheltered by a very high hedge, I saw a blue mug, an army tin mug, attached to the belt of one of our sergeants. "The poor fellow will not have any further use for it", I said to myself; he was lying there, waiting to be buried. He was probably one of the last that the courageous and over-worked stretcher-bearers had brought in. Those men could not take shelter in trenches or hide behind trees. On the contrary, they had to work out in the open, hoping that the enemy would respect the Rules of War and let them go about their errands of mercy. I had lost my mug in Lébisey Wood, near Caen, and ever since then I had had to borrow one or drink out of whatever I could find. This time I was determined not to lose *it. I have it still. It was very useful to me in the German prisoner-of-war camps.*

When we reached the garden we dug a new slit trench and spent the night in it. I shared my trench with another fellow who was 6 or 7 years older than I. His name was George Amos. We had been in the same section for about three weeks and had got to know each other quite well. We often had long discussions and arguments. I was not always able to understand him. There seemed to be some gaps in his life's story. He was a bit vague about it and did not want to give many details. However, he was a very brave soldier though perhaps a little too reckless.

I did not know many of the other fellows in my section; for the most part they were reinforcements from England without much combat experience. Many were young like me and a few hardly knew how to handle a rifle. It was obvious that they were poorly trained for the front line and especially for the infantry. Some of them came from the Regiment, others from the Artillery, from the Engineers and one of them had even been a chef in the Army Catering Corps! In order to pass the time, we made some chocolate and ate what we were able to heat up in the trench. We surreptitiously smoked cigarettes cupped in our hands and argued amongst ourselves as to who would stand guard first: one hour on, two hours off. The cook said he did not know how to use a Bren gun. "You'd better learn", I said to him, "it's now or never." I made this remark without thinking; we were all very edgy from lack of sleep. If I had known what was going to happen the next day I would have volunteered to stand guard all night myself because this was the last chance for these poor fellows to enjoy a decent night's sleep.

The night was short and dawn came quickly. Like the previous day and all the days before, we expected a lovely, hot day. That Monday was August Bank Holiday, at least for those who could enjoy it. We, however, didn't have much choice. We breakfasted on the rations we had. I remember that there was a tap near the house. I went to see if there was any water in it and after laying out my belongings on the rim of the trench, a box of cocoa, cooking utensils and such like, I washed myself.

It was rarely the practice of Headquarters to inform us of its intentions. Plans to seize the two buildings on the crest of the hill were undoubtedly made during the night and the artillery, as usual, gave us its invaluable support. At 1015 hours the order was given to be ready to move at half an hour's notice. This left us with little time to think about what was in store for us. It was better this way because at moments like this one feels like a condemned man. I quickly put a few essential possessions in my pockets, cigarettes and matches and also my tooth-brush, my razor and blades. Why these last three? I cannot say but later they proved to be very useful to me. They told us not to load ourselves down but to leave as much as we could in the slit trenches; we would be able to pick them up again once our objective had been taken. (If anyone found a box of cocoa and some cooking utensils they are welcome to them with my compliments!).

Everyone assumes that he will be all right in an assault. After all, you must rely on God to protect you because if you think that at any moment you are going to be killed you would never leave the security of your slit trench. How does one maintain this feeling of invulnerability? Is it man's instinctive nature that makes him believe that death does not exist for him even while he sleeps next to it? What force compels a man to get out of his trench, to leave its security and offer himself to his executioneers? Is it the discipline of duty or is it simply the dread of being a coward? I have often tried to understand this but I have never arrived at a conclusion. We all had fear, some more, some less, but we all went.

At exactly 1030 hours on this beautiful summer day our guns opened fire and the machine-guns beat down in the field directly in front of us. A few shells fell a bit short and we had to duck our heads. Some were smoke shells, sent over to hide our advance. They were offering us Monty's speciality, the artillery barrage, as a protective shield; in a way it was like the last cigarette you offer a condemned man. We had to follow close behind this monstrous rolling-pin that crushed everything in front of us as each salvo crashed down. If you stayed too far behind you lost its benefit. We all hoped that the German defenders would keep their heads down under this avalanche but, at the same time, some of us also knew from experience that there would be fanatics among them who knew what was happening behind the barrage and would shoot and shoot into the curtain of smoke. Their artillery also joined the action. Thus, in the usual way, we ran and walked, threw ourselves down on our stomachs, were knocked down and tumbled over, stumbled, swore and hoped that eventually we would reach our objective at the top of the rise. George Amos and I were covering the extreme right side of the field with our rifles. None of our comrades reached the crest but George and I did. The barrage stopped and we were alone.

We were lucky to find a German trench at the base of a hedge sheltered by a large tree. The other survivors of my section were strung out in a line across the open slope of the hill. Now the German defenders raised their heads. They left the building and counter-attacked with machine-guns. Every minute they swept the slope with their fire and we stayed put, waiting for further orders. There is an old English proverb, 'Curiosity killed the cat', but I'm afraid my comrades did not pay attention to it. We all wanted to see what the other side was preparing for us. George and I were able to peep out with some safety because we were sheltered by the trunk of the tree but any of our comrades who wanted to do the same raised their heads for the last time. One by one, they were shot like rabbits in a pen.

How long did we stay there, waiting for orders that never came? Half an hour? Three-quarters of an hour? Apparently no one else was left alive in our section except George and I so we discussed what we should do. Were we safe in our slit trench? Would they send reinforcements? Could we hold the Germans off? Our machine-gun was out of order and between us we only had four grenades. Neither of us was looking to win any medals, I less than George. I suggested that we get out of there as quickly as possible and get back down the field. This was not entirely to George's liking or, if it was, he hesitated for a moment before making up his mind. For those few moments of indecision he paid the supreme price. As for me, whether it was his hesitation or my own reaction I don't know but, in any case, my life was spared once again. For nearly every man there is a special moment or a period or an action that determines the course of the rest of his life. Although

Having forded the river, a tank commander studies his map before going through Vassy. (cf p. 135)

A soldier helps to keep the traffic moving at an important crossroads not far from the Main Headquarters of 11th Armoured Division.

French civilians present their identification papers at Montsecret. (cf p.140 et seq.)

I.W.M. #B9323

British and American M.P.'s meet in Tinchebray. 3rd Reconnaissance Regiment of 3rd British Infantry Division just beat the American 102nd Mechanised Cavalry to the liberation of the town. (cf p.141)

I.W.M. #B9295

Tinchebray had been evacuated and the city was deserted when the Allies arrived. (cf p.142)

I.W.M. #B9296

The British are welcomed to La Fontaine by civilians and members of the *Résistance*.
(cf p.282)

I.W.M. #B9286

The photographer poses a group of happy-go-lucky *Résistance* fighters as they go off on a hunt for German stragglers!

Be careful of the women of La Lande-Patry! They carry rifles — well, at least for the photographer!

Weary but happy refugees passing through Tinchebray on the way back to their homes. They use various means of transportation from overloaded perambulators to farm carts.

A Sherman tank raises a cloud of dust as it passes the church of Saint-Martin in Condé-sur-Noireau on the road from Flers. (cf p.149)

Désaunay, Condé-sur-Noireau

Infantrymen carrying out a sweep of the Rue du Chêne near the Hotel du Cerf in Condé-sur-Noireau. (cf p.149)

Sappers of 50th British Divisional Engineers putting up a Bailey bridge at Pont-Erembourg. (cf p.201)

I.W.M. #B9343

The remains of the railway bridge at Pont-Erembourg on the road from Condé-sur-Noireau to Saint-Denis-de-Méré.

Many of the inhabitants of Pont-Erembourg took refuge in a cave below the cliffs overhanging the village. Shown here are members of the Boisne family, well-known bakers in Pont-Erembourg.

I.W.M. #B9340

Madame Laignel between Captain Baden and Sergeant Martin of the 7th Somerset
Light Infantry. The two soldiers were making a reconnaissance of the factory
at Rocray when Madame Laignel insisted on having this photograph taken even
though the Germans were less than 100 metres away! (cf p.242 et seq.)

Collection of M. Albert Laignel

Sherman tanks in a sunken lane in the Bocage.

I.W.M. #B8588

Armoured cars of the Inns of Court in Gacé. (cf p.219 et seq.)

I.W.M. #B9644

All over the Bocage the Allies were given invaluable, detailed information by the locals. Here M. Duguey of Flers briefs the crew of a tank. (cf p.182 et seq.)

I.W.M. #B9297

I did not realize it at the time, that day in the field was the one on which I was the closest to leaving this world to rejoin my ancestors in heaven—or in hell! I have often thought about those last minutes and I have wondered and asked for the reason why I was spared to tell this story. I have never been able to find the reason except that a certain number of us must be allowed to survive!

So, I got out of the trench and ran down the hill as quickly as I could, making zig zags as we had been taught in training. When I got to the edge of the field, the familiar sound of an enemy machine-gun made me turn round. Standing on the slope, next to the tree, just below the trench, was a German soldier. He was very much on top of things while George Amos was dead, riddled with bullets. He probably only just saw the German in the last seconds of his life. Realizing that we were the only two with whom he had to contend or perhaps not even knowing that we were there, the German had leapt across the rows of beans and potatoes. He had crouched down close to the ground, taking his time to make sure of his prey. He probably heard me run and jumped up in order to fire at me from above. It was then that he was startled to find George at his feet, alone and defenceless. No doubt he was terrified so he lowered the automatic pointed at me and fired at my pal at point blank range. Perhaps the surprise at finding himself face to face with an enemy made him keep his finger on the trigger a little longer than he need have done but when he finally saw me and fired at me there was only one bullet left in the magazine; it found me and hit me in the leg. Instinctively, I threw myself flat on the ground and pretended to be dead. I had the impression that the bullet had passed through my leg and I wondered whether I was going to die from loss of blood. In falling, I had lost my helmet. I lay there, motionless, hardly daring to breath, not knowing what to do.

It was now about noon. It was very hot but I remained motionless. I knew that if they saw me move they would, without a doubt, fire at me again. But, it's a curious thing, I don't remember being afraid, not at all. I remember, very clearly, that I thought of my family and of all my friends in England. Although I don't believe in God I said a prayer for my mother. Then I thought

*of the possibility of our artillery resuming the bombardment of
the field when they realized that the attack had failed. Stretched
out in no-man's-land, without any cover at all, I felt like a condemned person waiting for the axman, or a mouse in the power
of a cat that is playing with it. Up to that time I had never been
alone but now I was alone and responsible for every decision I took.
There was no one to blame but myself.*

*A strange silence emanated from the other side of the road. Was
it possible that I was the only survivor or was there perhaps
someone else in a similar situation to mine? Below me was the orchard and after that there was the path bordered by hedges. Ah,
if only I could get there I would definitely be able to find a good
hiding place until nightfall. But night was far off; ten interminable
hours at least. I stayed put, forcing myself to make a decision,
examining my chances of survival, searching for the best way to
get away from there when, all of a sudden, German voices broke
the silence. They drew nearer and nearer. I heard the sounds of
their footsteps like the boots of a giant trampling the ground. The
noise was like thunder as they approached me across the meadow.
Having halted the attack, the enemy now wanted to make sure
that none of the attackers would trouble them again. Some of their
men, armed to the teeth and ready to shoot at the slightest movement, were inspecting the field. I had my face pressed to the ground
and could not see a thing around me but when the footsteps stopped I knew that some of the enemy were very near me, their fingers
on the trigger. They talked to one another, probably asking
themselves if I was still alive. As precautionary measure or, maybe,
simply out of curiosity, one of them turned me over with his foot.*

*There was no longer any point in pretending to be dead. I must
admit I was frightened by the sight of the small black hole at the
end of the rifle barrel knowing that it could spit out death and
at the long blade of the bayonet that could run me through and
through. Yes, certainly, I was scared because I did not know
whether they were going to finish me off or take me prisoner.
However, that only lasted for a short time. By changing my position my wounds were opened up and an expression of pain must
have replaced the expression of fear on my face. The Germans*

realized this and put their rifles away. I pointed to my legs; they helped me get up, assisted me across the field and led me into the building.

There I rejoined six of my comrades of whom one was a stretcher-bearer who had been taken prisoner on the other side of the road. Some minutes later they brought in Sergeant Fowler, our platoon sergeant. He was very seriously wounded. We did what we could for him but later I learnt that he died on the way to the hospital.

With a typical air of superiority and sneering with scorn and shrugging his shoulders, the SS Captain said to us, in English, "For you the war is over." I thought to myself, it's not the same for him because before the day is out he will undoubtedly have to face and repulse further attacks if he wants to hold on to his positions. However, I must tell the truth: fierce as our enemy was in combat, he was, contrary to popular reports, humane in the treatment of his prisoners.

Next an officer of one of the armoured regiments that had supported us during the attack was brought into the building. He had driven along the road in his jeep, not knowing exactly where the German positions were after the attack. Jeep and driver were machine-gunned, surrounded and taken prisoner.

We placed the stretcher carrying the sergeant on the jeep and, victors and vanquished together, pushed the vehicle in the direction of Chênedollé. We got to the top of the hill and there was no further need to push. As I had difficulty keeping up, I stopped walking. Suddenly, there was a short whistle and one of our shells fell on the road just in front of me, spun like a top and ricochetted viciously through the air. No one was hit and I realized that, once more, I had had a narrow escape from death.

Sad and dejected, we took the road to captivity ...

CHAPTER 7

BATTLES FOR
VASSY, MONTSECRET & TINCHEBRAY

THE POCKET TAKES SHAPE

After 7 and 8 August, most of the units of 11th Armoured Division were relieved and sent to the rear. However, they still stayed near the front in the role of a reserve force. Some of its regiments, like the Shropshires and the Herefordshires, had to go into action at Le Busq and at Bas-Perrier. The purpose of all these moves was to tidy things up and re-organize the positions of all the divisions that had arrived in the area at the height of the successful battles fought by General Roberts' men. The Guards Armoured Division, held up for a long time in its advance towards Montchauvet by German forces in positon on the heights of Saint-Pierre-Tarentaine and then on the heights of Drouet and Arclais, joined by 15th Scottish Division, attacked Estry. This attack dragged on until 13 August. In the meanwhile, 3rd British Infantry Division had taken over the positions won by 11th Armoured and had made contact with the Americans to the east of Vire.

The German plan was to counter-attack in the direction of Avranches and thus cut 3rd U.S. Army off from its supply base so they fiercely resisted the thrusts of 1st U.S. and 2nd British Armies in the direction of Vire. On 7 August, German armoured columns launched themselves from Mortain where the sector was held by the 4th, 9th and 30th American Infantry Divisions and the 2nd and 3rd American Armoured Divisions. These units fought valiantly and the Air Forces gave them great support. The Typhoons of 2nd Tactical Air Force, taking advantage of the good weather, dived on the enemy columns and, with their rockets, destroyed or damaged vast numbers of tanks and other vehicles. This effective cooperation of land and air forces ensured that the enemy attack was stopped in its tracks. In spite of this, the Germans persisted in their efforts to break through towards Avranches and the fighting continued for several days during which a number of new panzer divisions were thrown into the battle around Mortain.

By 12 August the enemy realized that he was not going to be able to attain his objectives and he started to make plans for a withdrawal. However, two days before, at a conference held at Bradley's headquarters, it was decided to seize the opportunity that the enemy's stubborness gave them and to encircle all his forces in that area. On 9 August, 15 Corps of 3rd U.S. Army had taken Le Mans and, without losing a minute, had swept on straight north behind the Germans who were fighting at Mortain. At the same time, 20 Corps, having penetrated beyond Châteaubriant, had reached the Loire and seized Angers on the 10th. On 11 August, driving up from Le Mans, 15 Corps was north of the Sées—Carrouges road. During the night of the 12th, 5th U.S. Armoured Division was in the suburbs of Argentan while Leclerc's 2nd Free French Armoured Division, having liberated its first French town, Alençon, reached Ecouché.

On 7 August 59th British Division had established a bridgehead over the Orne at Grimbosq, to the north of Thury-Harcourt, in order to give support to the Canadians pushing down south along the Caen—Falaise road. Villers-Bocage was finally taken after its complete destruction by aerial bombardment and 7th Armoured Division occupied Aunay-sur-Odon. 43rd British Infantry Division, which went into action in mid-July at the end of the bitter battle for Hill 112, had just chased the Germans from Mont Pincon.

The enemy's position was becoming desperate and his lines of communication and supply were more and more precarious. The time had come for 2nd British Army to launch a new attack so that it could take advantage of the near encirclement of the

German forces.

11TH ARMOURED TRANSFERRED TO XXX CORPS

The British Army's overall plan was, firstly, to advance to the south and the southeast from the line Caen — Villers-Bocage and along both sides of the Orne; secondly, to advance to the east with the forces situated between Vire, Estry and Mont Pincon; and thirdly, to renew the attack south of the line Caen — Troarn in the direction of Falaise. The second part of this plan was entrusted to the Army's VIII and XXX Corps on the right of the advance and to XII Corps on the left. Reading from west, the American sector, to east, the disposition of these units on 13 August was: VIII Corps with 3rd British Infantry Division to the east of Vire, Guards Armoured Division between Burcy, Viessoix, Chênedollé and Estry with Tinchebray as its objective; XXX Corps, with 11th Armoured Division as its spearhead followed by 50th and 43rd British Infantry Divisions, was to make for Flers and Condé as its immediate objectives, next destroy the encircled German forces in what was called the 'Falaise Pocket' and finally advance to the Seine. The task of the last-named two Divisions was to follow the tanks of 11th Armoured Division and mop up any pockets of enemy resistance left behind as the advance continued.

Up to this time, 11th Armoured had been under the command of VIII Corps. It had repeatedly given proof of its initiative and fighting spirit and it had always been in the van of the attack. General Horrocks, a personal friend of General Roberts, had just resumed command of XXX Corps after having recuperated from wounds suffered in North Africa. He could not have wished for a finer formation for the task he had been given. Thus, on 13 August the Division carrying the emblem of the Bull was made a part of XXX Corps.

THE ANVIL AND THE HAMMER

On 13 August, realizing the futility of its efforts at Mortain and that Hitler's stubborness in continuing the attack would allow the Allies to trap most of their forces in Normandy, the German High Command began to withdraw its armoured units in the direction of Argentan. First of all they hoped to save them from encirclement and then to use them to keep open the jaws of the pincer that were closing in on their 7th Army between Argentan and Falaise. In this way, most of the panzer divisions, the 1st, 2nd, 9th and 12th SS, Panzer Lehr, the 2nd, 9th and 116th Divisions were able to escape. However, most of the infantry divisions were trapped in the Falaise Pocket, the 326th, 353rd and 363rd, the 271st, 276th, 277th, 89th and 331st, together with some elements of 10th and 21st SS Panzer Divisions that were sacrificed. The enemy's retreat was well organized and, in the early stages, was carried out more or less according to plan even though the Allied Air Forces, with total command of the air, inflicted very heavy losses on the retreating columns. Now it was up to the Allies to speed up their attack, to throw themselves on the enemy and force him to do battle, to rough him up, to disorganize him and to hold him inside the Pocket so as to annihilate him completely and crush him. In order to do this, the Americans and Canadians between Falaise and Argentan were the anvil and XXX Corps, with 11th Armoured Division in the lead, was the hammer.

THE BULLS CHARGE AGAIN

In order to reinforce the bridgehead established some days before over the Orne in the vicinity of Thury-Harcourt, 15th Scottish Division was ordered to head towards that sector. Estry, the pivot of the German defence between Mont Pincon and Vire finally fell into their hands on 13 August. It had taken the Guards Armoured Division no less than a week to get to Estry and even after three days and nights of fierce fighting the Germans still held the town, supported by Tiger tanks buried in hull-down positions among the

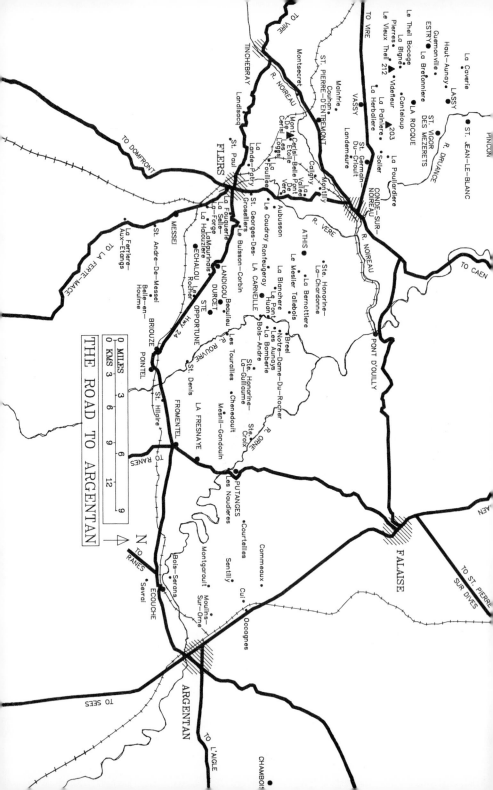

THE ROAD TO ARGENTAN

graves in the church cemetery. An entire brigade of infantry, a battalion of tanks, flame-throwers and flame-throwing tanks, a corps of artillery and an aerial bombardment that was almost continuous did not succeed in pushing them out. It was only when the German Army as a whole, realizing the desperate predicament it was in, started to retreat that the forces holding Estry abandoned it. By that time the village had been almost completely destroyed in the fighting; the ruins were left stuffed with the booby-traps the Germans always delighted in leaving.

THE ORNE OBJECTIVES

During the night of 13/14 August, 11th Armoured took up positions in the sector left vacant by 15th Scottish between Estry and Lassy. The mixed formations of tanks and infantry that had done so well between Caumont and the Vire — Vassy road were tried again. The composition of each of its two brigades was as follows: 159 Brigade had the 3rd Royal Tank Regiment and the 2nd Northamptonshire Yeomanry with the infantry of the 4th Kings Shropshire Light Infantry and the 1st Herefordshire Regiment; 29 Brigade had the Fife and Forfar Yeomanry and the 23rd Hussars with the infantry of the 3rd Monmouthshire Regiment and the 8th Rifle Brigade.

The two brigades started their advance at dawn on 14 August on two parallel routes of which the axes were, on the right, Estry — Vassy — Flers — Briouze, and on the left, Lassy — St. Germain — Athis — La Carneille — Putanges. Any places outside this broad advance path were left to the Inns of Court Reconnaissance Regiment to mop up. After having served so many masters they now passed entirely under command of 11th Armoured Division.

In passing, it should be mentioned that while the Division was stopped along the Vire — Vassy road on 6 August and while the German Mortain counter-attack was imminent, a daring plan was proposed at British G.H.Q. This was that the Inns of Court, together with the 2nd Household Cavalry, the other armoured reconnaissance regiment, should dash across the American line of advance towards Domfront. Once they arrived there they were immediately to head southeast for Alençon and then go north from the Alençon — Domfront road in the direction of Argentan and Condé-sur-Noireau. The purpose of this plan was to disorganize and destroy enemy supply convoys, in particular those bringing up gasoline and munitions, so as to weaken and paralyse enemy resistance still very strong around Vire, Estry, Vassy and Condé-sur-Noireau. Perhaps it was just as well that the major part of this plan was left to the Americans to carry out because they had the necessary troops in this sector and were much better placed to undertake such a hazardous mission.

DIFFICULTIES BETWEEN LE THEIL AND VASSY...

At dawn on 14 August, 159 Brigade, led by the Herefordshires who were supported by the tanks of the Northamptonshires, left Estry and seized Le Theil. Next, the Shropshires, supported by the 3rd Royal Tank Regiment, were to leap-frog over them and occupy the woods at La Herbalière. Finally, the Herefords were to pass through them and take Vassy.

The Herefords and the tanks of the Northamptonshires entered Le Theil by taking the main road and various side roads without encountering any opposition except for a few snipers and some mortar fire. However, on leaving Le Theil the infantry came under heavy fire that stopped them in their tracks. A squadron of tanks was sent to the right flank in the direction of Vieux-Theil but lost a lot of time trying to negotiate the narrow lanes. Another squadron was sent in the direction of La Bigne and Videfleur to help the infantry take their objective. The enemy reaction was vigorous. A tank was lost and they had to stop and wait for the Herefords to catch up with them and clear the area. That took up most of the afternoon and there was only just enough time before nightfall to mount an attack on Hill 212 and on the woods of La Herbalière where the enemy was stongly entrenched. It was not till nine o'clock in the evening that the attack was launched by two companies of infantry and two squadrons of tanks. By nightfall they achieved complete success although the Herefords, troubled by constant aggresive German patrols, suffered heavy losses. However, Vassy, that day's objective, was taken the next day.

...AND AT CANTELOUP

As far as 29 Brigade on the left was concerned, it advanced on two axes: the Hussars and the Rifle Brigade from La Caverie in the direction of Vassy, and the Fife and Forfar and 3rd Monmouths from Lassy towards La Rocque and Saint-Germain-du-Crioult. The Hussars were delayed along the Danvou — Vassy road by numerous obstacles, mines, felled trees and tanks dug in at the La Bretonnière intersection. The Hussars lost two tanks. In order to force the enemy to withdraw it was necessary to send the Hussars round by Guémonville and then across the fields and along narrow lanes while the infantry took the enemy in the rear as they were leaving the village of Haut-Aunay. By four o'clock in the afternoon they had covered only half the distance to Vassy. In order to make up lost time, a squadron of tanks and a company of infantry were sent towards the village of Canteloup where, in their turn, they were stopped after losing another tank.

Using the tactics of the Sioux and encouraging his men by his personal example, Lieutenant Bates stalked the village along a narrow path while the others approached it from the front. Night fell before the defenders abandoned Canteloup. They took advantage of the darkness and escaped from the village by sneaking past the Hussars and the Rifle Brigade who had encircled them and sprayed them with machine-gun fire from nightfall to daybreak.

AND ALSO AT LA ROCQUE...

Along the second axis of 29 Brigade, the one taken by the Monmouths and the Fife and Forfar, the precaution was taken of sending some sappers before daybreak to clear the road from La Caverie to Lassy of mines. While this was going on, patrols pushed

on up to the village which was found to be unoccupied. They seized a bridge over the Druance that had not been destroyed. At 0800
hours the infantry climbed on to the tanks and the column set off
without a care towards Lassy. The first tank had barely gone 100
yards when it ran over a mine that had been missed by the sappers, thus blocking all the traffic. Mine-clearing had to start all
over again, this time more thoroughly, before they were able to
continue on their way. After a detour across the fields, tanks and
infantry returned to the road at about noon, still going in the direction of La Rocque. They had not gone far when the lead tank was
destroyed at the intersection to the east of La Rocque by Germans
in position there with infantry, anti-tank guns, tanks and artillery.
'D' Company, supported by tanks, tried to bypass the enemy positions to the left. They sneaked along sunken lanes and managed
to get quite near to the intersection but were then greeted by a
hail of bullets from German infantry who had dug into the hedges
on the left side of the road. The Fife and Forfar tanks held steady
in all this confusion but unfortunately one of them was hit and
its commander, Sergeant Gale, was killed. Eventually, by eight
o'clock in the evening the intersection was firmly in the hands of
the Monmouths but communications between their 'D' Company
and the rest of the Battalion had broken down. Knowing that the
other companies had to be somewhere in the vicinity, the second-
in-command took two men with him and made off across the fields
in search of them. After crossing two fields he climbed up a slope
and suddenly came across about 20 Germans dug in along a sunken
lane. The Germans had their backs to him but, warned by the
noise he had made, turned their heads round and were as surprised to see him as the English officer was to see them. Thinking that
he must be accompanied by many more soldiers, they judged it
prudent to raise their hands and surrender. You can imagine their
surprise when, coming out of the lane one by one, they saw that
only two soldiers were with the officer.

All that day long, the Inns of Court, 11th Armoured Division's
Reconnaissance Regiment, patrolled in all directions: Pierres,
Vassy, Le Theil, La Rocque, Lassy and St. Vigor-des-Mézerets
where the men were plagued by mines and booby-traps.

VASSY IS CAPTURED

They were unable to capture Vassy that evening as they had hoped because of strong enemy resistance. The Shropshires had to wait in Estry until 2000 hours before taking up positions to the north and west of Le Theil. On the morning of the 15th they advanced again and occupied the La Herbalière woods that had been taken by the Herefords. From there they sent out patrols that reported that the roads were mined and barred by all sorts of obstacles and that the bridges on the stream that runs through Vassy had been blown up. Two platoons were immediately sent ahead to hold the intersection of the Montsecret, Flers and Saint-Vigor roads. They were soon reinforced by armoured cars of the Inns of Court that had succeeded in crossing the stream after a bulldozer had cleared a way across it. Vassy was deserted. The Shropshires and the Inns of Court continued their advance up to La Mainfrie in the direction of St. Pierre-d'Entremont where they settled down to pass the night.

THE ADVANCE TO ST. GERMAIN-DU-CRIOULT

The Hussars and the Rifle Brigade, unable to clear the village of Canteloup before nightfall, occupied it the next morning, the 15th. From there they headed towards the heights that overlook the valley and the Condé road to the east of Vassy and particularly Hill 203. Because of the advance of 159 Brigade on Vassy and the progress of their colleagues on the left towards St. Germain-du-Crioult, they were ordered to stop their advance; needless to say, no one objected to the enforced delay. Each man made himself as comfortable as possible for the night in spite of German artillery that was still very active.

The Monmouths and the Fife and Forfar, who had had a hard time seizing the intersection at La Rocque and had suffered heavy losses there, spent the morning of the 15th burying their dead. At the same time, the Inns of Court continued their reconnaissance probes towards St. Germain-du-Crioult. At about 1300 hours the

infantry climbed on the tanks again and, crossing the fields, occupied the area around La Poullardière.

Lieutenant Brownlie remembers: *We received orders to carry
a platoon of infantry on our tanks and to take a section of Engineers
with us; they were to inspect a bridge near the village of Solier,
to the northwest of St. Germain. We avoided the roads because
the enemy could have been lying in wait for us. This slowed us
down, particularly as the sappers only had half-tracks. We got to
the bridge without trouble through the village of La Painière. It
was mined and so were the approaches and we lost one of our
armoured cars there. While the sappers set to work to remove the
demolition charges I went on foot to the other side of the bridge
but saw nothing suspicious there. Soon the rest of the Regiment
arrived and took up positions on the south bank of the stream and
there they passed the night.*

SAD NEWS FOR THE NORTHAMPTONSHIRES

15 August was a sad day for the Northamptonshires. They had
just come back from patrolling along the right flank, trying to make
contact with the Guards Armoured Division who, as usual, were
treating 11th Armoured in a very snooty way, when they learnt
that their Regiment was to be disbanded two days later and their
Cromwell tanks sent to reinforce 7th Armoured Division who were
equipped with the same tanks. This was unavoidable because the
Northamptonshires had suffered very heavy losses on the Odon,
on the Caen plain and around Vire. Due to the lack of reinforcements, a common problem for many British regiments at that
time, they could not continue to function as a regular unit. Its
sister Regiment, the 1st Northamptonshires, was in the same
predicament and the amalgamation of the two regiments was decided in favour of 7th Armoured Division.

3RD INFANTRY DIVISION ATTACKS TINCHEBRAY

The Guards Armoured Division should have been on the right of 11th Armoured Division but, weakened by their losses in battling south from Caumont and around Estry, they were no longer spirited enough to keep up with the pace set by their neighbouring division. For three days, from 10 to 13 August, they fought without rest but also, it must be admitted, without enthusiasm although it is true that they were opposed by elements of 3rd Parachute Division, considered to be one of the elite German units. Nevertheless, their advance during these three days hardly amounted to more than a few kilometres between Burcy, La Botterie, Le Coisel, La Teinturerie, Le Val and Viessoix.

With the retreat of the enemy, after 13 August the Guards found themselves being squeezed into a corner between 11th Armoured on the left as they advanced on Vassy and 3rd Infantry Division on the right as they made for Tinchebray. General O'Connor commanding VIII Corps therefore decided to keep only 3rd Division in action, using them to maintain contact with the Americans on their right. The two brigades of this division, 8 Brigade on the right of the advance and 185 Brigade on the left, followed the axes of Highway 24 and the railway line from Vire to Flers respectively. The most severe fighting on the advance to Tinchebray took place at the intersections of Highway 24 at Coquard and at Saint-Quentin-les-Chardonnets, along the Coquard — Montfroux road, particularly between Coquard and Creuley, at the intersection of the railway line with the road from Bernières-le-Patry to Tinchebray and in the area between Bernières-le-Patry and Saint-Quentin-les-Chardonnets.

THE RESISTANCE OF THE GERMAN PARATROOPERS

On 12 August a very heavy barrage was laid down by the entire divisional artillery on the whole front of 8 Brigade. This Brigade, leaving from La Glaupinière, attained its objective, the important cross-road at Coquard, by about midnight. A few hours before

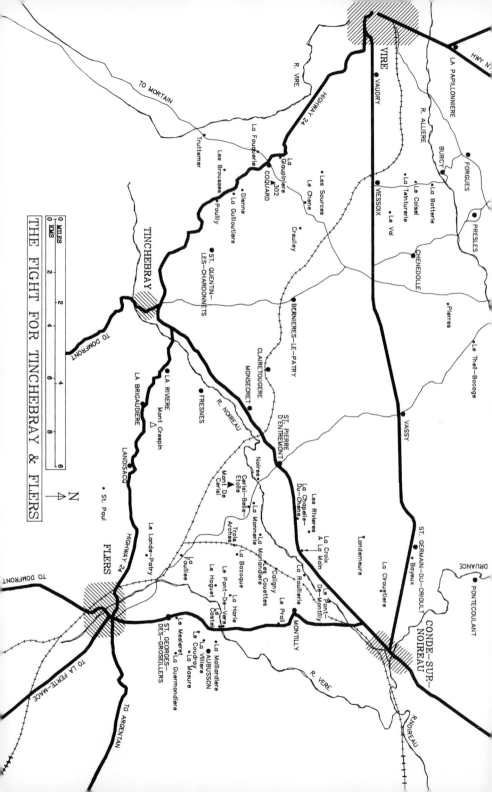

they had established contact with the Americans at La Fouquerie on the Truttemer road. The way was now open for an advance on Tinchebray the next day. However, the Germans of 3rd and 5th Parachute Divisions fought with tenacity and determination and 8 Brigade had to fight for two days and nights before they could advance along Highway 24 and take their objective. Supported by tanks, they had to capture, one by one and with heavy losses, the woods that overlook the intersection at Coquard from the east and the villages of Dienne, La Guilloutière, Brousses and Pouilly to the southeast.

On the left of the advance, 185 Brigade could not be supported by the divisional artillery for their attack from Hill 302 and the village of Les Sources but could only be covered by whatever mortars were available. Understandably, they attacked with less than their usual *élan*! It proved particularly costly to take the villages of Le Chêne and especially Le Creuley. At that time the Germans were still being very strongly supported by their artillery and mortars firing from the Vassy area. Although 27,000 rounds were fired in their support, 185 Brigade had to drop back from its start line because they had taken very heavy losses, particularly by the Warwicks. A new attempt was made, again by the Warwicks, this time supported by tanks. As soon as they approached the enemy positions they came under heavy automatic fire. At the start of the attack, 'C' Company lost its Commander, Major Baratt, the last of the Company Commanders who landed with the Battalion on 6 June. By the time they took their objective they had only 16 unwounded men left in the Company. With the help of tanks, they forced the enemy to withdraw beyond the stream that flows through the other side of Le Creuley. Their losses that day were very heavy: 10 killed and 48 wounded.

On 3rd Division's front, 14 August was reserved principally for the artillery who kept busy all day shelling the enemy positions, particularly those containing guns and mortars. After a day of this uninterrupted counter-battery work, the shelling started to produce results because by the evening the enemy stopped firing back. However, it was a sad day for 76th Field Regiment, one of 3rd Division's artillery regiments: their C. O., Lt. Colonel Foster, was killed by a sniper on the road between Viessoix and St. Quentin-les-Chardonnets.

TINCHEBRAY SPARED—BY MISTAKE!

During the night of 14/15 August, American and 8 Brigade patrols made contact. At four o'clock in the morning their reports confirmed that the enemy had started a partial retreat on the divisional front, leaving only rear guards.

At 0930 hours, a subaltern charged with taking water supplies to the Suffolk Regiment, arrived back at G.H.Q. late and rather shaken. He reported that on heading down the road to Battalion Headquarters he did not see that he had passed it and found himself on the main road to Tinchebray. He did not realize his mistake until he arrived at the heights of St. Quentin-les-Chardonnets. There he made a smart turn-around and came back without seeing anything of the enemy. As a result of this unplanned reconnaissance, the large-scale attack on Tinchebray that the South Lancashire Regiment was getting ready to launch with the support of artillery and tanks was called off. Thus, by a stroke of luck, the city was spared from destruction.

THE LIBERATION OF TINCHEBRAY & MONTSECRET

The rumoured enemy retreat now became a reality. Because most of 3rd Division's units had been in continuous action since the Invasion, the opportunity was now taken to let up a bit and to give them some rest. So, on the evening of the 14th, only the Royal Northumberland Fusiliers, the Division's reconnaissance regiment, were given firm orders to find out what was going on and to re-establish contact the next day with the fleeing enemy. They were to head towards Tinchebray and Montsecret, and beyond if possible because it was thought that these two built-up areas, crossed by streams and overlooked in the south by the heights of St. Cornier, Chanu, Mont-Crespin and Mont de Cerisy, would certainly be occupied by the enemy.

At first the advance towards Tinchebray made slow progress because the road was heavily mined but when they came in sight of the town they accelerated and the last mile was covered in record time. 'C' Squadron arrived there 10 minutes before their American cousins of 102nd Mechanized Cavalry. But the bridge was destroyed and covered by a rear guard so the Royal Northumberland Fusiliers* did not go much further.

'B' Squadron made rapid progress from St. Quentin and Bernières in the direction of Montsecret but, unfortunately, the approach roads they had to use were overlooked by high ground. The inevitable happened. As soon as they reached the bridges at Montsecret the leading elements came under very heavy bombardment and had to stop and take cover. By then it was 1530 hours and it was evident that the regiment, unlike the situation at Tinchebray, would not be able to advance beyond the stream. Suddenly, Major Gaskell appeared on one of the bridges to see what was going on and he urged a few of his armoured cars to push on to Flers. The enemy's reaction was immediate. Not only was the force that crossed over taken to task by the Luftwaffe (this was one of the few occasions on which they intervened) but one of the armoured cars ran over a mine. Major Gaskell himself was mortally wounded by a mortar bomb while he was on the bridge.

The area to the east of Montsecret was reconnoitred by 2nd Household Cavalry, the reconnaissance regiment placed under command of 3rd Division. Their Lieutenant Tabor distinguished himself in the vicinity of Montsecret — Clairefougères — St. Pierre-d'Entremont; in spite of fire from the enemy rear-guard that covered the bridges, he managed to disconnect the explosive charges that had been placed there for their imminent destruction. Feats of valour of this kind were undoubtedly why many bridges on the Noireau were taken intact. They also explain the violent reaction of the enemy artillery and Air Force in the Montsecret sector.

*The Royal Northumberland Fusiliers, the 5th Regiment of Foot, the famous *Fighting Fifth,* supplied troops for various duties. Their 8th Battalion formed the 3rd Reconnaissance Regiment (Royal Armoured Corp) of 3rd British Infantry Division. The Regiment also supplied the 2nd Independent Machine Gun Company attached to 11th Armoured Division.

CHAPTER 8

THE FIGHTING FOR FLERS AND CONDÉ

While the battle raged on the Noireau and on the heights of Berjou, all on 43rd Infantry Division's front,* VIII British Corps, on the extreme right of 2nd British Army, where they had made contact with the Americans, had only one division in action, namely, 3rd Infantry Division whose three Brigades had practically lost contact with the enemy. On the afternoon of 15 August, only its Reconnaissance Regiment was in action against the enemy whose rearguards stopped them on the line of the streams flowing from Tinchebray to Montsecret.

At Tinchebray, where their entrance coincided with that of the Americans, the bridges had been destroyed. The city had suffered relatively little damage and had been evacuated by its inhabitants since 7 August except for the old people living in the alms house and M. and Mme. Mermier who, with their gardener, M. Lecerf, hid themselves in a cellar. There were two other people who refused to leave their homes. They were M. Roulleaux, who was shot, and old Mme. Fortin, whose throat was cut. During the absence of the inhabitants the city was, as usual, pillaged by the Germans. Boxes of medicine, many carrying the labels of a Tinchebray pharmacist, were later found at Pont-Huan, between La Carneille and Notre-Dame-du-Rocher.

3rd Reconnaissance Regiment suffered some losses in scouting the road to Domfront. Among them was Trooper B. D. Robinson; he now lies in the cemetery at Tinchebray.

The bridge at Montsecret was blown up and the fords were

---

*See Appendix B, page 241.

covered by German artillery installed on the slopes north of the heights of L'Epivent and La Gaumonnière, between Landisacq and Cerisy. The British troops who ventured in the direction of Flers were forced to withdraw back into the Montsecret sector. 'A' and 'B' Squadrons, the two reserve squadrons of the Reconnaissance Regiment, together with 'C' Squadron of the Household Cavalry under command, passed the night on the road between St. Quentin and Montsecret.

OPERATION KITTEN

3rd Division's role was completely changed on 16 August, the day on which Operation KITTEN started. This Operation covered:

1. An advance towards the Seine, led on the right by the Americans, in the centre by XXX British Corps and on the left by XII British Corps.
   XXX Corps consisted of 11th Armoured Division and 43rd and 50th Infantry Divisions.
2. 11th Armoured Division was to lead the advance on XXX Corps' front from their start line, the Condé — Flers highway.
3. 11th Armoured Division was to advance in two columns, on two main axes:
   (a) Flers, Briouze, Ecouché, Argentan, Le Bourg-St. Leonard, Ste. Gauburge, L'Aigle.
   (b) Le Pont-de-Vère, Athis, La Carneille, Taillebois, Notre-Dame-du-Rocher, Ste. Honorine-la-Guillaume, Putanges, Bailleul, Exmes, Gacé, L'Aigle.

Because 11th Armoured Division was ordered to advance to the southern rim of the Falaise Pocket while the Americans came up from the south, it meant that VIII Corps, consisting, at that time, solely of 3rd British Infantry Division, had only one role left to perform, namely, that of a reserve force. From that day on, it was to employ itself as best it could but, as in the capture of Flers, it will be seen that it did not always act in accordance with its orders!

VIII CORPS' LAST FLING

On its last day of action, 3rd Division was given the job by VIII Corps of reconnoitring the enemy positions from the Tinchebray—Montsecret line, reached the day before, to the inter-Corps boundary on one side and the inter-Army boundary on the other.

At 0500 hours, 8 Brigade occupied the following positions: 2nd East Yorkshire Regiment at Montsecret and Fresnes; 1st South Lancashire Regiment at La Rivière; 1st Suffolk Regiment at La Brigaudière to the north of the main highway.

At 0815 hours, 185 Brigade received orders to begin moving towards Tinchebray at 1000 hours. They were to relieve V U.S. Corps and to occupy Hills 313 (between La Palluette and Chanu), 310 (between La Rivière and Chanu) and 248 (between Butte-Rouge and a position of the Tinchebray—St. Cornier road immediately after the crossroad at Yvrandes).

9 Brigade took up positions in the sector immediately to the east of Landisacq while the divisional troops went towards Chapelle-Biche and La Chapelle-au-Moine.

The role of the three Brigades of 3rd Division was, therefore, to occupy and clear a sector that, it was thought, had been evacuated by the retreating enemy. They were also ordered to get ready to make an opposed crossing of the Seine in case the enemy decided to turn and fight at that barrier. Numerous river-crossing training exercises were carried out in the Tinchebray and Chapelle-au-Moine areas and even a temporary bridge was built and put into use over the river at Flers by the Guards Armoured Division. Then, before these exercises were over, the news arrived that the Americans had crossed the Seine at Mantes and the British at Vernon. What a disappointment! However, they still had the Rhine to look forward to!

Prudence being the mother of security, the reconnaissance units of 3rd Division, the 8th Royal Northumberland Fusiliers and 'C' and 'D' Squadrons of the 2nd Household Cavalry, were ordered to patrol ahead in order to make sure there were no nasty surprises in store for the Division.

THE AMERICANS AND BRITISH MEET AT ST. CLAIR-DE-HALOUZE

At about 10 o'clock in the morning the two reconnaissance units set out on what turned out to be their last operation in France. 'C' Squadron carried out limited patrols in the area southeast of Flers. After going through La Chapelle-Biche, they left one of their vehicles, damaged by a mine, at La Helizière, not far from La Chapelle-au-Moines, and were welcomed by the population in the town square. 'D' Squadron sent out patrols in the direction of the Foret-de-Halouze where, at precisely 1654 hours, according to M. Emile Lambert, an eye-witness, they made contact with an American patrol that had climbed up from St. Clair-de-Halouze. The Germans had just evacuated this area and a certain number of prisoners were taken. However, 'D' Squadron lost a vehicle on one of the many mines that had been placed in the area.

ENTRANCE INTO FLERS

That morning, 3rd Reconnaissance Regiment received an encouraging visit from 'Bolo' Whistler, the Divisional Commander, who came to tell them that this was their last day of fighting and ordered them to continue to reconnoitre in the direction of Flers. So 'C' Squadron took Highway 24 while 'A' Squadron took the Montsecret road towards Le Café Bleu and La Lande-Patry, both taking many prisoners along the way. They were ordered to stop just outside Flers because that town had been given to 11th Armoured Division as their objective; 11th Armoured was on its way down from the north, from Vassy, St. Georges and Condé. On the outskirts of Flers they made contact with the Inns of Court, the reconnaissance troops of 11th Armoured, who had posted detachments all along the Vassy—Flers road to secure it for the imminent arrival of the tanks marked with the emblem of a black bull on a gold field.

'C' Squadron, coming along Highway 24, encountered so little opposition that it arrived at the entrance to Flers early in the afternoon. Its commander, Major Norton, asked for permission to enter the city. He got no reply. Impatiently, he asked again; did he or did he not have permission to enter the city? Still no reply. So, unable to resist the temptation and without waiting for orders, his men, supported by a few self-propelled anti-tank guns, entered the city centre in the middle of the afternoon. On the way they destroyed a German staff car that tried to sneak past them by taking a road underneath the Guilleux garage.

A small patrol, guided by André Lebreton of the *Résistance*, pushed on towards Charles-Mousset Street and just behind the Planchette factory came across a German vehicle that had blown itself up on one of its own mines.

THE FIGHT FOR THE CITY

Except for some intersections in the eastern part of the city that had been mined, Flers was not held by the enemy. As the historian of 11th Armoured Division recalls, with good humour, the only battle that took place for the possession of Flers was between two British units. The Northamptonshires of 11th Armoured were completely surprised to discover that they had been beaten to it by infantry patrols of 3rd Division. It took a lot of 'persuasion', couched, of course, in language more emphatic than diplomatic, before the redoubtable Major Norton would withdraw his men to Le Tremblay and leave the city to its rightful owners. However, at least he had the satisfaction of knowing that, for once, they had captured a city before its fall had been announced by the B.B.C.!

A REST AT SAINT PAUL

The next day, 17 August, the Royal Northumberland Fusiliers, 3rd Division's Reconnaissance Regiment, established their headquarters at Saint Paul. They stayed there until 2 September except for 'C' Squadron who were sent back to Monty's Headquarters there to be kept under the Field-Marshal's eagle eye for three weeks as a punishment for the breach of military etiquette they had perpetrated when, with more zeal than discipline, they had taken another unit's objective.* Operations were thus put in abeyance for this regiment except for two squadrons which, at dawn on 18 August, went into the woods at Messei to look into a report from the *Résistance* that they were full of German stragglers. By early afternoon they were all rounded up.

The rest period at Saint Paul was put to good use. The Regiment was trained in new methods of cooperation with the Artillery and the Engineers. Field firing exercises were frequently held. There was even a rumour that 'A' Squadron learnt a thing or two from a group of young ladies who, by chance, were near one of the targets. Lieutenant Rogerson asked himself what he would do if he ever met the owners of the buildings they were using so accurately as targets for PIAT training.

They rested, trained, carried out exercises and held sports and enjoyed shows put on at the Army Theatre in Flers by Flanagan and Allen and other entertainers. The Divisional band gave some concerts and the band of His Majesty's Life Guards provided a pleasant musical soirée.

The reception given by the French, both the country people and the town dwellers, varied as the fighting advanced across Normandy. The attitude of the farmers of Maltot or Esquay-sur-Seules, who had been under constant artillery fire, or of the inhabitants of the destroyed cities, such as Caen, was very different from the attitude of the inhabitants of Saint Paul who had hardly suffered at all from the war. There the English soldiers felt they were surrounded by friends to whom the *Entente Cordiale* was not just an empty phrase despite the hard times they had had to live through for four long years. The speech given by the Mayor and Curé of Saint Paul to the C.O. and officers of 3rd Reconnaissance Regiment in an official ceremony on 21 August is a good example of what the local population felt towards them.

Officers and men of the British Army! I have been asked by the Town Council and the Curé of this parish, a Chevalier de la Legion

---

*This was the story spread by their gleeful rivals but General Roberts remembers that at the time 3rd Division were short of transport to bring up supplies and that was why the Royal Northumberland Fusiliers (3rd Reconnaissance Regiment) were 'grounded'.

d'Honneur, *and by the entire population, to bid you welcome to our little village. Our first feelings are of relief and gratitude. We want to tell you what a great joy it has been to us to see the British soldiers chasing the Germans away. This is a very moving moment for us and in spite of all the trials we have been through we all remain the fervent friends of England and her Allies. We feel like old friends who, after having been shut up in a dark and damp dungeon, suddenly find themselves at liberty, out in the bright sun and fresh air.*

There could be no better place for this ceremony than right here. We are gathered around the monument raised to the memory of the brave sons of this village who, side by side with their valiant British and American comrades, gave their lives in the First World War for their country and for the cause of liberty all over the world. If they could see us they would be delighted that their children, in turn, brothers, sisters and friends, can now live in freedom.

During the last four years there have been some misunderstandings between our two countries. As you know, the entire responsibility did not rest on you alone; we had our part to play and it was not an insignificant part. But the burdens you have borne for the common cause, your victories and the return of your armies to the soil of France open up a new era of brotherhood and understanding. Although you are a peaceful nation you have gone to war in order to liberate France and Europe and to preserve the liberty of the entire world. We are sure that before long the sons of Normandy will be proud to join this crusade in company with the sons of Britain and with those of the rest of France and that, once they have been supplied with modern weapons, they will be eager to fight alongside you for the complete elimination of tyranny and for the restoration of Peace and Liberty throughout the world.

I bid you all welcome. Vive l'Angleterre! Vive la France!

THE BULL GETS READY TO CHARGE AGAIN

On the morning of 16 August, 11th Armoured Division occupied the following positions: 29 Brigade Headquarters in Bois l'Archer on the Vassy—Danvou road; two Squadrons of the Fife and Forfar Yeomanry with one Company of the 3rd Monmouthshire Regiment at La Faverie; the two other Squadrons of the Fife and Forfar with the three other Companies of the 3rd Monmouths at La Poullardière; two Squadrons of the 23rd Hussars and the 8th Rifle Brigade at the crossroads not far from La Croarde; 159 Brigade Headquarters in the sector Les Glivets—Botave; the 1st Herefordshire Regiment dispersed in the woods of La Herbalière, at Chateau, La Calbrasserie and La Tirlière; one Company of the Kings Shropshire Light Infantry at a place 500 metres to the northeast of Vassy on the Danvou road, another at La Rivière and the other two, which had come up the day before, at La Poterie and south of Hamel. Divisional Headquarters were at La Durandière, to the east of Le Theil.

CONDÉ UNDER THE SIGN OF THE BULL

11th Armoured Division had orders to get into position that same day on the Flers—Condé road so that they could lead XXX British Corps across the southern boundary of the Falaise Pocket in the direction of the Seine. Following their usual custom, the Inns of Court sent out patrols before daybreak in order to reconnoitre the country in front of the Division. 'B' and 'C' Squadrons went along the Vassy—Flers axis while 'D' Squadron took the axis Lassy—Condé.

Right from the start the latter ran into serious difficulties because of large numbers of booby-traps and mines scattered all along its route. At Cagny, on the Vassy—Condé road, about one kilometre from St. Germain-du-Crioult, the Germans had placed mines in shell craters. Sergeant Morgan's half-track tried to avoid them but couldn't and was blownup. The Sergeant and Troopers Perks and Hush were killed and were buried nearby while the other three occupants of the vehicle were seriously wounded.

Another patrol from the same squadron had better luck as it was the first British unit to get into Condé, or what was left of it. (One thing worth noting about this patrol was the fact that in it were the Tibbetts brothers, Joseph and Samuel, who served together throughout the war). Coming from the direction of Lassy, via Solier, the patrol passed through St. Germain-du-Crioult and took the lanes around Landemeure, La Rougetière and La Cirouetière to get to Condé via La Croix-des-Trois-Passes, La Conterie, Le Cimetière and La Conterie and Vire streets. During their patrol they managed to avoid the mines and booby-traps set by the enemy. Often, when something suspicious appeared on the road in front of them, one of the riders in the leading vehicle would get out to go ahead on foot and guide the driver through a heart-stopping slalom as he skirted death by inches.

Dawn was breaking when they stopped their engines on the highway in front of Mlle. Dumont's house. The four men were horrified by the extent of the destruction. The Lieutenant commanding the patrol decided to take Joseph Tibbetts and the driver with him to search for a way over the river. They passed by the ruins of the Ferodo store and by the Davout and Mollet houses and came out at the City Centre on the bank of the Druance river.

Standing alone in a desert of ruins and amid the silence of death, Samuel Tibbetts stayed to guard the armoured car while keeping in wireless contact with headquarters. He tells his story: *When I saw my brother and the Lieutenant and the driver disappear behind the ruined walls I was scared and sweat began to pour down my face. I could see the solitary bell-tower of St. Sauveur rising above the ruins. I imagined there were enemy snipers hiding there, waiting to pick off the patrol. Alone in this terrifying and oppressive silence, the sweat continued to bead on my face. Nervously, I looked to the left, to the right, behind me... All I could see were charred roof beams and piles of rubble with here and there a few sticks of furniture sticking out of the ruins. There wasn't a sound, nothing but a terrifying silence, not one person, not a solitary living soul, not even a bird! After an hour that seemed like a hundred years, the Lieutenant, my brother and the driver re-appeared and I breathed again. Thank God they were back. At that moment I knew how good it was to be alive!*

After sending a wireless report to headquarters that the state of the bridges and roads made it impossible for tanks to get through, the patrol returned.

11TH ARMOURED DIVISION PATROLS
IN FLERS AND ON THE RIVER VÈRE

While this was going on, the two other squadrons sent their patrols towards Flers along the same road up to St. Pierre-d'Entremont where they encountered their first mines. After working their way through this danger, most of the troop continued towards Noirée where they found that the bridge had not yet been blown up although the explosive charges were in place. A quick examination explained why: the detonators had either been removed or the Germans had not had time to attach them. Whatever the reason, the Division was glad of the gift of an intact bridge on an important road on the main axis of its advance. It would have been very easy for just a small rear-guard, entrenched on Mont de Cerisy, to hold up the construction of a temporary bridge for as long as they wanted.

The patrols continued towards Cerisy where they broke up into several groups. One went towards Café Bleu and Landisacq where it made contact with 3rd Infantry Division coming from Montsecret and Tinchebray. Another went towards La Fouillée, La Lande-Patry and St. Paul where further inter-division contacts were made. A third group, after crossing the river at Prieuré—there also the bridge had not been destroyed—headed towards St. Georges-des-Groseillers via La Bourdonnière and towards Flers and Le Hameau de Vère. Finally, a fourth group pushed on towards Caligny, where they ran into a German patrol near the bridge at La Frictière, and towards Montilly, where they had a look at the crossings over the Vère. The strategically important bridge at Pont-de-Vère had not been destroyed but, on the other hand, the patrol soon found out that it was covered by strong defensive positions and the Germans seemed eager to fight. All the other bridges the length of the valley of the Vère were unusable or were defended by tanks or 88mm's or by groups of infantry with mortars or by mines.

The patrols that came down from St. Pierre-d'Entremont towards Condé found all the intersections mined and all the bridges on the Noireau destroyed from La Monnerie to Condé.

The reports radioed to Division by the Inns of Court patrols brough out six main points: there were large numbers of mines, frequent demolitions, many booby-trapped road blocks, almost all the bridges on the Noireau had been destroyed, the same on the Vère and, finally, a defensive line had been established along the entire front of the Division. This line had been established on the high ground to the east of Flers and continued via Sottavie and Aubusson to the top of the slopes southeast of Pont-de-Vère. As far as the city of Flers itself was concerned, at 1425 hours the Inns of Court patrol sent back a message that, apart from the mined roads in the east of the city, there appeared to be no other enemy defences there. This report led 11th Armoured Division to hope that, in spite of all the obstacles it was going to meet, it would be able to attain that day's objective, i.e., to get its units on to the Flers—Condé road in preparation for a rapid pursuit the next day towards Briouze on the right and towards Putanges on the left. At one time it was even thought that it might be possible to establish 29 Brigade on the Flers—Athis axis but enemy resistance at Pont-de-Vère, at Aubusson and all along the valley of the Vère decided otherwise.

SAINT GERMAIN-DU-CRIOULT'S MEDAL

Early on the morning of 16 August, 29 Brigade, led by the tanks of the Fife and Forfar Yeomanry and by the infantry of the 3rd Monmouthshire Regiment, set out for St. Germain-du-Crioult. The night had been cold and damp and, because of the early starting time, the men had not even been able to have their usual 'cuppa char'. Disgruntled and numb with cold, they climbed on the tanks and tried to warm themselves on the hot engines. When they arrived at St. Germain they left their trucks and deployed themselves on each side of the road in order to capture the village of Le Pont de Montilly on the Condé—Tinchebray road.

The town of St. Germain-du-Crioult was emptied of its last inhabitants on Sunday, 13 August. On that same day the Germans warned the last occupants that they were going to blow up the bell-tower and that it was dangerous to remain in the neighbourhood. Madame Nicolet remembers the officer who warned her and urged her to take shelter. He said to her, in correct French: *This morning we blew up the bell-tower of St. Pierre-du-Regard. I'll never forget the grand spectacle it made and in which I took part. At the moment of the explosion the tower first shook and then crumpled and shortened as if it was breathing its last and then it crashed to the ground with the sound of falling rocks. I honestly believe that, above all the noise, I could hear the sound of the bells as they fell from on high. Then all disappeared in a cloud of dust.* C'est la guerre! *To-morrow we will blow up the bridges on the Noireau and then it will be the turn of the bell-tower of Montilly.*

A few people stayed in the village of Bayeux as they felt rather insecure away from the main road. In amongst them M. Maupas noticed a small patrol of British soldiers who were carefully searching the village. He was told by them that the main part of their force was in the town. Together with André Guesdon, they all returned to the town and there they encountered some civilians who insisted on the soldiers having a glass of wine. A German was found in the town. A few moments later a diminutive corporal found two others and proudly escorted them away.

M. Maupas recalls: *I remember that there was an ambulance in the square with a few wounded soldiers in it. At the time I had a boil on my arm and the Major insisted that I receive treatment for it. While they were dressing my arm an officer who spoke our language well and who was wearing a woollen bonnet with a pompom, tried to turn his tank round towards Pontécoulant. He was unable to do so because the road was completely blocked by huge pieces of granite that had fallen from the bell-tower.*

While all this was going on the patrol that had cleared the village of Bayeux returned to the road where it found M. Lainé milking his cows. A full bucket of milk was offered to the soldiers and was quickly emptied by them.

Although the author was born in a village near St. Germain he did not know that there was a very devout following of the Sacred Heart of Jesus in that parish. He only learnt this in October 1970 at a reception given by former soldiers of the 3rd Monmouthshire

Regiment at the Goring Hotel in London. One of the soldiers sought us out, the two French guests, Father Amiard and myself, and showed us a medal of the Sacred Heart of St. Germain-du-Crioult that he took from deep inside his wallet. *I was wounded there,* he said, *and the civilians who looked after me gave me this medal. Through an interpreter, they made me understand that if I kept it on me at all times I would come to no harm. I did this and I came through the rest of the war without another wound.*

THE BULLS REACH THE NOIREAU AT PLANCHES

The infantry set off in the direction of the Noireau, accompanied by some tanks of the Fife and Forfar and a few half-tracks from the Engineers. When they arrived at the cross-road near Landemeure a half-track blew itself up on one of the many mines the Tibbetts brothers had avoided a few hours before. This blocked the road completely. The column had to detour across the fields before returning to the Montilly road a hundred metres further on.

They reached the Noireau at the village of Planches. Jumping from rock to rock, the infantry managed to cross the stream but before going any further they sent a patrol into Montilly. As they arrived there two enemy armoured cars very considerately made themselves scarce. While this was going on, some of the tanks managed to ford the stream near the mill at La Rouillerie but most of the column, very wisely, waited for a temporary bridge to be thrown across the Noireau. It was six o'clock in the evening before the rest of the tanks crossed the stream not far from the factory at Les Fontaines while the wheeled transport had to make a detour through Noirée before going back to Montilly.

MONTILLY IS WELL GUARDED

Towards the end of the afternoon, the 3rd Monmouths, having passed through Montilly, where they were shelled and mortared, climbed up to Le Prail on the Condé—Flers road. There they were

rejoined by the Fife and Forfar tanks and took up defensive positions for the night.

Colonel Brownlie has this to say about that day: *Leaving St. Germain we lost a half-track on a mine. This forced us to make a small
detour. When we arrived at the stream we found that the bridge
had been destroyed so we made ourselves comfortable in the sun
while 'B' Squadron went off to find a suitable fording place. By
1800 hours the Engineers had built a bridge. We crossed over by
it but had some difficulties with the lighter vehicles; we had to
tow them through the mill-race to help them across. We got up
the next hill by taking country lanes. From there my friend Jim-
my Samson took a troop of tanks towards Pont Grat. He reported
that the bridge had been blown up and that an enemy tank fired
at him from the high ground. As it was so late he was ordered
to come back. He rejoined us while my crew was making repairs
to the track of my turret that had been damaged by the branch
of a tree. The Germans took this opportunity to shell us. As soon
as it was dark we retired to join the column near Montilly.*

ST. PIERRE-D'ENTREMONT, CERISY AND
MONT DE CERISY TAKEN WITHOUT A FIGHT

159 Brigade, advancing on the right along the Vassy—Flers axis,
was led by the tanks of the 3rd Royal Tank Regiment and the
infantry of the Shropshires. They took off at 0745 hours and by
0900 hours the column was descending the hill at Couhan. Three
quarters of an hour later it stopped at the entrance of St. Pierre-
d'Entremont while the Engineers cleared the booby-traps and mines
that abounded in the town. As soon as the road was clear, a few
Royal Tank Regiment tanks went on ahead as scouts and reached
Cerisy at 1100 hours. The area was empty of the enemy so the column went on, then stopped to reorganize itself.

This delay gave the Herefords, who were in reserve, the chance
to rejoin the Brigade near Noirée. They were immediately ordered
to reconnoitre the area of the bridge and to seize Mont de Cerisy.
Captain Wardman recalls: *I took some men and two tanks of the*

23rd Hussars with me and, after crossing the fields not far from the Noireau, we began to climb towards the crest. As we climbed I wondered what sort of a reception they were preparing for us at the top. Incredibly, however, this commanding position was not held by the enemy. On the crest there were only the burnt-out ruins of a chateau and the graves of 17 Germans.

At 1230 hours, three tanks of the Royal Tank Regiment, accompanied by a detachment of the Shropshires, spear-headed a new advance towards Flers. In the Les Loges—La Fouillée area they were delayed while they destroyed a German tank concealed in a lane near the roadside crucifix near Les Loges and chased away or captured the enemy infantrymen entrenched in the houses of these two villages.

THE BRIGADIER'S INITIATIVE

At 1500 hours Brigadier Churcher, commanding 159 Brigade, decided to change the itinerary of his Brigade. He had been study-ing the reports sent in by the Inns of Court as their wireless messages were received. He realized that, although the city of Flers was not defended, its capture at that moment only had propaganda value. On the other hand, if the bridge at Pont-de-Vère could be seized intact it would open up another route for the Division that they could use that same evening for a thrust forward on the left. He immediately ordered the troops at La Fouillée and those on the way there to make for Pont-de-Vère via Le Hoguet. In addition, he ordered those forces that had not yet left Cerisy to make for Pont-de-Vère via Caligny, Les Ramées and Le Perlyer.

By 1545 hours the Shropshires had reached the Caen—Laval railway line and had crossed the viaducts at Caligny, Les Couettes and Trois-Arches. From the last-named bridge they were able to take a disused path that enabled them to get across the railway cutting. It was by this route that the first carriers arrived in the vicinity of Pont-de-Vère. Unfortunately, after having crossed the Caligny—Flers road below Le Hoguet, the leading carrier got stuck between two tree stumps and could not be moved. It was abandoned but it meant that the rest of the column had to leave the cover of the sunken lane and cut across the open fields in full view of the enemy on the heights of Aubusson.

THE FIRST BRITISH TROOPS ARRIVE AT LA HARIE

When the order came to evacuate Caligny, recounts Germain Dufay who, only a few days earlier, had been forced to leave Cauville, *we did not want to be evacuated yet again so we decided to take cover in an animal shelter in the very middle of the fields. There were about twenty of us there but not all had the courage to stay till the end. However, it was a good place to be from which to watch as, day by day and hour by hour, the fighting drew nearer and nearer to us. One of the most spectacular sights was when the Air Force bombed the chateau of Mont de Cerisy. The flames were enormous and the smoke rose to a great height in the sky.*

During the night of 15/16 August we tethered the horses along the hedges and mounted a guard over them because we were afraid that the Germans would commandeer them. All night long we heard them leaving in the dark, taking the country lanes. The next morning all was calm; all the Germans seemed to have left. In the afternoon the first of the English arrived by the same lanes that the Germans had taken just a few hours before. Some of them left the lane and came across the field to where we were. They told us that they were only the advance guard and that the main body would be there in a few hours. Thinking that, at last, all was over, we went back to the house. At that very moment the German guns began to fire at the English troops, killing some of the animals in the field we had just left. We soon realized that the battle would now move in the direction of Pont-de-Vère.

...AND AT PONT-DE-VÈRE

The German guns opened fire just as the Shropshires, converging on Pont-de-Vère from Caligny and La Fouillée, reached the first houses of the village. W. D. Nind, one of the Shropshires, recalls: *Since that morning everything had gone well. We had left Vassy by road and made for a bridge that was said to be strongly held by the enemy. When we got past Caligny, the infantry got out of the trucks and advanced on foot in groups of eight to ten men along both sides of the road. I watched the progress of the infantry from the driver's seat of my truck.*

I had just driven over the crest of the hill (Le Breuil) and the head of the infantry column had just reached the bottom when the German guns opened fire. The descent to Pont-de-Vère was in plain view from Aubusson. A few soldiers were hit before they had time to take cover. I remember that one poor fellow had his head taken off by a direct hit just at the entrance to the Bazin farm. Everyone scattered into the fields on both sides of the road. I drove my truck into a narrow lane on the right at the bottom of the hill and eventually arrived at Pont-de-Vère. Our mortars soon took up the challenge and while a duel went on the rest of the Battalion came up and prepared to attack.

THE GUNS IN POSITION AT
ST. PIERRE-D'ENTREMONT & CALIGNY

In anticipation of the battle and drawing on the information sent back by patrols along the line of the river Vère, at 1430 hours the 151st Ayrshire Yeomanry was ordered to get their guns into position near St. Pierre-d'Entremont. Soon after, they fired their first 25-pounder shells in the direction of Aubusson, searching out the enemy positions on the heights dominating the River Vère that had been located by patrols. In addition, a Medium Regiment of tractor-drawn 5.5 inch guns went into action from a meadow near the village of Perlyer at Caligny.

Captain Garrett, a Forward Observation Officer of the 151st Ayrshire Yeomanry who accompanied the Shropshires, directed the fire of the guns, using his tank's wireless to give instructions to vary the direction of the fire to suit the tactical needs.

GERMAN PREPARATIONS AT
PONT-DE-VÈRE & AUBUSSON

As the Germans tried to escape encirclement by retreating eastward they left rear-guards to slow down the pursuing Allied forces. Accordingly, the lack of opposition to 11th Armoured Division on the morning of 16 August was reversed on subsequent days when the enemy showed that he was still capable of a planned, orderly retreat. He blew up all the bridges, scattered large numbers of mines everywhere and, wherever possible, set up defensive posit-ions each afternoon to hinder the advance of the Division.

The enemy forces opposing 11th Armoured Division that after-noon were two experienced Divisions, the 3rd Parachute and the 363rd Infantry, who, together, made up II Parachute Corps of 7th German Army. 363rd Division established itself to the east of Flers while 3rd Parachute Division defended the sector to the north of Flers from the heights around Sottavie up to Poirier on the Planquivon — Athis road. The German paratroops arrived at Pont-de-Vère and Aubusson at about three o'clock in the morning. The first thing they did was to turn out all the civilians and go looking for food. Then, dead tired, they fell asleep. But their rest was very brief. When their C.O. arrived the men were woken up and those who were not on their feet quickly enough were helped up with a kick in the pants. At daybreak, large quantities of mines, mostly anti-personnel, were scattered all over the river-side clothes-washing places at Pont-de-Vère, in the fields and ditches and intersections between La Maillardière and Les Soucettes and near the bridge of Desramé in the valley. The communities of St. Georges and Aubusson had not received evacuation orders so there were many civilians there; some were inhabitants and others were refugees from other villages. A few gathered nervously around a German officer and asked him what was going to happen. Seeing so many women and children gathered there from the farms owned by M. Sauquet and M. Lecornu at Le Castel, he said, "It's going to be a disaster! This evening there will be a terrible battle here and by to-morrow everyone will be dead."

Anti-tank guns were placed to cover the lane entering La Vallée; in the village of La Maillardière; on the road climbing from Pont-de-Vère to Aubusson; behind the school on the road to Flers; and also to cover the lanes from La Masure and La Villière. Other guns supporting the enemy troops fighting in Pont-de-Vère and Aubusson were strung out from La Selle-la-Forge to Ronfeugeray.

The paratroops began to dig their slit trenches and to place machine-guns and mortars to cover all the lanes between Pont-de-Vère, Aubusson, Le Coudray, La Croix-des-Aumones etc. The same thing was done in the villages themselves of La Guermondière, La Villière, Le Coudray, Le Clos de la Mare, La Maillardière, La Masure, Pont-de-Vère, Le Castel and the town of Aubusson. An observation post was set up in the presbytery at Aubusson. It was connected to the main headquarters in the cemetery and to other command posts in La Villière and La Maillardière.

THE ATTACK ON THE BRIDGE ON THE RIVER VÈRE

At about 1700 hours, 'A' Company of the Shropshires received orders to seize the bridge. It deployed itself in the fields and orchards of the villages of Pont-de-Vère and Le Castel. *They fought here in the evening of 16 August as we fought during the war of 1914-18,* reported M. Sauquet, the President of the Veterans of St. Georges-des-Groseillers. *The English infantry went through the orchards of Le Castel in short rushes, taking cover first behind one apple tree and then another, firing short bursts or tossing grenades ahead of themselves as they attacked the hedges and embankments.*

As soon as the first platoons, led by Captain Walford, reached the Condé—Flers road they were greeted by machine-gun fire and mortar bombs from positions hidden among the sunken lanes that spread out from the intersection of Le Castel and ran to the village of Le Coudray, passing behind the mill at Aubusson and the paddock at La Mare. These lanes, deeply sunken between high embankments, followed the main road for about a kilometre in the direction of Flers and provided the Germans with a perfect line of defence. Branching out as they did in all directions, they also served as ideal communication trenches between their different posts. They were able to use this network of sunken lanes to move in almost complete safety from Pont-de-Vère to Coudray or to the town of Aubusson, or to La Maillardière, to La Croix-des-Aumones or to La Masure.

The German paratroops made such good use of the terrain that 'A' Company was unable to take the bridge by itself. Two other Companies, 'B' and 'C', had to lend a hand. With the support of 'B' Squadron of the Royal Tank Regiment, the job was done by 1900 hours. It took two hours of fighting to seize the bridge.

FIGHTING ON THE SLOPES OF AUBUSSON

The enemy still occupied positions around Aubusson and, as before, the losses of the Shropshires were heavy. Right at the start of the fighting, Captian Walford was killed near the Laurent house while one of his men suffered the same fate near him, at the entrance of the lane to Le Moulin. Sergeant Jameson, who had placed his Bren gun in the ditch opposite the Lecornu house, near the intersection, was also hit.

Next the Shropshires received orders to clear the lanes and farms around Aubusson and the town of Aubusson itself prior to making for St. Georges-des-Groseillers. At 0745 hours the English artillery started firing a heavy barrage from St. Pierre-d'Entremont and the village of Perlyer behind which the infantry advanced, supported by the tanks of the 3rd Royal Tank Regiment.

REFLECTIONS ON THE BATTLE FOR AUBUSSON

Forty years after the event, Major 'Ned' Thornburn, MC, formerly O.C. 'D' Company of the 4th King's Shropshire Light Infantry, was asked to put his recollections of the battle for Aubusson on record. He wrote: *Since the majority of those who were killed there, and whose names are recorded on your Roll of Honour at St. Georges-des-Groseillers, were soldiers in my own Company or close*

*personal friends, it is perhaps fitting that I should do this in their
memory...I can only put in perspective the feelings of a particip-
ant, one who was called upon to make decisions affecting decisively
the fate of others.*

*The battle for Aubusson on 16 August 1944 was in many ways
the unhappiest of all my actions in France. It was an untidy battle in which we suffererd grievous casualties and paid a high price
for the ground we gained.*

*After 11th Armoured Division's brilliant break-through at St.
Martin-des-Besaçes and the Souleuvre Bridge, we had fought an
heroic battle on the Presles Ridge which unhinged the entire German defensive position in Normandy. As the German line started
to crumble the Division began a new thrust from Estry through
Vassy towards the Flers—Argentan main road. Vassy was occupied
by the Shropshires on 15 August, the Germans having withdrawn
from the battered town the previous day, and we dug in for the
night to the south of the town. The next morning the advance was
continued through St. Pierre-d'Entremont and Cerisy as far as La
Fouillée, but at this point a change of plan was decided upon. The
Shropshires were ordered to make their way across country in their
troop-carrying vehicles (T.C.V's) by way of a narrow lane down
to Pont-de-Vère. It was hoped that the bridge could be seized intact and the advance continued through Aubusson and perhaps
Ronfeugeray.*

*This manoeuvre had two unfortunate consequences. As has been
pointed out, the descent to Pont-de-Vère from the west was made
in full view of the Germans on the slopes of Aubusson so that any
surprise was thereby lost. Moreover, the narrowness and steepness
of the road created a bottleneck and made deployment difficult.
Too many vehicles were allowed to get too far forward, thus blocking the approach completely.*

*The attack was begun by 'A' Company at 1700 hours. Despite
stiff opposition they captured the bridge successfully with few
casualties and then began to advance up the slope towards
Aubusson itself. It was then that we really ran into difficulties.
The density of the tree-cover, coupled with the ramifications of
roads and tracks and the steepness of the slopes, made it difficult*

to pick one's direction and to pin-point the enemy positions, and even more difficult to see a clear objective. 'A' Company found it impossible to make further headway and (perhaps about 1900 hours) my own Company, 'D', was sent forward to reinforce and broaden the attack. Captain Walford, who had been leading 'A' Company, came back to meet me in a leafy lane near the foot of the hill (near the Laurent house) for the purpose of explaining to me 'A' Company's advanced positions so that I could plan my Company's attack up the slope. Thus there met on that ill-omened roadway myself, my Company Sergeant-Major Eddie Hughes, Captain Walford, Captain Peter Garrett*, the F.O.O. of the supporting artillery, and a fifth person whose identity I cannot now remember. A Sherman tank, which I have always believed was Captain Garrett's tank, was standing beside us on the roadway. We commenced planning the advance. The Germans were shelling us fiercely with their artillery but we were well used to that and I carried on with my instructions, keeping an ear open for where the shells were landing, some 25 metres, some 50 metres, some 100 metres away. Suddenly we heard a salvo of shells which we realized was coming straight on top of us. Captain Walford, Captain Garrett and Sergeant-Major Hughes dived into the roadside ditch, where they should have been safe. The fifth member of the group slithered quickly under the Sherman tank. I was too far from the ditch so I lay flat on my face on the road, a helpless target. The nearest shell landed with a crash, but in the ditch! It killed Captain Walford and Captain Garrett outright and gravely wounded Sergeant-Major Hughes. I, who should have been killed, escaped without a scratch. It has been said that God's ways are past find-

---

*On 3 August the pivot held by 4 K.S.L.I. at Grands Bonfaits was attacked by Tiger tanks and heavily mortared. Several of our own tanks were destroyed and the situation became critical. The Yeomanry O.P. officer with the K.S.L.I., Captain P. S. Y. Garrett, remained in his tank though that also was hit, and continued to direct the fire of the Regiment and also that of a Medium Regiment which was in touch with R.H.Q. Captain Garrett's shooting was so effective that the attack was eventually broken off and the situation restored. It was the opinion of the senior infantry commander present that the success of this action was almost entirely due to Captain Garrett's bravery and skillful shooting. Captain Garrett, who was killed in action shortly afterwards, received the award of the Military Cross for his part in this action. *(History of the Ayrshire Yeomanry).*

ing out but I have lived the rest of my life with the conviction that my own contribution to the common pool must be that of three men. Captain Walford was perhaps the best-loved officer in the Battalion and Captain Garrett, by his fearless devotion to his task of providing us with effective artillery support, had come to be regarded by our men as a member of their own Regiment.

This catastrophe (for so it undoubtedly was) gravely impaired the effectiveness of 'D' Company's attack. Some ground was gained but Aubusson was not reached before darkness fell about 2200 hours. The Germans then withdrew their rearguard from their positions at 2300 hours, as had presumably been their intention from the first, having by then delayed the British advance for half a day on the line of the River Vère. The following morning the Division resumed its advance against slight opposition for a further 15 miles before again bumping the enemy rearguards.

During the ill-fated attack on Aubusson I also lost one of my best senior N.C.O.'s, Sergeant Jameson, as well as the driver of my Company Bren-gun Carrier, Private Cole. All these casualties were to key personnel and I was left wondering uneasily just how vital was the objective which had cost the lives of so many valuable officers and men, or whether after the capture of the bridge the objective of harrying a crumbling enemy could not have been achieved just as effectively at less cost in human life.

Yet all was not on the debit side. Aubusson was the first action in which we came into contact with the French civilian population and we discovered a new facet of war. The local inhabitants suffered their own casualties from the shelling and mortaring (as well as from enemy mines) just as we ourselves did. Our Medical Officer, Captain Mearns, found himself treating civilian wounded in his Regimental Aid Post. And when, the next day, our Chaplain came to bury our dead he found himself supported by a number of people from the village who even took the time to make an enclosure round the graves and covered them with flowers, in spite of their preoccupation with their own dead. This spontaneous gesture of friendship and sympathy, which profoundly moved us when we heard about it later, was to be the beginning of a friendship which was to be consummated in the erection of the Divi-

sion's War Memorial and a lasting association between our Anciens Combattants and the people of this region.

As I mourned the loss of friends and comrades during that depressing night in August 1944 I little thought that 25, 30 and 40 years on I would be making pilgrimages to this self-same village.

And Lieutenant Wrenn of 8 Platoon, 'A' Company, 4th K.S.L.I. relates the following. *About 3 or 4 days before Aubusson my Platoon dug in in a new area along with Captain Walford.He had just pointed out where he wanted his slit trench dug when he decided to sleep in a farm building nearby. That night we had some very heavy shelling. A direct hit wiped out one of my three sections and another direct hit landed on where 'Buster' Walford would have been if he had stayed where he intended to dig his trench. Major Tom Maddocks, O.C. 'A' Company, told me of 'Buster's death and asked me to act as 2 i/c in his place but also to look after my own platoon.*

THE LIBERATION OF SAINT-GEORGES

While all this was going on the town of Saint-Georges welcomed the first British reconnaissance troops coming from La Bourdonnière. They were followed in the evening by 'A' and 'B' Squadrons of the 2nd Northamptonshires who had been held in reserve by 159 Brigade during its advance on Flers. They were given the job of clearing the area north of Flers where, according to a patrol of the Inns of Court, a few hundred Germans were waiting to surrender. The prisoners were rounded up at Mesleret and assembled along a path near the intersection. One part of 'A' Squadron headed for Les Groseillers and the other towards Aubusson by way of Le Coudray. 'B' Squadron made for Flers.

The fields and orchards were full of civilians and German troops. Some of the Germans wanted to surrender but others continued to fight fiercely, hiding in ambush behind hedges and on the high ground. It was very difficult to know which was which; while some came forward to surrender, others, at the same time, fired on the tanks from above. German guns also opened up and shells fell indiscriminately on friend and foe alike and also on some civilians who ran to the tanks for cover.

I was just a kid at the time, recounts Gerard Delaunay, *but I remember that from Mesleret the English saw some Germans crossing the Condé road at its high point near the Bonnesoeur café. A tank fired its machine-gun and I saw the bullets hit the corner of the garden wall where it stuck out into the road opposite the café. Some of the bullets kicked up a small cloud of dust, others sent up showers of sparks. While this was going on, with shells raining down around us, I and a few other tykes my age fought amongst ourselves to gather the empty cartridge cases as they fell from the tank's machine-guns.*

THE NORTHAMPTONSHIRES ARRIVE IN FLERS

German artillery continued to shell St. Georges-des-Groseillers and, in particular, that part of Mesleret where the Northamptonshires' tanks were. Some civilians were killed and there were also some casualties among the soldiers. It was obvious that the enemy was using a well-placed observation post from which he was directing the fire with great accuracy. 'B' Squadron, who had just received the order to push on to Flers, shelled the bell-tower of Aubusson, thinking that it was there that the observation post was situated. They scored a direct hit on the tower but unfortunately the German observer was not there. He was in the attic of the presbytery, a few yards away!

The Squadron continued on to Flers and, in its turn, sent in the same report as that sent in early that afternoon by the Inns of Court patrols, namely, there were no Germans in Flers.

THE FLOWERS OF LES GROSEILLERS

At about this time 'A' Squadron received orders to send out patrols towards Aubusson from the southeast. Some armoured cars left on this reconnaissance, going along the La Guermondière road.

The inhabitants of Les Groseillers stopped them and thrust flowers and wine on them. After an interval, Sergeant Titcombe and Corporal Smith continued on their way in their scout-car. They did not go far. At the next village they had a rendezvous with death. Their scout-car received a direct hit from a *panzerfaust* and was set on fire. Corporal Smith was killed instantly and Sergeant Titcombe, terribly wounded, died a little later. *We were broken-hearted,* said the villagers, *when we saw the unfortunate sergeant, burnt and bruised, go by on a bier. His battledress blouse was partially open and, falling out of it, we could see the flowers we had just given him.*

WHO FIRED AT US?

Another detachment went towards Aubusson via Le Coudray, gathering in German prisoners on the way. However, they were very unhappy when one of their tanks was hit, luckily, without any of the crew being hurt. Because they thought that they had destroyed the enemy observation post in the bell-tower, the Northamptonshires believed, for a moment, that the shells that hit them must have come from the tanks of another regiment of the Division approaching Aubusson from the north. They got on the blower and demanded an explanation. To cut a long story short, the other regiment gave them its exact position and, in turn, asked the Northamptonshires to disclose theirs by firing three red Very lights. This the Northamptonshires did and promptly attracted a new salvo of shells. Now they were certain that it was the enemy. The prisoners were left to fend for themselves, the infantry went in to clear the area and the tanks withdrew to a safer place.

A WARM WELCOME FOR A COLONEL AND A MAJOR

By nightfall the heights of Aubusson had not been cleared and fighting continued in the dark. The British artillery continued to fire right up to 11 o'clock. It was estimated that more than 2,500 shells were fired at the village, not counting mortar bombs.

'A', 'C' and 'D' Companies of the Shropshires were ordered to consolidate their positions around Aubusson while 'B' Company was told to occupy the heights between Le Breuil and Le Pont-de-Vère and, in particular, the track running through Montilly Wood.

The relief of the Shropshires by the 8th Rifle Brigade that had been planned for that evening after the fall of Aubusson and the support of the latter by the tanks of the 23rd Hussars who were getting ready to advance the next day on Athis, La Carneille, Taillebois and Notre Dame du Rocher, could not take place. Nevertheless, Lt. Colonel Hunter of the Rifle Brigade and Major Blacker of the Hussars did all they could to carry out the orders they had received that afternoon. When night fell they headed for Aubusson to try and find the place held by the Shropshires so that the relief could take place that night. The reception they received told them that the position was certainly strongly held, but by the enemy! The relief was put off to the next day.

THE INFIRMARY AT LE CATEL

It is difficult to estimate German losses during this fighting because, according to reliable witnesses, they took their dead with them for burial later. The civilians, as usual, paid a heavy price despite the care given to them by the English hospital set up in Le Pont-de-Vère. Dr. C. W. Mearns, who now practises in Northern Ireland, remembers that day very well. *I was the Medical Officer attached to the Shropshires. During the retreat of the Germans into the Falaise Pocket my Battalion was stopped by enemy fire from the other side of the Vère. Captains Walford and Garrett were killed in the fighting that ensued. A little later, after our men had taken the bridge, I went forward with my First Aid Post to be up close to the wounded. I clearly remember seeing two bodies on the side of the road, one of which I recognized as Sergeant Jameson of 'D' Company.*

There was an abandoned house just past the bridge, on the right, near the intersection. (This house belonged to the Lecornu family who had prudently decided to stay clear of the road). *I put my First Aid Post in it. Because our two companies had advanced by different routes on the left of the main road I thought it advisable to post a sentry during the night to take care of any eventuality. Then I began to attend to the wounded who arrived in a never-ending stream. Among them were some civilians and I particularly remember two women. One of them* (Mme. Mesrouze) *had part of her face blown off and the other* (Mlle. Trempu) *had her abdomen ripped open and the internal organs perforated. I did what I could for them and evacuated them as quickly as possible to a rear hospital but I don't think they could have survived their terrible wounds.*

TAKE THAT!... AND THAT!

When the battle was over and I was sure that all the wounded had been taken care of I decided to take a rest. My sergeant woke me up before dawn. While on guard he had heard a noise and voices not far from the house. It turned out to be a group of excited civilians who wanted to show us where more Germans could be found. While we were trying to understand what they were saying a prisoner arrived, escorted by one of our men with his rifle loaded and bayonet fixed. Before we could make head or tail of what was going on, one of the women in the group, Mme. Lebon, rushed at the prisoner and gave him two resounding slaps across the face. From this we concluded that the Germans were not very popular!

RESPECT FOR THE DEAD

A few hours later the other Brigade of our Division began to climb towards Aubusson and I gave the order to withdraw the First Aid Post to rejoin Battalion Headquarters situated a bit to the rear. Our chaplain, the Reverend Muir Haddow, a Scotsman, arrived to bury the dead in graves dug in a field near the road a few yards from the spot where these brave men had fallen.

*That same evening—and I will remember this till the day I die—
while our column was crossing the bridge to continue the advance,
we stopped by the side of the road. There, on a gently-sloping field,
we saw the graves of our dead comrades covered with flowers by
the local French people. This touched me very deeply because I
knew that the padre had carried out the burial service only a few
hours before and, although the population had their own dead
to mourn, they had first built an enclosure around our graves and
covered them with flowers.*

*I suppose this was the only way in which, at the time, the French
could show their gratitude. Unfortunately, we had to resume our
place in the column and were unable to express our thanks to them.*

Madame Lebon also remembers the burial of the two Captains
and the five soldiers. *Many soldiers took part in the ceremony and
all were deeply affected because the two officers were well liked
by the men. Some of them cried and most of the civilians who were
there were unable to hold back their tears. It so happened that,
just as the burial ceremony was over, the postman arrived with
the mail; there were letters for those who had just been buried.*

Somewhere in Great Britain a mother, a wife or the children
who had, very probably, scribbled some words at the bottom of
the page, did not yet know that the letter would never be read
by her son, her husband or their father.

MORE TRAGEDIES

Before ending the account of this battle from the memories of those
who took part in it, we should mention three incidents that,
tragically, happened either during the fighting or the next day.
The first concerns Captain Bennett who, on arriving to take the
place of the gallant Captain Garrett, just killed a few hours before,
was himself accidentally shot by an English sentry, a raw recruit
with too nervous a trigger-finger, who had arrived as a replacement just a few days before. Hit in the stomach, Captain Bennett
was attended to by Dr. Mearns at Le Pont-de-Vère before being
evacuated in a critical condition. He did not survive his wounds.

The second incident took place the next day. A woman went to the river-side washing place at Le Pont-de-Vère to wash some clothes in the stream. The Germans had booby-trapped the place. When he heard the explosion, her husband, knowing instinctively what had happened, ran to her aid — and to his own death; he too set off a booby trap.

Father Amiard lifted the remainder of the mines in the washing area so that other people would not fall victim to those diabolical devices. This was the start of a new 'career' for M. L'Abbé. He formed a team and during the next few months risked his life daily in order to save the lives of others. He was continually summoned from every direction to de-fuse or lift explosives, was always working in difficult conditions and, sometimes, even in comical circumstances. His courage was only equalled by his modesty. His devotion was known to all. These few lines will have to suffice to tell what he did but really, in order to do him justice, an entire book should be written about him so that nothing is forgotten.

The third incident concerned a civilian, a young girl, Jeanne Devolder. Together with other refugees, she was taking cover from the shelling in a sloping field near La Masure. A shell exploded on top of a nearby hedge, seriously wounding Jules Betton, who bled to death, and killing Jeanne instantly. The unfortunate child did not know that, in death, she was going to join her brother, Roger, who had been savagely murdered the previous day by the Germans just a few hundred metres from there.

These were the circumstances of the murder of Roger Devolder. He and Marcel Montaufray, both from Montilly, accompanied the Lebailly family when they left Caligny for Bellou-en-Houlme. On 15 August, just a day before their liberation, the two men, together with Arthur Lebailly, decided to return to their villages to see what damage had been done by the recent shelling. When they arrived at Aubusson they were stopped by the *feldgendarmerie*. They were lined up against the wall of the Fouquet bakery where they were searched, beaten and robbed of their bicycles and money. They were then taken in the direction of Les Clos. At about 1300 hours the truck that transported them stopped in the village of La Corbellière, at the farm of M. Avice. Gestapo headquarters were there. The three young men were taken out of the vehicle and led before two or three non-commissioned, or, maybe commissioned, officers who had their office in the kitchen of the farmhouse. After a very brief interrogation, they were driven to the entrance of M. Avice's orchard between the farmhouse and the entrance gate. Each of them had both arms raised except for one who, because of his injuries, could raise only one arm. There, they were made to take off their shoes and, barefoot, they were backed up against the apple trees. Next they were spaced out along the wall of the farmhouse, their arms still raised, their heads resting on the wall.

Then the young men were handed over to the tender mercies of the forty or so soldiers in the orchard. Despite the precautions that had been taken to prevent them from seeing what was happening, Mme. Avice and Mme. Gémy witnessed the horrible scene and described it thus. *The Germans tried to prevent us but we saw how the ghastly massacre of the three unfortunate young man was done. They were hounded to the far end of the orchard by the unleashed pack of these ferocious brutes who, giving way completely to their most bestial instincts, beat them unmercifully, especially on the faces, with sticks, fists and boots. When they came to the orchard boundary hedge about 150 metres from the house, torturers and victims disappeared from our sight and no one will ever know what happened to the boys at the end.*

Some days later, when crossing his fields, M. Avice was intrigued to see some freshly-dug earth in a corner of one of them. He did not have to remove much soil to realize that he had found the grave of the unfortunate young men. He then undertook the sad duty of telling their families.

Supported by one's faith, one knows that forgiveness, like mercy, brings peace of mind both to him who grants it and to him who receives it but how can a mother, or a father, or a wife forget? *Pas possible!* It is impossible!

However, some comfort can be taken from the fact, and a good example drawn from it, that the nephews of one of the martyrs, in the course of their language studies, were received into German homes and that their families, in return, welcomed young Germans into theirs.

MEMORIES AND TESTIMONIES OF THE
INHABITANTS OF AUBUSSON

M. Guibout gives the following account of what happened at La Villière. *On 16 August 1944, when we woke up, we were surprised to see a detachment of machine-guns installed in our house; it was commanded by a German officer. Two more machine-guns and four automatic rifles were also in M. Horion's orchard, opposite his house. An anti-tank gun had been placed in the entrance to the cellar and it was aimed at the road, ready to fire.*

During the course of the morning we saw only one German tank. As it climbed towards the town, one of its tracks caught the entrance stairs of the house. Towards early afternoon, when the English artillery started their barrage on Aubusson, we and our neighbours took shelter in M. Horion's cellar. There were 25 of us. At about half past six in the evening, taking advantage of a break in the shelling, two SS soldiers came to turf us out. Seeing me in the entrance to the cellar, one of them ordered me, in good French, "Get out of here at once; you had better go back at least 2 kilometres." Although I was determined not to leave the shelter, I pretended to agree when suddenly the barrage started again. My two gallants said nothing more but quickly rejoined their comrades. All that evening and all that night we stayed in the cellar.

On the 17th, at five o'clock in the morning, curious to know what was happening outside, I stuck my head out. There were the Germans, their hands held high in the air, under the guard of a very welcome Englishman. When I returned to my house later in the morning I found a basket full of grenades in the cellar and also an anti-tank mine. An English officer came to de-fuse them. Some time later, Father Amiard also came searching for explosives of this kind.

René Seigneur and Henri Garnier of La Guermondière had the following story to tell. *All of us from that time, young and old alike, will remember that 16 August forever. In the early afternoon, four batteries of German guns shelled St. Georges from Ronfeugeray. At about 9 o'clock in the evening a scouting Allied armoured car arrived at the bottom of the hill at La Guermondière via the lane from Les Groseillers. During the course of the after-noon a German had arrived at the farm of M. and Mme. Pierre Seigneur saying, in distraught French, "I'll shoot the first one of the enemy to show himself." This he did by taking up a position behind an embankment and firing at and hitting the armoured car, killing a soldier named 'Smith'. We buried the Englishman right there. We covered his grave with flowers and the inhabitants of Groseillers tended it for several years. His companion was ter-ribly burnt but he managed to get out of the armoured car and escape.*

Most of us spent the dreadful, long night of 16/17 August huddled together in our slit trenches though some chose to stay in their houses. Shells burst on all sides as the artillery fire shortened its range and crashed down on the village. The first of the English arrived in the small hours of the morning of 17 August. A Ger-man surrendered near M. Seigneur's house, a Jugoslav and a Czech near M. Garnier's. At last we were liberated and, most incredibly, without a single civilian being killed or wounded.

Maurice Briard has his memories of 16 August at Coudray. *The weather was fine and two Coudray families left to go to Bellou, on the other side of the Paris—Granville railroad tracks. On the other hand, there were many refugees, some from as far away as Calvados county, who could go no further. We were all set to use the mechanical binders from the farm for transport but, in the meanwhile, we waited. By 10 o'clock nothing had happened and we grew bored. We decided to harvest the barley in the field below the cemetery. We had to go by Le Chemin au Loup and found it occupied by German soldiers who were preparing to defend it. We then passed by Georges Mollet's orchard and started to work on the harvest. Two cherry trees had been blasted to pieces in the northern end of the field. A few soldiers had dug in in the nor-thwest corner of the cemetery. Others had dug fox-holes that covered the lane to La Croix-des-Aumones from the road to La Villière. These fox-holes (the remains of some of them are still visi-ble to this day) were so placed that the soldiers manning them could not leave their posts during the fighting and they also prevented any movement along the lane.*

*At about 1230 hours we heard artillery-fire from the direction
of Cerisy and machine-gun-fire from Caligny. We decided to return
to our house. At the intersection of the lane with the road to La
Villière we were stopped by German soldiers who would not allow
us to take the road; they said it was mined. A camouflaged command post with an anti-tank gun or a mortar had been placed
about 30 metres from the lane. We were brought before a very
young German officer who told us, in very good French, that a
battle was imminent and he offered to escort us so that we could
return without danger. About 40 soldiers came with us up to the
farm and then returned to the village. A spandau was placed in
a corner of the barn and another machine-gun at the end of M.
Mercier's garden wall. Other soldiers came to the house for a drink
and urged us to get out. We crossed to the orchard on the other
side of the road but that was all we could do.*

*I then left on a bicycle, going towards St. Georges. Everyone
seemed to be waiting on the edge of their slit trenches and a little
later I saw the first English vehicles arrive. I tried to tell them where
the German defences were but they did not understand me. I asked
Jean Delcroix of Flers to help me and between us we were able
to make ourselves understood to the crew of the tank that led the
column. On the map, I traced the German positions that I knew
about for the tank commander. They then continued on their way
but I was unable to follow them. A little later we heard from Le
Mesleret that there had been some sharp fighting on the road to
La Guermondière and between Le Pont-de-Vère and Aubusson.*

*Shells began to fall all over the place and many of them were
of large calibre. When I was eventually able to return to Coudray
the Germans had left. Just a few machine-guns rounds had been
fired from opposite M. Mercier's house by an English armoured
car. I found only a dozen small calibre shell holes in the village
and its surroundings. No one had been killed except some of the
English soldiers coming from Pont-de-Vère.*

The Vardon family was also caught up in the maelstrom at La
Maillardière. *During the afternoon of 16 August 1944 we were at
the house of our parents, M. and Mme. Henri Vardon, at La
Maillardière. With us were some refugees from Flers, making a*

total of about 20 people. The Germans had been very busy since morning and we got the impression that they were in a panic. They came and went in all directions as their orders became more and more hysterical. Some of them had discarded their well-known field-grey uniforms and had taken to wearing French civilian clothes, hoping to deceive their enemies, of course.

The trenches we had dug for our own protection were occupied by Germans. They had turned them into a defensive strong-point. We did not think we would be safe in the house so we took shelter in the barn a few paces away. Suddenly, about 100 metres away, we saw the low profile of English tanks coming from Le Pont-de-Vère. Yes, at last, they were our Liberators!

The first tank reached the house. It had a beautiful engine; my, what power! It went past us. Suddenly, we heard several explosions. A German gun, camouflaged a little further on under a medlar tree, had opened fire. Two shells hit the tank and destroyed it. Its two occupants, horribly burnt, were killed. Now aware of the danger from enemy resistance the other tanks withdrew towards Le Pont-de-Vère.

A little later our long agony of fear and suffering began. The British guns opened up in order to dislodge the enemy from our area and a rain of shells beat down on us from all sides. The repeated explosions tore the trees apart, pulverised the roof tiles and spattered the walls and the ground. In the very first hour of this hell a shell smashed the door of the barn. Mme. Trempu was killed outright, her daughter, Yvette, aged 14, was mortally wounded and so also was Mme. Mesrouze. Her grand-daughter, Gabrielle, aged 4, had an arm torn off and the same thing happened to Mme. Vardon. In terrible pain, our wounded lay on the straw for many hours. What could we do for them? Where could we find help? Outside, shells whistled overhead all the time. A German soldier placed a machine-gun near the wall and fired without cease in the direction of the valley. The English infantry, preparing to mount an attack, were pinned down by this fire. All evening long, violent fighting took place in the village, at times hand to hand.

Later, taking advantage of a lull, M. Vardon and M. Trempu, who had been wounded by a shell, hurried down the road to Le

Pont-de-Vère to look for help. It was a long time before they return-
ed. Not till 11 o'clock in the evening did an English ambulance
arrive to evacuate the wounded who, by that time, were un-
conscious. The unforgettable nightmare brought on us by the war
as it swept over us ended on the evening of the 17th, leaving us
utterly stunned. At last we were free from the 4-years-long Ger-
man occupation but at what a price!

The 4-year-old Gabrielle Mesrouze and Mme. Vardon survived
their evacuation to a rear hospital. Many weeks late their families
found them in a French hospital in Caen; each had had an arm
amputated.

CHAPTER 9

TOUGH GOING TO
BRIOUZE AND PUTANGES

POSITIONS AND ITINERARIES

At dawn on 17 August the positions of 11th Armoured Division and its units were as follows: Divisional Headquarters was in the village of Hamel, very near the Headquarters of the Inns of Court at La Halboudière, midway between Vassy and St. Pierre-d'Entremont; 29 Brigade Headquarters was at Le Prail (Montilly), with 23rd Hussars at Cerisy-Belle-Etoile, 2nd Fife and Forfar Yeomanry and 3rd Monmouthshire Regiment on the heights between Damecent and La Cornière (Montilly) and 8th Rifle Brigade between La Harie and Le Breuil (Caligny); 159 Brigade Headquarters was in St. Pierre-d'Entremont, with 3rd Royal Tank Regiment at La Fosse (Montilly), 2nd Northamptonshire Yeomanry in the village of Caligny and 1st Herefordshire Regiment and the 8th Northumberland Fusiliers scattered among the hamlets of La Fouillée, La Bazoque, L'Aubrière and Le Mesleret. Finally, the 4th King's Shropshire Light Infantry, having fought for part of the night, occupied the heights from Aubusson to La Guermondière.

During the night the decision had been taken for 11th Armoured to advance on two main axes, i.e. 29 Brigade to the north, via Aubusson, towards Athis, La Carneille and Notre-Dame-du-Rocher and 159 Brigade to the south, via Flers, towards La Selle, Echalou, Bellou, Landigou, Durcet, Ste. Opportune, Les Tourailles and Briouze.

THE JOYS OF PATROLLING

As usual, the patrols of the Inns of Court were the first in action. It was 'A' Squadron, in reserve the previous day, which left camp first, going along the road from Cerisy to Caligny. They crossed the River Vère in broad daylight and climbed towards Aubusson where they split up into several groups. It was soon after this that the first of them, *les premiers Anglais,* were received as liberators. They were covered with flowers and plied with the best bottles of wine reserved for just this occasion. Conversely, by nightfall they found that their stocks of cigarettes were very low!

THE FIRST INTO RONFEUGERAY

At 0720 hours the first group signalled that it had arrived at the intersection of Le Carrefour-Champian on the Athis — Flers road. At 0845 hours it entered Ronfeugeray. Vic Truss was in this group and recalls: *As the reconnaissance unit of 11th Armoured Division, up to that time we had been used solely to look for the weak points in the German lines where resistance to a break-through would have been feeble but when we reached Flers we realized that we were leading the break-through!*

I remember Ronfeugeray very well. I can still see myself driving through the village in pursuit of the German infantry, then getting down from my scout-car and chasing after them with my Bren gun. After that we returned to the village to catch our breath and to radio our report. It was at this moment that the villagers gave us our first welcome. Some of them brought us wine, others brought us something to eat. I have saved the photographs we took at the time and I have preserved them carefully because it was after this experience that we got the impression that the hard and bloody battle of Normandy were over. We hoped that this was the beginning of the end and that we would soon be able to return home in one piece.

A few days later one of Vic Truss' comrades had both legs blown off by a mine.

A little later the patrol continued on its way to the intersection at La Blanchère and arrived at La Carneille at 1010 hours, after signalling that German infantry was in the north of the town, near the village of Les Bruyeres. Next it made for the bridges at Bois-André and Pont-Huan. M. Victor Ballon met this patrol about half an hour later on the old lane called Le Roc-Creux. None of the English spoke French but, with the help of his son, he was able to make them understand that about 20 Germans held positions in the village of La Berthelotière and that the town of Carneille had been abandoned by the enemy. This information was immediately radioed to regimental headquarters.

From La Blanchère another patrol headed for Taillebois and signalled back that they had had a brief skirmish with the enemy at Les Naudries. At 1130 hours they reached the crossroad at Taillebois and early in the afternoon they sent a message to say that the bridges at Bréel and Taillebois had been destroyed.

ONE GOOD TURN DESERVES ANOTHER

While this was going on, 'D' Squadron was ranging to the east of Flers. A patrol coming down the Athis road stopped at the Little Sisters of the Poor where an American nun gave them a letter and probably a few holy medals also. Sister Marie Michel remembers: *The previous day it had been very hot. Some tired and thirsty Germans, on their way through the village, told us they were going to mine the nearby intersections, at La Planchette, the toll station on the Paris road, Les Douets and so on. "Whatever you do, don't let your old men go anywhere near them," they told us. We had pity on the soldiers and gave them a drink of cider. They repaid our kindness because the letter handed to the English soldiers the next day by the little American nun gave full details of where the mines had been placed.*

THE DEATH OF A FRIEND

The story of the letter and the mines is absolutely true. In view of the information in the letter, the patrol contacted their head-quarters and was ordered to make a half-turn and get back to the Paris road at Buisson-Corbin thus avoiding the mines and by-passing an enemy strong-point that had been pointed out to them by the inhabitants of La Fouquerie. The patrol, made up of the Tibbetts brothers, who had been the first in Condé the day before, and Corporal Baines, then headed for Briouze. On the way they marked the mines that had been placed at the crossroad at Landigou.

Twenty-five years later the Tibbetts brothers followed the same route. They left the highway after the intersection at Le Rocher and, going by the village of La Saussaie, reached the Briouze — La Forêt-Auvray road not far from the bridge at Saint-Denis. *After crossing the road we went into a large field on the right that slopes down to the Rouvre. We hid our Daimler under a hedge. Corporal Baines went forward to the stream and, standing up in his armoured car, examined the condition of the bridge through his binoculars. A shot rang out and we saw our comrade drop down on the seat of his scout car. His driver immediately turned around and came back to us. We were unable to do anything for our comrade: he had been killed instantly by a sniper. Sadly, we return-ed. Some hours later the body of Corporal Baines was buried in the cemetery of a small village near Flers where our Squadron's headquarters was at the time.*

The Regimental Chaplain found M. Joseph Turmel, the gravedigger of La Selle-la-Forge, and asked him if he would dig a grave. The burial service took place in the afternoon at about 1400 hours. The Corporal was taken to his resting place by a delega-tion of about twenty of his comrades, four of whom carried the body on a bier. At least 250 civilians followed the cortège. The villagers had gathered all the flowers from their gardens and about 30 children followed Corporal Baines' coffin, their small hands full of the bouquets they later placed on the grave. In the even-ing, a flag-led procession of veterans, accompanied by their families, came from the villages of La Rivière, Fumeçon and Les Aclos to pay their last respects.

When the veterans of 11th Armoured Division returned to Flers for the first time in 1970 the ceremonies organized for that occasion included, first of all, a visit to the cemetery of La Selle-la-Forge where Corporal Baines still lies. It, and the village of Sevrai, are the only villages in the county of L'Orne that have a grave of a soldier of the Division. The British filed by silently, one by one, passing by the headstone of the grave and then took their places back in the cars. All except two; they were the two Tibbetts brothers who, pale and in tears, had come back after 25 years to find the place where their comrade had been buried.

Other patrols of the same Squadron headed towards Briouze via Bellou-en-Houlme, Messei and St. Andre-de-Messei. They made contact with American patrols from V U.S. Corps between Bellou and La Ferrière-aux-Etangs and at Saires-la-Verrierie, about 1500 metres to the southwest of Briouze. They exchanged information and 11th Armoured Division was assured that the Americans did not intend to occupy Briouze that day.

THE RECEPTION AT FLERS

159 Brigade, advancing on Briouze, was led that morning by the tanks of 'C' Squadron of the 2nd Northamptonshire Yeomanry escorting the infantry of the 1st Herefordhsire Regiment. The first tank that entered the city came from Le Mesleret and carried a well-known passenger, Bob Bernier, head of the *Résistance*; he certainly deserved this great honour. The population who, the day before, had already had a fore-taste of liberation, overwhelmed the British troops with flowers, kisses, wine and so on. The historian of the Northamptonshire Yeomanry writes: *The crowd was delirious. Everyone wanted to thank the soldiers, to hug them or to shake their hands. This did rather tend to slow down the advance of the column.*

Another troop of tanks entered the city by the Cerisy road. M. Duguey, Mayor of Flers at the time, recalls how he greeted them.

On Thursday, 17 August, I was told that the English troops would be entering Flers that very day by the Vassy road and along the Rue de la Banque so I got ready to welcome them in the name of the City of Flers and to place myself at their disposal. I waited a little further down Rue Charles-Mousset and soon saw the first tanks appear. I asked for the officer commanding the detachment. I was told that the officers were in the vehicles that followed and I was soon introduced to them. Among them were two French officers, a Major and a Captain. After a few words of greeting I invited them to my house on the Rue de la Banque to celebrate their arrival. There we drank champagne toasts to Liberty and to Victory.

TROUBLES AT LANDIGOU

The mines that had been placed at the toll station and at the crossroad on the Paris road were lifted without anyone getting hurt. However, when the lead tank arrived at about 11 o'clock at the intersection of the road to Landigou, near the Bruyères' crucifix, it blew itself up on one of them. The column had to stop while the sappers cleared the mines. M. Touzé and M. Prodhomme, his employee, recall the scene as follows. *At nightfall on the 16th the Germans mined the intersection and the lanes round about. We had to be more than usually careful where we put our feet when we went to tend the livestock the next morning. While we were milking the cows there was the first explosion—and the first victim, a young girl who was going along the path below the crucifix. She was seriously wounded. At half past seven there was a second explosion. This time it was a German ambulance coming from Flers. It was carrying munitions which went on exploding in the flames for a long time. One German was killed. His two companions, apparently unhurt, managed to drag him out of the vehicle before he was completely burnt but then abandoned his body in the middle of the road. We buried him that evening near the crucifix. There was a third explosion and a third victim, this time a dog. Finally, just before noon, there was a fourth explosion, this time set off by the tracks of an English tank. What happened was that at about 10 o'clock, while a column was coming in our direction from Flers, a jeep with four men on board drove up. They questioned us and we told them that the intersection was mined. They turned round and stopped the column just before it arrived at the intersection. By this time, in anticipation of their arrival, large numbers of civilians had gathered there. An old lady, a refugee from Caen, offered the men flowers and glasses of cider, busily rushing to and fro. Then, ignoring our warning, the column set off again. The jeeps passed through without trouble but the first tank blew up just opposite the roadside crucifix. Two of its crew were wounded.*

The intersection was cleared by pushing the tank off the road into an orchard. After the mines had been lifted, the remaining tanks and the infantry continued on their way to Briouze, accompanied by French civilians on bicycles, many of them proudly displaying the letters F.F.I. on their sleeves. M. Moulin turned over three German prisoners to the English; he had caught them trying to make their escape in a cart. In addition, thanks to information supplied by the population, about 15 other Germans were picked up at various farms in the area. Ferdinand Lebailly, who had never hidden his hostile feelings towards the occupiers, made a big show of climbing on to the hood of a jeep and guiding it to the village of Les Landes in order to pick up some Germans there. He found 5 of them seated round a table, ready to enjoy an omelette. As they sadly raised their arms he took pleasure in asking them, "What's the matter, have you lost your appetite?"

A FUNNY SORT OF RECEPTION

The other Squadrons of the 2nd Northamptonshires, 'A' and 'B', were also sent off in the direction of Briouze except that they went via La Halouzière, Echalou and Bellou-en-Houlme. As they went forward, their line of advance gradually paralleled that of 'C' Squadron on Highway 24. They sent patrols across to maintain contact when they arrived at major intersections on the Paris and

Les Halzes roads.

Maurice Lefaivre remembers the reception the English gave him not far from the intersection at Beausoleil. *I and a few members of our group left from Messei for La Carneille hoping to rejoin the çolumn that was heading towards Bellou. When we passed the Luchaire factory we left the road and cut across the fields in order to save time and also to make sure that no Germans were hiding in the area. We had only a few hundred metres to go to reach the Flers—Echalou road when a machine-gun opened up on us from the column. The bullets whistled past our ears. This was certainly not the kind of 'liberation' we had been praying for. We did not stop to tell them that we were not the enemy; we just got back to the Messei road as quickly as possible.*

Undismayed, I set off again, this time on a bicycle, and reached Beausoleil by road without further incident. There, at last, I made contact with the English. I couldn't restrain myself from telling them that their reception a little earlier had seemed to lack a certain warmth! An officer begged me to accept his apologies and explained that the Germans used all sorts of tricks to get near the columns in order to inflict losses on them. His men thought we were the enemy and decided to open fire rather than risk being caught in an ambush.

FIGHTING AT DURCET AND AT SAINTE-OPPORTUNE

After meeting up at the Les Haizes intersection, 'A' Squadron of the Northamptonshires was ordered to make for Durcet and, if possible, to reach the River Rouvre at Tourailles. They arrived at Durcet without incident just as a German truck was leaving from the Avenue du Chateau. Its occupants were taken prisoner and some of the inhabitants began to celebrate their liberation. But the rejoicing was of short duration because very soon shells began to rain down on them. Someone blew a whistle and all the drivers scrambled back into their tanks while the infantry dived into the ditches on both side of the road to Les Tourailles. The intersection at Beaulieu was strongly held by enemy infantry. In the meanwhile 'C' Squadron continued towards Briouze; they also ran into strong enemy resistance, first of all from infantry in the neighbourhood of Le Rocher and then from 88mm anti-tank guns positioned on the high ground at the village of La Saussaie. It became more and more evident that the German rearguard intended to fight along the line Durcet — Ste. Opportune — Briouze so as to halt the advance of 159 Brigade for that day. Seeing no point in risking the same heavy losses they had taken the day before at Aubusson and knowing that there were a large number of Germans in the area, especially at Ste. Opportune, it was decided to lay on a heavy artillery barrage before launching an attack.

While this was going on, a few minutes before 1600 hours, the infantry of the Shropshires and the tanks of the 3rd Royal Tank Regiment were ordered to head towards Briouze itself and then to capture the bridges on Highway 24 between Pointel and the intersection at St. Hilaire. They set out immediately and by 1700 hours the headquarters of the Royal Tank Regiment had reached the intersection at Les Haizes. At 1730 hours Brigadier Churcher of 159 Brigade was told that there were approximately 900 SS troops in the Ste. Opportune area. It did not take him more than 10 minutes to decide, first of all, to call off the advance on Briouze that evening and, secondly, to clear Ste. Opportune instead. At 1800 hours Colonel Silvertop of the 3rd Royal Tank Regiment and Colonel Reeves of the 4th Shropshires went off together on a reconnaissance and established their headquarters at the La Maurinais intersection on Highway 24. An hour later Brigadier Churcher joined them and they prepared plans to attack Ste. Opportune immediately. A quarter of an hour later, General Roberts, always leading from the front, arrived and approved the plans they had made.

Accordingly, at 1930 hours 'C' Squadron, together with the Shropshires' infantry, prepared to leave from between the driveway to the chateau of Durcet and the intersection of Le Parsauque. Headquarters of the Royal Tank Regiment was placed at the entrance of the chateau's driveway while 'A' and 'B' Squadrons were on the high ground at La Maurinais. As had happened in the village of Durcet, all these movements and preparations attracted the attention of the German artillery and soon shells fell very near the columns as they waited for the hour of departure, wounding a few men.

MASSIVE SUPPORT FROM THE ARTILLERY

The artillery of 11th Armoured Division was soon ready to play its part. 151st Ayrshire Yeomanry had been in position about one kilometre north of Flers since noon and in the early afternoon they started ranging in the direction of Landigou. 125 Battery of this Regiment placed its guns at the exit of Les Hautes-Folletières while the other batteries were strung out along the highway, the southernmost being near La Provotière, not far from the Landigou road.

Assuming that the enemy had tanks in the area, 117 Battery of 75th Anti-Tank Regiment was attached to the Shropshires and the 3rd Royal Tank Regiment for the attack on Ste. Opportune. A little after 2000 hours, the entire artillery of 11th Armoured Division, attached to 159 Brigade, opened fire, first of all in the direction of Beaulieu and Ste. Opportune and the surrounding area. The tanks of the Northamptonshires and the infantry of the Herefordshires succeeded in dislodging the enemy hidden in the ditches and hedges around the intersection at Beaulieu without too much trouble. After that the guns concentrated on Ste. Opportune for a long time. Next they shelled the area along Highway 24 from the Le Rocher intersection to Briouze to the southeast and then the area along the Rouvre up to Les Tourailles to the northeast. Later in the evening the batteries increased their fire in order to answer the German batteries hidden in the woods of La Mousse and beyond. While this was going on, the Royal Tank Regiment tanks in support of the Shropshires passed through them and prepared to attack the village itself.

As it happened, the opposition they encountered was very weak because, according to the locals, the Germans had been so shaken by the intensity of the shelling that they withdrew in confusion, defying the orders of their officers. By the time the infantry had finished clearing Ste. Opportune and taking up their positions for the night it was completely dark. Before dawn brought an end to the operation they had added another 20 prisoners to the 20 they had taken in the evening of the previous day.

GOOD-BYE TO THE 2ND NORTHAMPTONSHIRE YEOMANRY

At 2200 hours, in compliance with orders received three days before, all the tanks of the 2nd Northamptonshire Yeomanry were gathered together in order to be withdrawn from the Division. They were replaced by the 15/19 Hussars who arrived straight from England. The Northamptonshires and their Cromwells sadly took the road to Bayeux having been transferred, together with their 1st Regiment, to 7th Armoured Division. In a special Order of the Day, Major-General Roberts expressed his regrets that a formation that had carried out every task assigned to it so brilliantly was now leaving the Division and he wished them good luck for the future.

And so it turned out that one of the last tasks accomplished by the 2nd Northamptonshires was its participation in the fighting of 16 August, the day on which one of its Squadrons was the first into Flers and the day on which it suffered its last casualty, Corporal Smith, killed at Groseillers.

THE TACTICS OF THE RETREATING ENEMY

The tactics employed by the enemy in controlling its retreat towards the Pocket were to pull back each night for about 15 to 20 kilometres and then prepare a position at some place that favoured the defence, such as a stream, or in a valley or on the crest of a hill, and rest there during the day till nightfall. In such good defensive country, where just a handful of resolute and well-armed men or even a single, well-placed anti-tank gun could hold up an entire armoured division, it is not surprising that they managed, in large measure, to slow down the speed of the British aadvance.

Because of the Germans' skillful retreat, 11th Armoured Division was generally unable to outflank the enemy and thus open the way for the infantry divisions that followed behind it. Each day, along the entire length of the road, it alone was available to deal with the enemy rear-guards. On its left axis of advance that had been code-named DIAMONDS, was 29 Brigade. (The right axis of advance was named CLUBS). The left axis was led by the tanks of the 23rd Hussars and the motorized infantry of the 8th Rifle Brigade and also included the tanks of the 2nd Fife and Forfar Yeomanry and the infantry of the 3rd Monmouths. On the evening of 17 August they came up against a strong enemy rear-guard well entrenched on the slopes of the high ground that dominates the River Rouvre all the way from Notre-Dame-du-Rocher to Bois-André.

WHICH DIVISION WILL TAKE ATHIS, 11TH ARMOURED OR 43RD INFANTRY?

On reaching La Carrefour-Champian the first group headed towards Athis with orders to stop one kilometre short of the town because, at the time, it was still, officially, the objective of 43rd Infantry Division who were coming up from Berjou via Ste. Honorine-la-Chardonne. The second group continued beyond the same intersection in the direction of Ronfeugeray and La Carneille.

The Inns of Court patrols had been sending back such favourable reports all morning that each column made rapid progress, taking far fewer precautions than usual. 214 Brigade of 43rd Division, which had captured its objectives so brilliantly at Berjou and Cahan, had just been relieved by 129 Brigade of the same Division. At 0800 hours on 17 August, 129 Brigade was ordered to attack Ste. Honorine which had been shelled the day before by the English artillery. After that they were to attack Athis. At 1000 hours the 5th Wiltshires of 129 Brigade advanced very carefully on Ste. Honorine but met no serious opposition. At 1100 hours the 43rd Reconnaissance Regiment of 43rd Division got into the town and reported that the intersections were mined. By 1145 hours the 5th Wiltshires finally entered Ste. Honorine and liberated it.

However, by 1030 hours some units of 11th Armoured Division had arrived at the outskirts of Athis. They received permission to enter the town and promptly did so. They posted a few tanks to take care of anything coming from the valley of the River Vère (the *Résistance* was mopping up German stragglers there), sent out patrols along the road to La Carneille and then headed, first of all towards Ste. Honorine and then split to the right towards La Bernottière to take Taillebois.

THE ORDEAL OF A GERMAN PRISONER

The crossroads at La Bernottière had not been swept for mines so, before going through it, the tanks stopped at the village of Le Meslier. There a German prisoner from La Bourdonnière was brought to them. His story is worth telling.

The inhabitants of La Bourdonnière passed the word on to the English that an anti-aircraft battery had been in place for about 10 days near the farm; this attracted the first enemy shells on 15 August, after lunch. We cleared out that same evening. The next day some new troops of ours installed their guns there but they were soon spotted. This brought down another bombardment followed by another evacuation. In the afternoon, the munitions dépôt near La Gresillère blew up. In the evening, while the guns rumbled in the direction of Aubusson, we fled in disorder, most of us on foot but some on bicycles. Some of us were in farm carts, others had their bleeding feet wrapped in scraps of cloth instead of boots while others, absolutely exhausted, curled up and slept at the side of the road in spite of all the noise and confusion. Those who were stronger staggered along behind any moving vehicle, holding on to it with one hand. As we watched this pitiful sight we realized that we were witnessing the rout of the last of our troops. One of our soldiers on a bicycle said to a Frenchman, "To-morrow the Tommies will be here; for you the war is over."

The night of 16/17 August was calm. The morning also passed quietly until the noise of engines growing louder announced the approach of a column of troops on the road from Athis to La

Bernottière. The local people immediately rushed to the main road to greet the English — and to smoke their cigarettes! Eventually they returned to their farms happy that their liberation had taken place with so little damage.

A little later, one of the last of the fleeing Germans, armed with a revolver, burst into one of the farmhouses and demanded civilian clothes. The owner of the farm was away and the women were alone. They gave the German what he asked for. Hurriedly, he changed in a corner of the room, quickly getting out of his uniform and hiding his revolver away. He said he was hungry. They gave him some bread and dripping and while he ate he took a photograph from his wallet and showed them his wife and children; they were somewhere in Germany, at the mercy of the Allied air raids. The women couldn't help but pity him and this eased their sense of guilt at helping a German get away.

At this very moment the head of the family returned to the house where he was very surprised to see his new guest. He wanted to know what was going on and insisted on learning all the details. Addressing himself to the de-frocked German soldier, he made him understand, in no uncertain terms, that he himself had been in the Great War and that it was wrong for a soldier to disguise himself as a civilian. Why, if he had done that in 1914-18, the French Army would have put him in front of a firing squad. He went on to say, "The English are at the end of the driveway. I will give you two minutes to get back into your uniform and then I will take you to them as a soldier."

Accustomed to obeying commands and realizing that he had no other choice, the German got back into his uniform and followed his guide. Everyone was silent. The German was pale. When the two of them came near the column rifles were levelled at them. Arms raised, the German was briskly searched and an Allied soldier interrogated him in his own language. A few minutes later he left for the rear under escort to join other prisoners who had been lined up along the wall of the Crédit Agricole d'Athis building before being led off into captivity.

A-HUNTING WE WILL GO—WITH BAYONETS!

While an English patrol was having a look round the intersection, an inhabitant of Le Meslier told them that some Germans had passed the night in a field bordering the road on which the column waited and that perhaps a few were still there, ready to open fire on them from behind the sheaves of wheat. Electrified by this information, a burly sergeant immediately gave orders for the field to be searched. A Bren gun was placed on a nearby mound and the infantrymen took up positions all along the road on the edge of the field. A tank swung its turret round to cover the field with its heavy machine-gun. When all was ready, three soldiers fixed bayonets and, at the command, as if they were on bayonet drill, dashed into the field and attacked the wheat sheaves, one after the other. They found nothing there, not a thing. Back they came, strolling along at a more leisurely pace and chatting to one another as if they had been out hunting rabbits, still under the guns, and jeers, of their comrades.

THE BRIDGE OF TAILLEBOIS

As the road was clear, the tanks of the 23rd Hussars and the carriers of the 8th Rifle Brigade continued their advance towards Taillebois and arrived there at 1340 hours. A battery of self-propelled guns immediately went into action at the intersection. One hour later the infantry started to fill the bed of the stream with branches and logs in order to get the light vehicles across while the Engineers began to build a Bailey bridge more than 30 metres long. Just then the first enemy shells began to fall among them, giving warning that the battle for the slopes of Notre Dame-du-Rocher was about to begin.

THE ARRIVAL AT LA CARNEILLE

The column made good speed on its way to the Champian intersection in the direction of La Carneille and arrived there without incident. Colonel Brownlie, who was a Lieutenant at the time, gives the following account of this journey. *Knowing that the enemy was on the run, we realized that we did not have to slow down our advance to take the usual precautions. So my Squadron Commander and I decided to have a race between our troops of tanks to see who would get to La Carneille first. We went through Ronfeugeray at a gallop and saw some of the enemy on the road at La Blanchère but they got out of the way, obviously not wanting to interfere in the race! My Squadron Commander won the race handily and we then realized that we had left the rest of the Regiment far behind.*

Our arrival at La Carneille was marked by some very touching scenes of welcome when the inhabitants realized just what had happened. I remember seeing a butcher dancing up and down outside his shop, his carving knife in his hand, swinging his arms and waving us on.

We were ordered to carry on straight to the River Rouvre. Soon after we had left, the enemy started to shell the town and later we learnt that some of the civilians had been injured.

COURAGE IN A CASSOCK

In passing we should pay tribute to the courage of a young priest, L'Abbé Creusier. In company with the Touzés, father and son, (such a trinity had to be under the special protection of Le Bon Dieu) he devoted himself, body and soul, to finding food for his flock. Later, in spite of the awkward cassock that was still in fashion at that time, he turned himself into an acrobatic fireman and put out several fires in the town. He then went on ahead of the Allied tanks that had stopped at La Blanchère and passed back further information to them. This helped the column to resume its advance and in recognition of his services the English honoured the courageous priest by placing him on the first tank that entered La Carneille. But still L'Abbé Creusier had not done enough for that day; he went on ahead to Le Bois-André and came back with two prisoners and the next day brought in three more.

THE BRIDGE AT PONT-HUAN

Colonel Brownlie continues with his reminiscences: *While we were on the road, the Commander of my Squadron and I were told to await the arrival of the infantry before approaching the stream. However, we knew that it was still some distance away so we went on, side by side, until we found a way over. The bridge that I used was partly destroyed and a munitions truck had fallen into the stream and was still burning. A little later the Engineers started to build a 'scissors' bridge. * Just then we spotted an enemy patrol that had been watching us from the woods on the other side of the stream. We opened fire on it and it disappeared.*

M. Prieur of Le Pont-Huan remembers this incident. *While the soldiers were in the process of raising the bridge, some Germans came to spy on them. They were very close, just opposite, on the other side of the stream. As soon as they were spotted they were machine-gunned and they took off immediately. No doubt they carried back a detailed account of what the English were up to because a little later mortar bombs started to fall on the village and the approaches to the bridge.*

That evening a furious battle broke out at Le Pont-Huan between the advance units of 11th Armoured Division and the German rear-guard. It was vital to the retreating enemy to slow down the Allied advance and, taking good advantage of the terrain, they did so and inflicted heavy losses on the Division.

---

*A small, box-girder bridge, carried on an AVRE (Armoured Vehicle Royal Engineers), used to span short distances. It unfolded like a pair of scissors.

A BATTLE FLARES UP AT NOTRE-DAME-DU-ROCHER

Early in the morning of 17 August, recalls M. Godier who lived in the village of Aunays, near Notre-Dame-du-Rocher, *several hundred Germans, well armed with grenades, rifles, machine-guns, mortars and* panzerfausts, *were assembled in the middle of my farm. Their commander harangued them for some time after which they went off in small groups to their battle stations, some in the field just below the house. At the beginning of the afternoon we saw some English soldiers on the slopes on the other side of the stream; they were watching the movements of the enemy and trying to pin-point their defences. German mortars were already bombarding the approaches to the bridge. In anticipation of the reply that the British were sure to make before launching an attack and knowing that we would soon find ourselves in the middle of a battle, I led my family and all the refugees who were with us into the cellar.*

Madame Hebert who, at the time, was a school teacher in Notre-Dame-du-Rocher, remembers: *That day I was at the village of La Gaillardière, situated between the village and the Taillebois bridge. Early in the afternoon I saw about 20 English soldiers arrive at the hamlet having come from Taillebois by a dirt road. They hid themselves among the farm buildings. I went up to them to tell them that there were no more Germans at La Gaillardière. Those who had been guarding an important munitions dump for some weeks, a dump hidden in the woods of our farm, had left the day before in the evening, taking all their trucks but leaving some of their equipment behind. Others, among them SS troops, after blowing up the bridge at Taillebois a little before 9 o'clock in the morning, had also left. What I did not know at the time was that a large number were still well dug in in another part of the village.*

PROGRESS IS SLOW AND DIFFICULT

Supported by the tanks of 'C' Squadron of the 23rd Hussars, 'H' Company of the 8th Rifle Brigade crossed the stream by the make-shift bridge and established firm bridgeheads up stream and down stream from there. They were immediately followed by 'G' Company, commanded by Noël Bell, and by the tanks of 'A' Squadron of the Hussars who continued to advance towards Notre-Dame-du-Rocher. 9, 10, 11, and 12 Platoons of the Rifle Brigade, the troops previously mentioned by Mme. Hebert, arrived at La Gaillardière where they were heavily attacked by enemy mortars and machine-guns. The tanks of the 23rd Hussars had to fight all afternoon to get into the village because the German rearguard resisted every inch of the way. The enemy was supported by a few tanks but also by some large-calibre self-propelled guns that, very prudently, were well in the rear and so well camouflaged that it was impossible to find them. Leaving 9 Platoon to guard the hamlet, 10, 11 and 12 Platoons headed for the village in order to help the tanks clear it. Night soon fell and tanks and infantry had to withdraw to Notre-Dame-du-Rocher and spend the night very near La Gaillardière. They stayed there under heavy and accurate enemy mortar fire, suffering some casualties.

Madame Hebert adds: *Fighting started in the early afternoon and went on all night with a terrifying intensity. It did not stop until 0500 hours the next day. My family and I spent the night in an underground shelter at the lower end of the farm. In the morning we emerged safe and sound and discovered, to our horror, two English soldiers who had been killed very close to us just on the other side of the hedge. They were buried by their comrades in a copse at the side of the road.*

The two soldiers were Captain Hart of the 24th Lancers who had been transferred to the 23rd Hussars less than 10 days previously and Private Abrahams of the 8th Rifle Brigade.

RESISTANCE FIGHTERS ARE CAUGHT IN AN AMBUSH

As soon as the village of La Gaillardière had been liberated, Robert Lebon, 31 years old, a member of the *F.F.I.*, took up his rifle to help the Allies. Together with Roger Seunot of Berjou, 32 years old, and Louis Porée of Ste. Honorine-la-Chardonne, he set out to look for German stragglers. When they arrived at the village of Souquet they were caught in an ambush set by some of the enemy who were still full of fight. The first two were killed and the third was wounded.

THE FIGHT FOR PONT-HUAN

While the bridge was being built at Pont-Huan, the rest of the column had made up time and had rejoined Lt. Brownlie's troop, taking up positions all along the road that led to the stream. Two companies of the 3rd Monmouths, 'A' and 'B', were ordered to cross over and establish a bridgehead on the other side of the rivulet. A soldier from one of the platoons who had taken up a position in the middle of the millhouse advised the Ferouelle family to go into the cellar because, he said, they would soon be in the middle of a battle and an artillery barrage would engulf them at any moment. The very steep, rocky ground on the other side of the stream slowed the infantry down and they were almost immediately brought to a halt by enemy mortars and machine-guns placed on the high ground at La Bomberie and Les Aunays. From those two places the enemy could observe and counter all their movements.

Lieutenant Brownlie continues: *In the evening my troop of tanks crossed the bridge with a company of infantry. The Company Commander and I made a quick plan to attack the hill on which the enemy defences were situated. While we got ready to attack, the rest of my Squadron arrived and joined in the attack. All went well until the tanks reached the top of the hill where they were stopped by enemy fire. The lead tank carrying the troop leader received a direct hit and Lt. Munro was killed instantly. His driver, terribly wounded, had to spend the entire night in agony under his tank because every time an attempt was made to rescue him it was stopped by enemy machine-guns firing from the nearby woods.*

THE GROUND FAVOURS THE DEFENCE

Major Todman, who commanded 'D' Company of the 3rd Monmouths, recalls: *At 6 o'clock in the evening I was ordered to
attack with 'C' Company on my left. We were supported by Fife
and Forfar tanks. A very quick plan was made because no reconnaissance had been possible. It was simply agreed that once the
bridge had been crossed the Companies would follow behind the
tanks, each on its own side of the road. A signal for the advance
was agreed on with the Squadron Commander. As soon as the signal
was given the first infantry units set off.*

*As the tanks approached the summit two of them were hit and
the others were stopped by very accurate enemy fire. As soon as
the first platoons of my Company crossed the Pont-Huan—La
Bomberie track in order to attack the high ground overlooking
a very large, rock-strewn field, a well-aimed barrage of mortars
crashed down on them. My Company had to stop its advance and
although we took shelter behind a hedge and a stone wall, 6 of
my men were killed. 'C' Company, led by Major Keyes, was taken
in enfilade by enemy machine-guns while advancing along the left
side of the road. Major Keyes was hit and died a few hours later
and 17 of his men were killed or wounded.*

Some attempts were made to infiltrate along the flanks but they
failed. However, a few tanks advanced across the fields on the left
of the road and by the end of the day they had reached the
L'Aunays farm where they found several of the buildings on fire.
They went through the orchard there in order to attack enemy
positions established along the path from the roadside crucifix at
Notre-Dame-du-Rocher to the La Mousse woods. At that moment,
tanks of the 23rd Hussars, coming from the Taillebois bridge and
followed by the infantry of the 8th Rifle Brigade, reached the village
itself. It was too dangerous to continue the advance in the semi-
darkness — friendly units were already firing at each other — so
the attack was called off. The tanks withdrew and the 3rd Monmouths settled down for the night in defensive positions made very
uncomfortable by enemy artillery fire that went on late into the
night.

As soon as it was dark they started to evacuate the wounded. Because there were so many of them, a First Aid Post was set up a little to the rear and ambulances were sent up to bring the wounded back from the forward assembly points. Unfortunately, when the ambulances arrived at the bridge, they were unable to cross over to the other side as their wheels would not fit the bridge that had been built for tracked vehicles only. This meant that the unfortunate wounded had to wait until 3 o'clock in the morning before they were evacuated.

Major Todman continues: *The enemy withdrew during the night and at dawn we had the sad task of bringing in the dead. Twenty-five years later I was able to examine the place where the enemy positions had been established and I said to myself that we had been very lucky not to have suffered much heavier losses that day.*

At this point we should note that, from Normandy to the Dortmund—Ems Canal in Germany, the 3rd Monmouthshire Regiment suffered 1100 casualties, of which 267 were killed, thus holding the unenviable record for the heaviest losses among all the units of 11th Armoured Division. It was also one of the two Battalions to receive the Victoria Cross, the highest British military award for valour. This award was made to 25-year-old Corporal (later Sergeant) Edward Chapman of 'D' Company, the same Company that Major Todman commanded at Pont-Huan, for his part in an action on the Dortmund—Ems Canal on 2 April, 1945.

The other award of the Victoria Cross to a Battalion of 11th Armoured Division was to 32-year-old Sergeant (later Company Sergeant Major) George Eardley of 'A' Company, 4th King's Shropshire Light Infantry, for his part in the battle at Overloon, Holland, on 16 October, 1944.

M. Constant Noel gives his account: *The artillery fire from both sides ceased towards the end of the night so at dawn I risked going out to see what had happened. That was when I saw my first English soldier who told me that he was looking for some Germans who were said to be still hiding in the area. True, we were liberated but the damage to the buildings in the village and the area round about caused by the fighting was enormous. Next I went out to one of my fields and there, in the middle of my herd that had been killed by machine-gun fire, I saw a wrecked tank near which lay a body, on its back, its arms crossed over its chest. Shocked by the sight, I turned back. When I reached the gate to the field I saw another body of an English soldier curled up in the bushes on the slope; I had not noticed him when I first arrived. They and five of their comrades were buried in that same field, near a well.*

Two other graves were dug in the Touzé field, close to the road, in the shelter of a stone wall. It was Mme. Ferouelle who prepared the bodies for burial and later tended the graves.

SORTING OUT THE BOUNDARIES

On 18 August, in the small hours of the morning, the K.S.L.I. finished clearing Ste. Opportune: the previous day's heavy bombardment had persuaded the enemy to get out. However, even before 159 Brigade had completed this task, 11th Armoured Division received orders at 0230 hours to chase after the enemy in the direction of Briouze. Before 6 o'clock that morning, Colonel Silvertop, commanding the 3rd Royal Tank Regiment, brought his Squadron Commanders together. He ordered 'C' Squadron to continue the chase on the left through Ste. Opportune, rejoining Highway 24 at the crossroad at St. Hilaire, and 'A' Squadron, accompanied by the Herefords, to take and by-pass Briouze along the main road.

At this time, the inter-Army boundary between the British 21st Army Group with 11th Armoured Division forming the spearhead of XXX Corps on the right flank and the Americans was an imaginary line running from La Ferrière-aux-Etangs to Ranes, through Sées and then to the south of L'Aigle. However, with the tacit approval of the high command, the American 9th Infantry and 3rd Armoured Divisions, together with General Leclerc's 2nd French Armoured Division, had advanced beyond this line and had reached Highway 24 from Briouze to Argentan and had even gone beyond it in a few places, such as, for example, between Fromentel and Ecouché. But, officially, the imaginary boundary between the two Armies remained unchanged.

11th Armoured Division had a rather unpleasant experience resulting from this mix-up. 'A' Squadron, moving through the fog that covered the countryside and limited visibility to less than 50 metres, arrived at Briouze at 8 o'clock that morning. Its advance elements had passed through the town when a barrage of shells and mortars that seemed to come from the south stopped them between the railway bridge and the bridge over the stream near Pointel. It took half an hour to clear up the confusion before a more friendly contact was made in Briouze between the English and the Americans. The latter had occupied the general area the previous night and they now hurriedly called off their artillery bombardment.

It was essential for 11th Armoured to have sole use of Highway 24 but in order to do so the Americans and the French would have to agree to withdraw south of this line. At nine o'clock, Brigadier Churcher, commanding 159 Brigade, met his American counterpart, Brigadier Charmon, commanding 9th Infantry Division, in the market square at Briouze. A few minutes later they were joined by General Roberts and the three of them agreed that the situation on Highway 24 could only be cleared up at a higher command level because it concerned the two Allied Armies.

At 11 o'clock a message was received from 2nd Army Headquarters, from Monty himself, requesting that 11th Armoured be allowed sole use of Highway 24, code named CLUBS.

A TRAFFIC-JAM IN FLERS

In the meanwhile, 11th Armoured Division had to contend with other troubles in Flers. After clearing the valley of the Druance and building Bailey bridges at Condé and at Pont-Erembourg, 50th British Infantry Division had received orders to assemble in the area of Saint-Germain-du-Crioult — Vassy so as to be ready to follow the advance of 11th Armoured. At 10 o'clock, well before their appointed hour, 61st Reconnaissance Regiment of 50th Division arrived at Flers. Because of the hold-up of 159 Brigade at Briouze, the last vehicles of 11th Armoured Division had not yet gone through Flers so the M.P.'s directing traffic put Flers out of bounds to 50th Division until the last vehicle of 11th Armoured Division had gone through the town.

A BRIEF REST

While waiting for the confusion on Highway 24 to be sorted out, the units at the head of 159 Brigade got up as far as the heights of Pointel. There the men of the 3rd Royal Tank Regiment and the Herefords made good use of the delay to tidy up, to get some sleep and to bathe in the nearby stream. The 4th K.S.L.I., who had covered the distance from Ste. Opportune to the west entrance of Briouze on foot, did the same. They were all delighted to learn that they could rest until 1900 hours.

ALL-ROUND PATROLLING

Oblivious of all these activities, the Inns of Court sent out their usual morning patrols. 'C' Squadron left at 6 o'clock to cover the area round Briouze and then in the direction of Ecouché and Argentan. When its day's work was done, the Squadron withdrew for the night to the neighbourhood of Fresnaye-au-Sauvage. 'B' Squadron was up even earlier and at half past four it headed towards the bridge at Taillebois in order to cross the River Rouvre and carry out a reconnaissance of La Forêt-Auvray, Chênedouit, Putanges, Ecouché and Fromentel.

THE BRIDGE AT PUTANGES IS BLOWN UP

A little after 10 o'clock, Lt. Thomas entered Putanges only to have the bridge blown up in his face. A few moments later, while he was inspecting the ruins of the bridge, Lt. Grierson was hit by a sniper and died on the way back to his Squadron's headquarters. He was buried at Notre-Dame-du-Rocher. Lt. Hird, who brought him back in his armoured car, was, in his turn, also wounded by a shell that landed near his vehicle while returning to Putanges.

Father Leroux, Vicar of Putanges at the time, recalls: *For three nights in succession and up to 8 o'clock that morning, what we dreaded most was the attention of the R.A.F. The Germans were in retreat and were queuing up to cross the old 15th century bridge in single file. On 11 August the R.A.F. tried to destroy the bridge for the first time but their bombs fell wide, destroying a near-by house from which the occupants escaped unharmed. On 15 August when they made a second attempt we were having lunch and pieces of the ceiling, loosened by the explosions, fell into our plates — a little extra tidbit to celebrate the feast of Ste. Marie! I did not say Mass that day in Pont-Ecrépin. Next the American artillery took over from the Air Forces and, firing from the direction of Yveteaux, caused a number of civilian casualties. On the morning of the 18th I was across the road from the church, talking to the policeman, when a tremendous explosion shook the area. The bridge had been blown up. The pendulum of the clock broke and it stopped at the exact hour of the explosion: the hands marked the time as twenty minutes past ten o'clock.*

CONTACTS WITH THE 2ND FREE FRENCH ARMOURED DIVISION

A number of enemy tanks, still active in the rear of the advancing column, caused trouble before being put out of action by the guns of the 75th Anti-Tank Regiment. Some Panthers, holding positions on the far bank of the Orne to the south of Putanges, held up 'B' Squadron of the Inns of Court when it tried to move in the direction of Fromentel and Ecouché. It tried again and succeeded, coming this time from Briouze. At 1415 hours the Squadron entered Ecouché and at 1600 hours it made contact with the 2nd Free French Armoured Division.

HIGHWAY 24 IS CLEARED UP TO ECOUCHÉ

At 1500 hours the two American divisions that had crossed over the inter-army boundary withdrew to the south of Highway 24 from Briouze to Ecouché. The leading elements of 159 Brigade, who had been held up all morning around Briouze, could now resume their advance towards the assembly area just to the west of Ecouché. The first to arrive were the tanks of the Royal Tank Regiment followed by the Herefordshire infantry transported in lorries and accompanied by 117 Battery of 75th Anti-Tank Regiment. This was a wise precaution because there were still many enemy tanks prowling around northwest of Ecouché. German artillery was also active from the heights of Montgaroult along a section of about 5 kilometres of Highway 24 to the west of Ecouché. One of the Herefords' trucks was hit and set on fire but its occupants got out safely. As night fell, the occupants of another vehicle, which was serving as a Command Post, were not as lucky when a shell exploded very near them; it killed two sappers while they were digging a slit trench nearby and wounded both the Second-in-Command and the Adjutant of the Regiment. Buried immediately on the spot, the bodies of the two engineers were later moved to the communal cemetery at Sevrai where they lie to-day. During the night three other infantrymen were also mortally wounded.

In order to avoid further losses, the Shropshires, the tanks of the 15/19 Hussars, the guns of the Ayrshire Yeomanry and a party of divisional troops were diverted to the southwest of Ecouché. They made a detour from Fromentel south along the roads in the American sector and eventually arrived at the assembly positions near Ecouché via the Rennes road. The traffic along these roads was so dense that it was near daybreak when the 15/19 Hussars and the Shropshires finally arrived at their destination.

During that same night the German airforce dropped large numbers of parachute flares that lit up the whole area but, fortunately, no bombs.

OBJECTIVE PUTANGES

During the night of 17/18 August the enemy withdrew from Notre-Dame-du-Rocher in the general direction of Putanges. The next morning, 'B' Squadron of the 23rd Hussars led 29 Brigade, accompanied by 'F' Company of the Rifle Brigade and followed by 'C' Squadron. All along the road they saw the unmistakable signs of a disorganized, hasty retreat. Abandoned equipment, destroyed and disabled tanks, tired, dirty, demoralized prisoners — all this told them that they were approaching the Falaise Pocket that the Brigade would soon have to cross. Burning *panzers,* destroyed trucks and large numbers of dead horses littered the sides of the road and filled the ditches into which they had been pushed in order to clear a passage. At noon, 'B' Squadron arrived at the heights overlooking Putanges to find that the bridge over the Orne had been destroyed. Those who had taken part in the savage fighting around Hill 112 just 6 weeks before could hardly believe that 11th Armoured Division could now cross the same river barely 60 kilometres further away with practically no opposition.

SHARING A PEACE PIPE

Still accompanied by the Rifle Brigade, 'B' Squadron of the 23rd Hussars went off to the south of Putanges to see if they could find another route. They soon met heavy opposition but this time no blood was shed; they had to battle their way against an American column that was coming down from Fromentel on the same road but going in the opposite direction. Just then orders came through for the Americans to drop back to the south of Highway 24. Major Wigan of the 23rd Hussars was invited to a pow-pow by the American commander and they discussed the new orders over a peace pipe!

THE LAST BRIDGE OVER THE ORNE

While this was going on, 'C' Squadron was called on to undertake a more delicate task; they were ordered to tackle the enemy who had taken up positions between the road from Ste. Honorine-la-Guillaume, Putanges and the River Orne and who still had some guns and tanks. Accordingly, they made for the bridge at Ste. Croix which was the only remaining bridge over the Orne by which the last of the enemy could escape. However, this bridge was covered by a rearguard strongly entrenched in and around the village of Launay. After several tentative attempts to attack it from the front and to outflank it, unsuccessful attempts that went on all afternoon, the Squadron withdrew and the bridge was left in the hands of the Germans who eventually blew it up.

A NEW TASK FOR THE 3RD MONMOUTHS

The only thing 29 Brigade could do in order to get across the Orne was to establish a bridgehead at Putanges before building a Bailey bridge there. Just before noon, the 3rd Monmouths, who had spent the morning licking the wounds they had suffered the day before, left Notre-Dame-du-Rocher for the assembly area a little beyond Mesnil-Gondouin. There they met up again with the guns of the 13th Royal Horse Artillery who had stopped on the road east of Chênedouit to shoot off a few rounds in the direction of Ste. Croix, and with the tanks of the Fife and Forfar Yeomanry.

The job of establishing a bridgehead to cover the construction of a Bailey bridge was given to the 3rd Monmouths. Their C.O. and his Company Commanders took their jeeps into Putanges at about 1500 hours in order to make a plan for crossing the Orne. In driving down into the town they received unmistakable evidence that the enemy was not very far back from the other side of the stream because they were fired on by an anti-tank gun hidden somewhere on the opposite bank.

A TOWN OF THE DEAD

The historian of the 3rd Monmouthshire Regiment recounts that the officers were appalled by the sight of the village. *Putanges was a town of the dead. Most of the houses had been destroyed and looted and only one or two inhabitants, frightened and dazed, were encountered.*

PLANS FOR THE CROSSING OF THE ORNE

They decided that they would make the crossing the following night. Because the destroyed bridge was undoubtedly covered by enemy guns, two crossing points, one above and the other below the destroyed bridge, were chosen. Two companies would cross at each point and then re-group on the other side to form a semi-circular bridgehead within which the Engineers could immediately start to build the Bailey bridge.

The stream was about 30 metres wide and the banks were steep. The men spent the rest of the afternoon lashing branches together to make rafts.

A COUNSEL OF CAUTION

Brigadier Harvey agreed to the plans for a night crossing on three conditions: (1) the artillery and all available anti-tank guns must be in position to give support; (2) until the guns could be placed on the other side of the stream the bridgehead must be kept as narrow as possible; (3) they must be very careful; if there was any opposition and the enemy mounted a counter-attack the advance troops must withdraw.

The guns of the 13th Royal Horse Artillery and the 75th Anti-Tank Regiment got ready for action while Noël Bell, 'G' Company Commander of the 8th Rifle Brigade, who was also given command of a platoon of machine-guns from another Company and a troop of self-propelled guns, disposed of all his forces on the heights overlooking Putanges in preparation for a possible enemy counter-attack the next morning.

A DIFFICULT NIGHT OPERATION

They went about their attack very carefully having learnt their lesson at Pont Huan the day before. At 11 o'clock in the evening the 3rd Monmouths covered the few kilometres to Putanges in Indian file, carrying their make-shift rafts with them. When they reached the city two small groups of good swimmers, each with protective patrols, went to the two selected crossing points and swam over, taking ropes with them to pull the rafts across. The two groups landed on the opposite bank without opposition. The night was pitch dark. The only light was a reddish glow from houses burning in Putanges that reflected in the water. Not a sound revealed the presence of the enemy on the other side of the river.

By 2 o'clock in the morning, 'C' and 'D' Companies had managed to get about 30 men over but not without loss. The rafts proved to be too small and difficult to steer and they sunk under the weight of the men. Two men were drowned and two others owed their lives to a courageous wireless operator of 'C' Company who rescued them and pulled them to the bank. Although there was no opposition from the enemy, the crossing proved to be much more difficult than had been anticipated.

'A' and 'B' Companies ran into even greater difficulties and decided to abandon their crossing point and go back, instead, to the bridge. They got hold of some long ladders and a number of thick oak planks that they scrounged from nearby and built a causeway from one rock to another and, in that way, crossed without trouble. 'D' Company Commander, not wishing to risk the lives of the rest of his men, used the same crossing.

WHAT A SURPRISE FOR A GERMAN CONVOY

By 3 o'clock in the morning the four companies held a semi-circular bridgehead on the east bank with a radius of about 1 kilometre.

By that time the men were very tired; many had difficulty staying awake and alert. For this reason, when they heard a large convoy of horse-drawn carts coming down the Falaise road towards them they did not, at first, realize it was an enemy convoy but rather thought it was a British one that had crossed the river at some other place. It was a huge surprise to the front sections when they suddenly realized that the convoy was a German one but no greater than the surprise of the Germans when they found themselves surrounded by Bren guns spitting at them from all sides at point blank range. Taken completely by surprise, the convoy dispersed in disorder, several of the carts going the wrong way and ending up among the 3rd Monmouths who took them prisoner.

A RUDE RECEPTION

Artillery support was immediately called for in order to hasten the convoy on its way but whether the wireless sets had got wet in the crossing or whether conditions for radio contact were bad or whether the gunners, snug in their positions on the heights overlooking the city, were dozing, when they eventually opened fire half an hour later, the shells, incredibly, went in the wrong direction! Instead of landing to the north of the Putanges road the shells fell south of it. Just at that moment, as dawn was breaking, a large group of German soldiers carrying white flags decided to come across the fields to surrender to 'A' Company. The shells fell right in the middle of this group of candidates for captivity. They quickly scattered into nearby woods and, less than pleased with the rude way in which their surrender offer had been received, they did not renew it.

The soldiers in the bridgehead at Putanges were able to see the devastating effects of the R.A.F. attacks on the retreating enemy columns. German army vehicles and equipment clogged the ditches on both sides of every road. The bodies of German soldiers were scattered everywhere, lying where they fell, for the retreating enemy did not have time to bury them. The roads were torn up with bomb craters and the fields and meadows were so heavily pock-marked that they looked as if they were covered with bee hives.

A BAILEY BRIDGE IS BUILT AT PUTANGES

The sappers of the Royal Engineers started building a Bailey bridge at 5.30 in the morning. After a quick survey of what was involved in putting up a bridge at that difficult site, they said that they thought that the bridge would be ready by 1400 hours. According to what M. Robine, President of the local *Union Nationale des Combattants,* and M. Paul Guedon, a former hairdresser, told us, the Royal Engineer officer who was in charge of the construction of the bridge was drowned while the bridge was being built and his body was swept away in the Orne. This was confirmed many years later when the Martinelli contracting company was rebuilding the bridge. The remains of an English soldier, identified by his uniform, were found wedged between the huge granite blocks near one of the abutments of the old bridge. The remains were transferred by the local authority to the British War Graves Commission which is responsible for all British military cemeteries in France.

A VALIANT MAN FROM FLERS

Before ending this chapter we wish to record that it was in this sector of the fighting that a 17-year-old *Flerien,* Michel Morel, who, shortly before, had escaped after being arrested by the Germans, was granted permission to fight in the ranks of 11th Armoured Division. This was the start of a distinguished military career that, after three wounds, earned him, in addition to a citation signed by General Roberts, the British Military Medal and several French decorations including the *Croix de Guerre des Theatres d'Operations Exterieures* (he fought at Suez, in Algeria and in Indo China), the *Valeur Militaire,* the *Croix du Combattant,* the *Legion d'Honneur* and the *Chevalier de l'Ordre National du Mèrite.*

CHAPTER 10

INTO THE FALAISE POCKET

RELIEF OF 2ND FRENCH ARMOURED DIVISION AT ECOUCHÉ

Before 159 Brigade could continue its advance from Ecouché, around which it had concentrated the previous day, it had to liaise with 2nd French Armoured Division who had held the city since 13 August and who had captured the bridge over the River Orne undamaged. The French were anxious that some other formation should take over from them so that, with the permission of Bradley and Eisenhower, they could make a dash for Paris. It did not take much to persuade them to give up their sector to 11th Armoured Division and they gladly passed on all the information they had about the enemy positions in front of them.

Once these formalities were over, on the morning of 19 August, 'A' Squadron of the Inns of Court, who, in conjunction with the infantry of 3rd U.S. Armoured Division, had liquidated all the enemy pockets that were holding out to the southwest of the Orne between Ecouché and Putanges, was recalled and sent towards the Forêt de Gouffern, a few kilometres to the east of Argentan, in preparation for the next advance of 11th Armoured Division in the direction of L'Aigle. They arrived there very quickly by taking by-roads that skirted Argentan to the south. At St. Christophe-le-Jajolet their itinerary took them through the sector held by 2nd French Armoured Division and 80th and 90th U.S. Infantry Divisions who gladly made way for 11th Armoured to go through.

WAITING FOR THE LIBERATION OF ARGENTAN

But now the 'charge' became bogged down because, going as it did from west to east, it cut across the northward advance of V U.S. Corps as it battled for the possession of Argentan. As it was, all the usable roads going east passed through Argentan so 159 Brigade could not continue its advance in that direction until the city had been captured and the roads opened up.

TOWARDS MONTGAROULT AND SENTILLY

On the morning of 19 August, 159 Brigade was, therefore, occupied in patrolling and reconnoitring the heights to the north of Ecouché from whence the enemy had been shelling them heavily from the time of their arrival there the previous evening. During the night the enemy withdrew most of his forces so at about 1300 hours the Brigade was able to advance of the axis Ecouché—Montgaroult—Sentilly. The Herefords, supported by the 3rd Royal Tank Regiment, met only weak opposition on the outskirts of Montgaroult. However, their Major Phillips, commanding 'C' Company, who, instead of taking cover inside the tank was sitting on the outside giving orders, was seriously wounded by a shell that hit him on the shoulder.

When Montgaroult had been occupied, the 4th K.S.L.I. took up the advance and reached Bois-Sérans without difficulty; there they took up positions for the night.

A TOUGH LESSON

During this same afternoon, the tanks of the 15/19 Hussars were assigned to protect the right flank of the Brigade. They had advanced about three kilometres to the west of Argentan and had reached Moulins-sur-Orne when they received their baptism of fire from a Panther. This threw the untired formation into a panic. Retreating hurriedly, they abandoned 8 of their tanks and 2 scout cars. Four of their men were killed and a dozen wounded. Their first day of battle had taught them that war is not a gentle game!

MAJOR MITCHELL'S GOOD LUCK

Directed by an observation plane, the guns of the Ayrshire Yeomanry slammed their shells repeatedly into the enemy columns fleeing from Montgaroult and Sentilly towards the east. Many of the enemy vehicles were destroyed or set on fire and soon completely blocked the road on which they were trying to make their escape. Going forward in his jeep in order to reconnoitre new positions for his guns to the northeast of Ecouché, Major Mitchell hit a mine. His jeep was completely destroyed but, by a miracle, he was not even wounded.

From their new positions the guns of the Ayrshire Yeomanry covered the Argentan — Falaise road, causing heavy casualties to the enemy forces who still had to use or cross it.

"I HAVE WAITED A LONG TIME FOR THIS DAY"

While the sappers were building the bridge at Putanges, the tanks of the Fife and Forfar Yeomanry managed to cross the Orne by a ford near Naudière and started to enlarge the bridgehead. Some enemy stragglers and deserters were taken prisoner but most of the organized resistance in this sector had dissolved. At 1500 hours the bridge was ready and the first to go across were the Headquarter vehicles of the 3rd Monmouths. While the column drove down to the bridge a gallant lady, Madame Guédon, who had run a café in the Rue de l'Eglise, deeply moved, asked to speak to the officer in charge. Someone directed her to Colonel Orr's staff car where the Adjutant, Captain 'Claude' Davey, was standing. With tears of joy and emotion the lady gave him two small flags, one French and the other English; she had made them some time ago in anticipation of this day of liberation. "I have waited a long time for this day so that at last I can give these flags to you," she said to Captain Davey.

Captain Davey took good care of the flags and eventually brought them back to England at the end of the war. On 10 May, 1970, at the end of the banquet that closed the first reunion of the veterans of 11th Armoured Division, Major Davey, as he then was, explained how he had come to own these two small flags and the importance of what they represented. He then presented them to the City of Flers. To-day they are exhibited in the Museum in the chateau at Flers dedicated to 11th Armoured Division.

ALONG THE ARGENTAN—FALAISE ROAD

After having enlarged and consolidated the bridgehead establish-ed by the 3rd Monmouths, the Fife and Forfar were relieved by the tanks of the 23rd Hussars and the infantry of the 8th Rifle Brigade. Together they pushed on towards the Argentan—Falaise road, right up to Courteilles, without encountering any opposit-ion. On the way they caught up with a convoy of horse-drawn carts and a company of anti-tank guns which they took prisoner with all their equipment and supplies. In the space of a few minutes a flood of prisoners was making its way to the rear.

MORE NURSES THAN PATIENTS

One party of tanks and infantry took up positions to pass the night around Commeaux. On their own initiative, 'B' Squadron of the Hussars and 'G' Company of the Rifle Brigade, taking advantage of the last daylight hours, carried on the pursuit up to Cui where the lead tank was destroyed. Its crew was taken prisoner but escaped the next day. There the Rifle Brigade found an important hospital which contained many wounded Germans and also a high-ranking medical officer who slipped on a Red Cross armband just as they arrived. There seemed to be more male nurses than patients in this hospital. The astute riflemen soon realized that many of the 'nurses' wearing Red Cross armbands were really fighting troops who had assumed this disguise hoping for better treatment in captivity. The men of the Rifle Brigade spent the rest of the evening trying to sort things out when they received orders to withdraw from the village and to pass the night in a quieter sector.

Meanwhile, another group of tanks and infantry reached the Argentan—Falaise road. A Panther which covered the road hit the two leading carriers, killing 8 men of the 8th Rifle Brigade. The group did not stand on their rights but made a quick turnabout and rejoined the main force.

All that afternoon the 3rd Monmouths were in reserve and did not go into action. At nightfall the Battalion held positions between Commeaux and Sentilly.

Towards the end of the evening contact was made with the American V Corps in order to establish their common boundaries and the places where 29 Brigade, in its advance the next day to the north of Argentan, could go through the American lines without disturbing the American attack on that city.

AN UNHAPPY SITUATION AT CUI

At dawn on 20 August, the Hussars and the Rifle Brigade resumed their advance towards the northeast. At Cui the situation was the same as on the previous day except that the arrival of *les Tommies* was not greeted this time by gun fire from the enemy. The situation there has been well described by the historian of the 23rd Hussars. *The German hospital captured at Cui had been installed in a beautiful chateau that that morning had lost almost all its beauty. It had the same air of desolation and neglect that was seen on all the other battlefields. Most of the windows had been blown out by the bombardment of the previous night. At the main gate there was a group of convalescents who seemed to be exhausted and utterly dispirited. The main avenue down which the tanks of 'A' Squadron drove presented yet another example of the ravages of war. In a nearby ditch, a Sherman, set on fire the previous day, lay on its side. Tank tracks had gouged and torn up the grass of the lawns and the gravel of the driveways. The neglected lawns were strewn with German bodies which were mostly shrivelled up or terribly mutilated. We tried not to look at the three dead horses near the gate, grotescuely swollen by the August heat, their entrails oozing out over the gravel. Personal belongings of dead Germans or of Germans who had fled were everywhere, an indescribable jumble of clothes, mess tins, helmets etc. But worst of all was the stench, the acrid smell of a burning Sherman, the nauseating stench of decomposing bodies and, in particular, the sharp smell that was peculiar to German troops and that clung to everything that belonged to them. All these smells combined to produce an effect that is impossible to describe.*

Scenes like this were common all over the place while the Allied armies encircled the Germans trapped in the Falaise Pocket and the Allied Air Forces pounded them unmercifully. This was where the completely disorganized and defenceless enemy was annihilated.

BUT SOME OF THE ENEMY ARE STILL DANGEROUS

However, there were still a few *panzers* which refused to give in and which had enough ammunition and fuel to try to delay the encirclement and to hold some passages open through which the last of their forces could escape. Just when patrols of 'B' and 'C' Squadrons of the 23rd Hussars crossed the Argentan—Falaise road, two Panthers, hidden in the edge of the Forêt de Gouffern, opened fire on the leading tank, hitting it and killing two of its crew. The remaining tanks immediately attacked the two Panthers and wreaked their vengeance by destroying both of them.

A TERRIBLE PUNISHMENT

The two Squadrons went into the forest accompanied by the infantry of the 8th Rifle Brigade. The historian of the 23rd Hussars writes: *There was abandoned equipment everywhere, ammunition dumps, burning half-tracks, Volkswagens, tanks. Most had been destroyed by the retreating Germans themselves but one could see that our Airforces had made a sizable contribution also. We were no longer appalled by the sight, now familiar, of disembowelled horses, smashed carts and scattered equipment. Here and there, lying in the ditches, were burning trucks and other vehicles machine-gunned by our fighterbombers. Sometimes one could see a shrivelled, blackened cadaver inside a truck while other bodies, smashed and mangled, were strewn around. We had inflicted a truly terrible punishment on the Wehrmacht.*

A MAGNIFICENT CATCH

It took 'G' Company of the 8th Rifle Brigade and 'A' Squadron of the Hussars about four hours to come to the relief of their colleagues after leaving the hospital at Cui. They crossed the Argentan—Falaise road at Occagnes, entered the Forêt de Gouffern and headed towards Bailleul but they did not reach it until the evening because the infantry constantly had to leave their carriers and, under the protection of their tanks, assure themselves that the enemy tanks lying on both sides of the road had really been abandoned or put out of action. Furthermore, the Engineers often had to come to their assistance to clear the numerous mines and remove trees that had been felled across the road.

Just then, 12 Platoon of 'G' Company landed a magnificent catch in their net: they seized the first German General captured by 11th Armoured Division together with his entire Headquarters. This was General Kurt Badinsky commanding the 271st Infantry Division. This is how Major Noël Bell, who commanded 'G' Company at the time, tells the story. *12 Platoon of my Company was advancing on foot when an elderly lady ran up to them to tell them that there were some Germans in her manor house. The men approached the place and when they saw a General at one of the windows they pointed their rifles at him and immediately surrounded the house. They quickly lined up the Headquarters staff officers together with the secretaries and other personnel and briskly searched them. The old General did not seem to understand just what had happened to him but as he no longer had a Division to command he agreed to surrender, but only to an officer. He refused to believe that Michael Anderson, the Lieutenant commanding 12 Platoon, was an officer. When, in due course, I arrived on the scene I had the greatest difficulty in convincing him that I was not just an N.C.O. He could not believe that, in combat, a British Army Major looked just like his men and when the Colonel arrived, all covered in dust and looking like the rest of us, it was the last straw for the old man. We allowed him the favour of saying goodbye to his staff. After much clicking of heels, salutes and even hugs, the first German General that any of us had ever seen was hurried back into captivity leaving behind two magnificent staff cars, a Lincoln Zephyr and a Horch, which were promptly claimed by the Colonels of the Hussars and the Rifle Brigade.*

During the afternoon, supported by the tanks of 'C' Squadron of the Fife and Forfars, the 3rd Monmouths also went through the Forêt de Gouffern but a little further south than their colleagues. Although they did not have the good luck to run into a German General they did capture an entire German field hospital containing nearly 200 wounded men, many of them British and American soldiers.

A despatch-rider enters Flers by Highway 24. (cf p.145)

I.W.M. #B9291

An infantry patrol arrives in Flers at the lower end of the *Rue de la Banque*, near the intersection with the *Rue de la Boule*.

I.W.M #B9294

About 10 British soldiers were killed during the battle for Le Pont-de-Vère. Among them were two officers who are buried side by side with their men in the British Cemetery at Tilly-sur-Seulles. The officers were Captain Peter Garrett (151st Ayrshire Yeomanry) and Captain 'Buster' Walford (4th King's Shropshire Light Infantry).

Author's collection

A general view of the Cemetery in which they rest. (cf p.163 et seq.)

Author's collection

Temporary graves in M. Sauquet's field at Le Pont-de-Vère. This photograph was taken during a ceremony organized by Roger Dubois during which the children of St. Georges-des-Groseillers placed flowers on the graves. The bodies were exhumed in 1946 and reinterred in permanent graves. It is in this exact place that the Monument was raised to the memory of all the soldiers of 11th Armoured Division who were killed in France and North-West Europe from June 1944 to May 1945. (cf p.314 et seq.) *Author's collection*

The 11th Armoured Division Monument at Le Pont-de-Vère. (cf p.314 et seq.)

L'Orne Combattante

The officers of 123 Battery of 151st Field Regiment (Ayrshire Yeomanry). The officer on the extreme left is Captain Peter Garrett who was posthumously awarded the Military Cross for his bravery during the German attack on Grands Bonfaits. (cf p.163 et seq.)

The Proud Trooper

Mine-clearing Engineers at work on the *Rue de la Banque* in Flers ...

... so that patrols can make their way in safety. (cf p.145)

Soldiers and civilians chat it up and toast one another in the *Rue de la Banque* in Flers.

The first Sherman tanks of 11th Armoured Division pass through *Cinq-Becs* in Flers. *Cinq-Becs*, the place where five roads converge, was lit, before the war, by a five-branched gas lamp-post. After the war it was first re-named *Place Centrale*. In 1972, on the death of de Gaulle, its name was changed again to to-day's *Place de Général de Gaulle*.

I.W.M. #B9330

A Cromwell tank of 'C' Squadron, 2nd Northamptonshire Yeomanry passing through Flers. The next day, this Regiment, having suffered very heavy casualties, was disbanded and replaced by the 15/19 King's Royal Hussars. (cf p.188)

A tank, loaded with infantrymen, makes its way from *Cinq-Becs* towards *La Grande Rue* in Flers.

While a Military Policeman waves on an approaching line of 11th Armoured Division tanks on its way to *Cinq-Becs*, a daring lady makes a dash across the road in front of them with her wheelbarrow.

I.W.M. #B9324

Flers having been liberated, the refugees, who have had a very hard time, start to return to their homes while a tank passes them on the Paris road.

I.W.M. #B9358

Civilians cheer on their liberators as tanks drive along the road near the churchyard in Flers.

I.W.M. #B9351

At *Cinq-Becs* a fireman, perched on the rubble, gives out the good news of their liberation to the joy and applause of the town folk — but look what has been done to their town!

The rapid Allied advance by-passes German stragglers all over the countryside. Here M. Née Louis escorts his prize, 7 prisoners found on a farm near Landigou. They were handed over to the British near Buisson-Corblin. (cf p.184)

In Flers, members of the *Résistance* bring in a jeep-load of German prisoners.

I.W.M. #B9327

A single British soldier marches German prisoners along the *Rue des Calvados* in Flers on their way to a prisoners-of-war camp.

I.W.M. #B9338

The French Forces of the Interior of the Flers region together with their leaders. Bob Bernier is in the centre of those seated in the second row, 6th from the left. On his left is Guy Mollet, then an official in the Department of Civil Affairs, later Prime Minister of France from 1950 to 1957. (cf p.182)

CHAPTER 11

THE CAPTURE OF GACÉ AND L'AIGLE

FROM LIBERATED ARGENTAN TO LE BOURG-ST. LÉONARD

After passing the night in the neighbourhood of Montgaroult and Sentilly, 159 Brigade spent the morning of 20 August resting while the men of the 15/19 Hussars, with great daring, went off in search of the tanks they had abandoned the day before. All the tanks, except two that had been destroyed, were recovered.

By 1700 hours, Argentan was finally in the hands of the Americans who soon opened a passage through the city. Then 159 Brigade, followed by Divisional Headquarters, went through the suburbs and headed for their assigned assembly area near the town of Le Bourg-St. Léonard where they all passed the night in a drenching rain storm.

OBJECTIVE GACÉ

The next day, 21 August, 29 Brigade crossed the city in its turn and arrived at Le Bourg-St. Léonard just after the last vehicles of 159 Brigade had left with orders to capture Gacé. The itinerary that 159 Brigade had to take angled northwards to D13, the road from Trun to Gacé, which it was to meet a little to the east of Chambois going via Avenelles and Omméel.

Advancing behind the patrols of the Inns of Court who had rested the previous day in the Forêt de Gouffern, sometimes leaving the narrow, twisting roads in order to go across country, 159 Brigade was first led by the 4th King's Shropshire Light Infantry mounted on the tanks of the 3rd Royal Tank Regiment. They were slowed down by mines, demolitions and destroyed bridges. 'Scissors' bridges had to be built to the west of Villebadin and at Omméel where, moreover, some enemy resistance had to be overcome before they reached Highway D13. In order to protect the left flank, the Shropshires were sent towards St. Pierre-la-Rivière. They were supported by the tanks of the 15/19 Hussars who led the column into the forming-up area for the attack on Gacé.

THE GERMANS RESIST SOUTH OF GACÉ

While this was going on, 29 Brigade left Le Bourg-St. Léonard with orders to take Exmes, Croisilles, Echauffour, Ste. Gauburge and L'Aigle. At first they were led by the tanks of the 23rd Hussars still accompanied by the infantry of the 8th Rifle Brigade. They soon reached Exmes and found that it had been liberated by 2nd French Armoured Division. The tanks of the Fife and Forfar went to the head of the column after they passed Croisilles and ran into trouble just as they arrived at the Gacé—Ste. Gauburge road to the south of Gacé. The crossing of the Touques river was particularly difficult. Only a few tanks managed it; one was destroyed, two men were killed, seven wounded and two were reported missing. Seeing that there was still enemy resistance in this sector, the rest of 29 Brigade, the 23rd Hussars and the 8th Rifle Brigade, were diverted from Croisilles via La Castelle and Authieux-du-Puits towards Echauffour. They stopped about 6 kilometres from this last place and spent the night there.

THE ATTACK FROM THE NORTHWEST

At 1700 hours the two Brigades of 11th Armoured Division were still held up outside Gacé by enemy infantry armed with anti-tank guns and *panzerfausts*. Because the Fife and Forfar had encountered strong resistance in the south of the city it was decided to attack it from the northwest. A Squadron of tanks of the 15/19 Hussars took up positions on the heights to the west of the city from which they could overlook the valley and opened up an accurate fire on the enemy positions situated on the opposite slope. The Germans were able to observe the preparation for the attack from the east of the city and started to plaster the assembly area with mortars. Sergeant Lawrence of the Hussars was killed and a number of the Shropshires who were getting ready for the attack were wounded. At the same time, Lieutenant Richards of the Inns of Court and his driver had left Highway D13 in order to carry out a reconnaissance of Gacé. Their armoured car got stuck in a narrow lane and was blown up. Both men were killed.

FORTUNE FAVOURS THE BOLD

'A' and 'D' Companies of the Shropshires led the attack on the city with 'C' Company following up. Colonel Silvertop, commanding 3rd Royal Tank Regiment, sent in a troop of tanks which, after first going through the city, took up positions on the heights in the east of Gacé while the infantry got on with the clearance of the city. To say the least, this was an extremely dangerous move for the tanks but Colonel Silvertop, with a sixth sense sharply honed by much fighting, instinctively knew what to do in such a situation. In any case, he got away with it and the city was taken without much trouble. When the job was over the infantry counted 150 prisoners. Its task had been greatly simplified because, thanks to the daring dash of the tanks to the east of the city, the Germans had been caught between two fires. The only place where they put up any resistance was at the railway station. When it was all over General Roberts, commanding 11th Armoured Division, sent the troops involved a message of congratulations.

"CHARGE! GO LIKE HELL THROUGH THE CITY"

Major Langdon takes up the story and tells how, all on their own, he and his tanks made their audacious dash through the city. *In the evening of 21 August my unit, the 3rd Royal Tank Regiment, which had been in reserve for most of the day, was ordered to relieve the 15/19 Hussars who were held up just to the east of Gacé. We were ordered to capture the city. Colonel Silvertop gave the job to 'A' Squadron commanded by Major Close and he appointed No.1 Troop, which I commanded, to spearhead the attack. I first went, on foot, to the Colonel of the Hussars who quickly filled me in on the situation. From his headquarters I could see the road that ran straight ahead, down one hill and up the next, as it crossed the city. Returning to my troop I quickly gave orders to each of my men. I took the lead, followed by Sergeant Elstob. I shouted to my driver, "Charge! Go like hell through the city."*

As we charged down the hill an enemy armoured car that seemed to be abandoned blew up just as we passed it and slewed across the road, blocking off the rest of my troop. However, I did not see this until later because by that time we had arrived at the first houses. Suddenly there was a series of violent explosions and I knew that my tank had received a direct hit. Knowing what armour-piercing shells can do from my experience in the battles around Caen, I ordered my crew to abandon the tank because I expected it to burst into flames at any moment. We flattened ourselves between the tank and the wall of the house where it had stopped. The shelling went on for a while and then I realized that the enemy were not using armour-piercing shells. The shells that had hit the tank had caused little or no damage so we got back in, feeling much safer, and continued our advance towards the intersection. We next came to the main thoroughfare which leaves the city to the east. While we bowled along on this double-laned avenue, I saw two nuns who ran to take shelter in a house. They were the only people I saw.

When we arrived at the exit of the city we took up a position so that we could cover the approaches. I listened to the conversations going on between the rest of my Regiment on the wireless.

After a while I gathered that they were still held up by the armoured car that had slewed across the road, barring it, when it blew up. When there was a break in the wireless chatter I came on the air and sent off my report on the chance that it would be heard, explaining that I was all alone at the other end of the city and, please, would someone come and reinforce me quickly.

After a while I saw Sergeant Elstob's tank coming towards me. He was soon followed by my troop and then by the rest of 'A' Squadron. No sooner had they arrived and taken up positions than an enemy half-track burst on to the road very close to us and came right at us. The machine-gunner of Sergeant Elstob's tank left his seat. With his Sten gun he wiped out the crew of the half-track and the rest of the Germans withdrew hurriedly.

When night fell the tanks withdrew into the centre of the city and were relieved by the infantry who guarded the entrances into the city. Later I learnt that many prisoners had been taken in Gacé.

THE FIGHTING AROUND GACÉ

M. Jean Grandin was one of the few civilians who had stayed in the city. When the Shropshires and the 3rd Royal Tank Regiment arrived he was at the Trégaro school. This is how he describes how they waited a long time to be liberated by the arrival of 11th Armoured Division in Gacé.

Anyone who visits Gacé to-day gets the impression that this town was lucky to have been spared by the last war. However, its bell-tower was an artillery target when the German hordes crashed through our defences to the north of Montfort on 17 June 1940. This small town of some 2500 inhabitants has recaptured its former charm but only after suffering terribly in 1940 and in 1944. The trouble is that Gacé has always been considered a town of great strategic importance.

Nestled as it is in a valley overlooked by wooded heights, Gacé is hardly a good defensive position but its strategic importance is as an important communication centre of a network of roads between Tours and Rouen, Argentan and L'Aigle and Vimoutiers and Mortagne. The annihilation of the 7th German Army in the Pocket at Chambois, just about 15 kilometres to the east, between the high ground at Montormel and Exmes, made the enemy, fleeing in the direction of Tancarville and Rouen, take a desperate chance. The stakes for Gacé were well worth the risk.

The Allies had started their advance on Gacé as early as 13 August. In spite of stiff resistance on the line Coulmer—Croisilles, the liberators reached the town of Coulmer. In the evening they seized the intersection at La Boulaie on the road from Exmes to Gacé. They were no more than four to five kilometres from the city as the crow flies. The enemy became jittery and vicious. That very day he arrested a group of us in the middle of the city as partisans while searching a school where one of our colleagues, a much-wanted Résistance fighter, was hidden. On that same day also several men of the F.F.I. were executed. The next day he tried to re-take the intersection at La Boulaie. Three days later, during the night of 16/17, he renewed his attacks and made ground near the crossroad at Son near which he set up defensive positions. He became more and more savage as he suspected that the underground was actively working for the liberation of the city. We expected that he would resist fiercely. Men of the 20th Panzer Division lay in wait in scattered positions in the woods and in fox-holes along the roads leaving Gacé towards Croisilles and Coulmer. The bridge that crosses the River Touques on the road from Exmes, a large one, about 7 metres long, was mined. We were warned that it would be blown up at 1100 hours on the 17th. An 88mm gun was placed about 50 feet from the intersection of Highways 138 and 132 and aimed towards Coulmer. Beyond that, on the roads towards Echauffour and Mortagne, in the terraced fields of the village of La Chapelle and in the hedges bordering the apple orchards the enemy lay in wait in small groups. We sensed that he knew that this was a delaying tactic while the main battle was taking place around Chambois. There were signs of confusion everywhere. Near this road, in the basement of an old distillery, 50 soldiers in field-grey uniforms were under command of a Luftwaffe Lieutenant, easily recognized by his clean, dark-blue uniform as he anxiously scanned the Allied position with his field-glasses thinking they were 6 kilometres away.

Previously, on two occasions, on the 13th and especially on the 14th, at about 1700 hours, the centre of Gacé had been hit by artillery fire which engaged the German guns posted on the heights to the north, towards Montfort, La Trinité-des-Laitiers and, above all, in the woods of Saillière. Again, on the evening of the 17th, at about 2200 hours, the artillery of the American 70th Infantry Division pounded the town.

Since the 13th, a large part of the population had been evacuated to the nearby villages to the north and east and to the hamlets of Madrilly and St. Evrouit-de-Montfort. The experiences of 1940 and also the sad processions of refugees from Calvados who, since 12 June 1944, had sought shelter by the hundreds in the Trégaro and Durvie schools, warned them that a similar exodus would give the retreating Germans a chance to ransack the houses. Later, on the 16th, an order was issued forbidding them to stay in their houses while the Allies were so close except between 1100 and 1300 hours. The fierce German resistance around Le Bourg-Saint-Léonard — it changed hands four times between 16 and 18 August — and the determined defence of the Germans at Chambois up to the evening of the 19th stalled the liberating troops and delayed the entrance of the Allies into Gacé. Although the liberators were at Croisilles and Coulmer, Highway D13 between Chambois and Gacé remained very dangerous with the risk of ambushes in the valleys through which it ran. The enemy was able to dig himself in on the wooded heights that dominate the road that climbs up to Avernes-sous-Exmes (Hills 277 and 288). Closer at hand, the Germans held the intersection at Son, about 3 kilometres from Gacé, from 14 August. Chambois had to await its liberation until 19 August at 1930 hours while the enemy tried to avoid encirclement by retreating. Isolated mopping-up operations went on all over the place. It was not till 20 August at about 1800 hours, after a violent barrage that caused the death of two people in La Fangeaie (2 kilometres northeast of Gacé) that the fugitives managed to reach the Rouen road on foot. At nightfall a large group of the Boches, about 50 men of the once-fearsome Wehrmacht, stumbled along, each armed with nothing but a rough-cut staff, looking more like

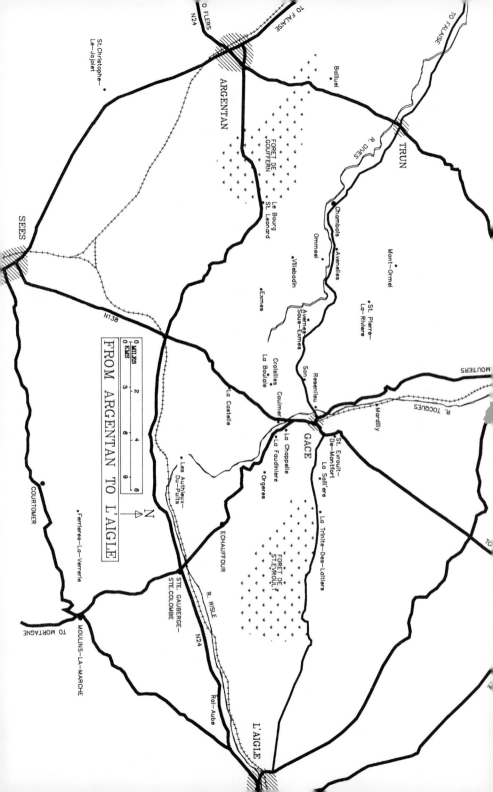

FROM ARGENTAN TO L'AIGLE

old men or fearful medieval pilgrims ready to defend themselves against robbers than modern soldiers. How Hitler's glorious army had changed its tune!

However, on the morning of 21 August, Allied planners were still nervous of possible enemy resistance in Gacé. In spite of the reports from an observation plane flying over the area, the Air Force could not attack because of low cloud. In the early afternoon there was some desultory shelling of enemy guns hidden in the woods of La Saillière. A few defenders had dug in in Touques, under the trees in the southwest of the city. Enemy positions on the sides of the roads from Croisilles, Coulmer and Orgères had hardly changed since the 17th. A few of their infantry withdrew further back to the heights at La Chapelle and to the Favrils farm, first blowing up the bridge on Highway 138, the Exmes road, in the early afternoon. It had been mined for the previous four days.

In the afternoon the Allies were also able to advance up to Résenlieu, about 600 metres to the west, the last of the wooded heights that overlook Gacé. After getting rid of the enemy still scattered between the intersection at Son and the woods at Résenlieu, they made better progress. However, some small groups of Germans still held out in the south, supported by a few guns firing from the edge of Highway 832 near the village of La Faudinière, on the heights of La Chapelle to the south and, going still deeper inland, from the plateau of La Saillière to the east of Gacé.

In the evening, the sound of engines, punctuated by gun fire, came from around Résenlieu. Eventually, two tanks appeared near the church at the top of the road to old Résenlieu. This was a dangerous place for an advance party. The ground is completely bare for about 300 metres as it falls to the Touques stream and the nearest cover is the line of hedges that border the railway line nearby. They would have to move fast when crossing this open ground if they were not to become targets of the German snipers hidden along the edge of the stream. The stream itself, about 3 metres wide, twists and turns and its banks are about 2 metres high. Fortunately, a short distance from the city boundaries, the stream narrows above the bridge that connects old Résenlieu to Gacé and there one can get across more safely. Just then we heard the sharp crackling of a fire not far from the level crossing near the former Sadac dairy. Two enemy trucks carrying munitions were ablaze and every so often rounds of rifle ammunition would explode like fire crackers.

By now the advance party had crossed the Touques. They took advantage of an alley about 100 metres long between some houses. Our liberators made their grand entrance into the city by coming in from the west past the hen house of the Trégaro school! There was no doubt that these soldiers, wearing helmets camouflaged with sprigs of leaves, were from 11th Armoured Division for the insignia of the Bull could be clearly seen on their shoulders. After sharing a toast with us of a white Bordeaux specially saved for this wonderful occasion, the Captain leading this contingent, of medium height with brown eyes, asked me for details of the enemy positions and what sort of opposition they were likely to meet. After telling them about the disorganized flight of the feldgrau *the previous evening, I volunteered to lead them across the city. The small group, which up to then had been waiting quietly on the right side of the road, now silently climbed the avenue leading to the railway station, the Rue du Nouveau-Monde, and then took part of Highway 138 — to-day it is called the Avenue de Tahiti — into the very heart of the city. Ever alert, each man had his rifle ready. The last possible defensive position in the city left to the enemy was at the junction of the Rue de Lisieux and the roads from Vimoutiers and Chambois. Fortunately, we met no opposition there. Some of the enemy who had taken off towards the north were run to earth near the Hospital of Sainte Marie. It was all over. Gacé owed its deliverance to the 4th King's Shropshire Light Infantry who, without pausing, went on towards St. Evroult-de-Montfort and, more particularly, in the direction of L'Aigle.*

While this was going on some other tanks had come down the hill from Résenlieu. They skirted the old chateau, now the Town Hall, and came out on the Rue de L'Eglise near the Cenotaph. The first Sherman was commanded by a Lieutenant-Colonel with five bars on his shoulder. Standing in the turret of his tank, he examined his map. I told him of the enemy positions in the village of La Chapelle, at the junction of the roads from Exmes, Coulmer and

Orgères and, in particular, of the 88mm gun at the intersection of Highways 138 and 832. He then continued on his way.

The enemy turned at bay and trained his guns towards Gacé from whence the tanks were coming. Fortunately, most of them were able to advance without any trouble. However, at the end of the day, the enemy still clung to his positions dominating Highways 138 and 832. Near La Faudinière an anti-tank gun scored a direct hit on the turret of a Honey tank that was coming across the fields from Coulmer. Three men, a sergeant and two of his crew, were killed outright. A little later they were buried on the side of the Orgères road near their destroyed tank. At last the fighting stopped. Gacé and its suburbs were free!

Tanks continued to come into the city all through the night so that by the morning of 22 August there were long lines of them in the streets from the railway station and from the lower end of the city all the way up the road to Rouen. At last, life returned to normal. The Gacéens returned to their houses after eight long days of terror. They were delirious in greeting their liberators, each one trying somehow to talk to them. On this day, even though the bell in the bell-tower could not be rung, an official and happy reception was held at the Town Hall around 10 o'clock. The Commander, who spoke some French, after making a few comments about the Allied troops, handed the city back to the Mayor, M. Trigoust. At last, the orders of the German Kommandantur and all the restrictions imposed on us by our barbaric enemy were ended. We were free and it was in the name of Liberty that the four of us at the Gacé Town Hall ceremony — the English Commander, the Mayor, the Town Clerk and myself as interpreter — toasted each other in friendship and mutual admiration.

ON TO L'AIGLE

At dawn on the 22nd, the tanks of the 15/19 Hussars, carrying two companies of the Herefords, left Gacé with orders to clear that part of the road that crosses the Forêt de St. Evroult in the direction of La Trinité-des-Laitiers. Some of the enemy still remained to be rounded up there but this work was not really suited to tanks and they found it long and tedious. During the afternoon, 11th Armoured Division's tanks and infantry had to leave the road clear for 50th Division who had orders to attack towards the Seine on this axis. The Hussars and the Herefords then headed towards Echauffour; it had already been cleared that morning by the Fife and Forfar Yeomanry and the 3rd Monmouths.

Tanks of the 23rd Hussars had passed the night near Authieux-du-Puits and they now took the lead and made for L'Aigle by two different routes. Two squadrons went along the north bank of the Risle and rejoined Highway 24 at Aube while the other headed for Ste. Gauburge where they found that the bridges had been blown up and all sorts of mines and obstacles scattered around.

In the afternoon of the 18th, guided by the *Résistance,* a few Americans managed to get into the centre of Ste. Gauburge and from there they fired on nests of German *spandaus.* This action lasted three quarters of an hour. The Americans then withdrew in the direction of Ferrière-la-Verrerie. A few German shells, coming from batteries installed in the forest of St. Evroult, landed in the neighbourhood of the parsonage and the Jeanne-d'Arc Memorial Hall and also along the length of the road to Courtomer. After the American attack, the Germans, who had already blown up the bridges on the roads to Gacé, Grande-rue and Faubourg-St. Jacques, now thought it more prudent to reinforce their defences and so strewed mines at the entrance of the city opposite the Fichet house and Faubourg-St. Jacques.

A patrol found a shallow ford a little way down-stream but the ground was very swampy and several tanks, including the Colonel's, got stuck and could only be pulled out with great difficulty. However, the rest of the Squadron managed to get through and charged towards L'Aigle on Highway 24. The enemy had laid mine-fields all over the place and as the Engineers were still stuck in the swamp the tank crews had to clear them themselves. They were not very happy about this but, finally, some of them lassoed the mines with ropes and pulled them out of the way. The sappers eventually caught up with them just in time to clear the last of the mines. The Hussars noted, with great interest, that they used exactly the same technique — except that they used a longer rope!

As it was impossible to get through Ste. Gauburge easily until a Bailey bridge had been built, at about 1600 hours it was decided to send the rest of 29 Brigade round by a northern route which, though blocked by felled trees and mines, proved to be the most practical. Nevertheless, the tanks of the 23rd Hussars that had succeeded in going through Ste. Gauburge, where the welcome was very warm, were the first troops of 11th Armoured Division to reach L'Aigle. At about 2000 hours they were relieved by the 3rd Monmouths who took possession of the city, occupying the main intersection and the roads running east and southeast from it. It was the first important city the Welshmen had taken over since their arrival in Normandy.

Although German artillery continued to shell the city and their tanks prowled around in the suburbs, the night passed without incident. In the morning of the 23rd, 50th British Infantry Division entered the city, taking over from 11th Armoured Division, and continued to chase the retreating enemy.

That afternoon the 3rd Monmouths withdrew from L'Aigle and went to rejoin the other units of the Division who had gone to Rai-Aube to take a well-earned rest. The Bull had been charging across the southern part of the Falaise Pocket for 12 days, not stopping once, cutting the enemy to pieces, disorganizing him, not allowing him any rest, shaking and tossing him without mercy right up to the end when, on 23 August, the last German was eliminated in the Pocket. But now the men who had fought almost continuously since 23 June were tired. The few days' rest they were granted was very welcome. Reinforcements in men, materiel, vehicles and tanks arrived to make good their severe losses. Many soldiers and officers who had been wounded in previous battles were warmly greeted when they now rejoined their units.

On 28 August, 11th Armoured Division got ready to leave Normandy after having taken part in every major action that had been launched by 2nd British Army in the historic Battle of Normandy. But this redoubtable honour meant that they had to leave 868 of their best men behind them buried in Norman soil. This was nearly half the number of those who fell during the whole of the year from June 1944 to May 1945 during the course of the campaign in Northwest Europe.

CHAPTER 12

FROM NORMANDY TO THE BALTIC

THE CHARGE RESUMES

50th and 43rd Infantry Divisions, the two other Divisions of XXX Corps of 2nd British Army, relieved 11th Armoured Division. The first continued the chase from Gacé and L'Aigle up to the Seine; the second established a bridgehead across that river at Vernon. At nightfall on 27 August, the first elements of 11th Armoured, the 3rd Royal Tank Regiment, crossed the river, followed by the Fife and Forfar Yeomanry and then by the 23rd Hussars. The Division, whose task it was to resume the offensive against the enemy who was hurrying back to his own frontiers, had now been reorganized into its original formation. It was thought that this would be better suited for accomplishing its new objectives. 29 Armoured Brigade, consisting of all the tank regiments and including 8th Rifle Brigade, the only motorised infantry in the Division, took the lead. 159 Infantry Brigade, comprising all the other Battalions, followed the tanks, ready to come to their assistance if necessary. The Division was also reinforced by having 8 Armoured Brigade placed under its command. Two days of fighting against weakening opposition took 29 Armoured Brigade to Marseille-en-Beauvaisis and 8 Armoured Brigade to Beauvais. There, its job done, it gave way to the Guards Armoured Division who led the next day on the right flank of 11th Armoured.

THE CAPTURE OF AMIENS

In the evening, Lieutenant-General Horrocks, commanding XXX Corps, came to talk to Major-General Roberts about a night advance by 11th Armoured Division to Amiens so that they could seize the bridges over the Somme before the enemy had time to blow them up. Although it was obviously a risky venture it did not deter 'Pip' Roberts who agreed all the more readily when General Horrocks assured him that he had laid on a full moon for that night! Unfortunately, the moon did not obey either the General or the calendar and the night was as black as ink. But despite that, and a pouring rain, 29 Armoured Brigade covered the 50 kilometres that separated it from Amiens that night.

All went well in spite of a few mix-ups and accidents to some of the vehicles because their weary drivers had trouble keeping their eyes open. Along the way, many additional vehicles kept arriving from side roads to join the column and eventually it was necessary to wait for daybreak to sort things out. Only then was it seen that some enemy tanks had also joined the convoy during the night believing they were travelling with their own. They were promptly dealt with.

The 3rd Royal Tank Regiment entered the suburbs of Amiens at dawn. Half an hour later they captured, intact, the railway bridge which spans the Somme and at six o'clock they arrived at the centre of the city. There they captured a long column of Germans whom they surprised marching off to have breakfast.

The *F.F.I.* gave the Allies enormous help. A few hours later, with their assistance, the 23rd Hussars, together with the 8th Rifle Brigade and the Fife and Forfar Yeomanry, captured two other undamaged bridges.

ANOTHER LUCKY CATCH

Before entering the city, 'A' Squadron of the 23rd Hussars shot up a convoy of enemy staff cars. Major Blacker, the commander of the Squadron, searched one of them and found maps that showed,

NORTH SE[A]

LONDON

READING

ALDERSHOT ● GUILDFORD

CANTERBURY

DOVER

SOUTHAMPTON
PORTSMOUTH   BRIGHTON

STRAITS OF
DOVER

MIDDLEB[URG]

FLUS[HING]

OSTEN[D]

CALAIS
Pas-De-Calais
BOULOGNE

● YPRES

ISLE OF
WIGHT

LILLE ●

ENGLISH CHANNEL

● ARRAS
CAMBRAI ●

CHERBOURG

DIEPPE

AMIENS

● S[T.]

HAVRE

BEAUVAIS

BAYEAUX

ROUEN

● COMPIEGN[E]

ST.LO   CAEN

R. SEINE

VIRE   FLERS   L'AIGLE ●

VERNON

PARIS

ALENCON

VERSAILLES

FROM NORMANDY TO THE BALTIC

in the greatest detail, the exact positions the enemy hoped to be able to establish that very day from Switzerland to the Pas de Calais, in particular along the lengths of the Somme, the Marne and the upper reaches of the Moselle. Two things were obvious: the destroyed cars were from the Headquarters of a very high-ranking officer and the plans he had prepared had been made useless by 11th Armoured's audacious night advance. These two facts were confirmed less than an hour later when the Fife and Forfar Yeomanry captured the most important prize yet taken by any of the Allied Armies — General Eberbach himself, the Commander of the 7th German Army.

ANTWERP FALLS, INTACT, INTO THE HANDS OF 11TH ARMOURED DIVISION

After Amiens, enemy resistance practically disappeared. The Charge of the Bull became a full-speed chase, liberating on the way a large number of cities where the welcomes were fantastic and capturing the first V1 rocket launching sites from which the bombardment of England had been going on for many months. Skirting Arras to the northwest, 11th Armoured crossed the mining country near Lievin, Lens, Carvin and Seclin, then, pushing to the east in order to avoid Lille, which was left to 50th Infantry Division, their advance units crossed the Belgian frontier between Cysoing and Tournai. They rushed at full speed across Belgium, leaving Brussels to the Guards Armoured Division, and, driving north, reached Antwerp on 4 September, capturing the port intact.

The Division had covered a distance of 550 kilometres in little more than six days and of that distance the last 150 kilometres had been covered in 26 hours. From the time it started its attack south from Caumont-l'Eventé on 30 July it had fought its way over nearly 1000 kilometres.

THE FIRST VICTORIA CROSS

Although 11th Armoured Division did not play a leading role in the battle of Arnhem, nevertheless, its part was important because it had to cover the right flank of the advance on the Eindhoven — Nijmegen road. This necessitated a night crossing of the Wilhelmina Canal by the Fife and Forfar Yeomanry and the Herefords. Then, turning south, it had some difficult fighting to do in the swampy country to the north of Overloon.

It was there that Sergeant George Eardley of the 4th King's Shropshire Light Infantry earned the first Victoria Cross awarded to a soldier of the Division.

After Overloon the Division was engaged in liquidating the Meuse pocket that is cut through by numerous canals. The sappers had to build 7 bridges in 8 kilometres!

The onset of winter led to a slackening of fighting for the Division and this was put to good use by 29 Armoured Brigade who were ordered to exchange their worn-out Shermans for the new Comets. However, this change of 'mounts' was slightly interrupted by the German offensive in the Ardennes which forced the brigade to re-mount their old tanks so that they could take part in the defence of Namur, Dinant and Givet.

THE SECOND VICTORIA CROSS

Towards the end of the winter, 11th Armoured Division took part in clearing the country between the Meuse and the Rhine and helped in clearing from this sector the enemy paratroops who fought very stubbornly now that they were on their native soil. Then came a period of rest around Louvain, immediately followed by a new 'charge' in the course of which, having crossed the Rhine, they burst into the plain of Westphalia. They then crossed the Dortmund — Ems Canal and climbed to the high ground of the Teutoburger Wald which was stoutly defended by cadets from the Military Academy at Hanover.

It was in the course of this stiff fighting that Corporal Edward

Chapman of the 3rd Monmouthshire Regiment earned the second Victoria Cross awarded to the Division.*

As it happened, this was the last battle fought by the 3rd Monmouths. Exhausted by the heavy casualties it had suffered all the way from Normandy, its place in the Division was taken by the 1st Cheshire Regiment.

After crossing the rivers Weser and Aller and engaging in further fierce fighting, the Division found itself in the small village of Belsen. There it discovered one of the first of the concentration camps, the existence of which was to make the world recoil with horror and disgust.

Continuing its advance, 29 Brigade was the first British unit to reach the Elbe. A week later it captured the Hamburg—Lubeck *autobahn* and this enabled it to reach Lubeck in record time. There they took nearly 80,000 prisoners, including 27 Generals. The capitulation of the entire German Army took place a few days later. Immediately after the surrender, Grand Admiral Doenitz was allowed to form a provisional government with which to rule the country. Germany was in such chaos that at first the British thought that this was the only way in which to restore some semblance of law and order. However, it was soon realized that this was a mistake because many wanted Nazis found places in this interim Government. So the Allies decided to put an end to it. This was the last task assigned to 11th Armoured Division in Europe. It was accomplished by 159 Brigade who had been stationed at Flensburg since the Armistice. On the morning of 23 May, 1945, the last of the former leaders of the Third Reich, Doenitz, Jodl, Speer, Rosenberg etc. (Von Friedsburg managed to kill himself with cyanide) were arrested and sent into captivity. The operation was a complete success because the Germans were taken by surprise. On that day, 756 persons were arrested, among them many Nazi leaders.

*The Victoria Cross posthumously awarded to Corporal Sidney Bates of the 1st Royal Norfolk Regiment though earned while his Battalion was under command of 11th Armoured Division at the Battle of Perrier Ridge on 6 August 1944, is 'credited' to 3rd British Infantry Division, his parent Division.

Other, less spectacular tasks were given to the soldiers: the control and disarmament of all the German Army units; the collection of tens of thousands of refugees, displaced persons and prisoners of all races; the repatriation of those who had a country to go to, such as the French, Russians, Italians, Poles, Balts and so on.

In January 1946, 11th Armoured Division was disbanded and its units were first distributed among other formations before being demobilized in their turn. The only one of the old units still active to-day is the 3rd Royal Tank Regiment.

FINALE

No better ending can be offered for this story than the words written in 1954 by Major Joe How, MC, the author of *The History of the South Wales Borderers and 3rd Monmouthshire Regiment.*

It cannot be said that these memories are happy ones for the immediate presence of the stark tragedy of war hung as a black shroud over the period; but they are memories of a true, deep comradeship which can only be experienced by those who live under the dark shadow of danger. They are memories of perils braved in the company of others, and friendships which, quickly matured under the common risks endured, grew in a few weeks and even days to a depth and intensity of sincerity which is incomprehensible to the uninitiated. In a world where man seems intent on destroying himself and all that he has created, in a world of violence, death and agony, where man's finer feelings are submerged in the turmoil of modern battle, the one flower which pushes its way up through the welter of debris to bloom radiantly above the orgy of destruction is the devotion of the soldier to his comrades.

ORDER OF BATTLE

11TH ARMOURED DIVISION
Major-General G. P. B. Roberts

29TH ARMOURED BRIGADE
Brigadier C. B. Harvey

23rd Hussars
2nd Fife and Forfar Yeomanry
3rd Battalion Royal Tank
Regiment
8th Battalion The Rifle Brigade
(Motor)

159TH INFANTRY BRIGADE
Brigadier J. B. Churcher
(from 28 June 1944)

3rd Battalion The Monmouthshire
Regiment (to April, 1945)
4th Battalion The King's Shropshire Light Infantry
1st Battalion The Herefordshire
Regiment
1st Battalion The Cheshire Regiment (from April, 1945)

DIVISIONAL TROOPS

2nd Independent Machine Gun
Company (Royal Northumber-
land Fusiliers)
The Inns of Court Regiment
2nd Household Cavalry
Regiment
2nd Northamptonshire
Yeomanry (to 17.8.44)
15th/19th King's Royal Hussars
(from 17.8.44)
Royal Army Service Corps
Royal Army Ordnance Corps
Royal Army Medical Corps
Royal Army Chaplains
Corps of Military Police

Royal Artillery
13th Royal Horse Artillery
151st Field Regiment
(Ayrshire Yeomanry)
58th Light Anti-Aircraft
Regiment
75th Anti-Tank Regiment
Royal Engineers
13th Field Squadron
612th Field Squadron
147th Field Park Company
10th Bridging Troop
Royal Corps of Signals
Royal Electrical and Mechanical
Engineers

THE BATTLES OF 43RD (WESSEX) DIVISION

THE CROSSING OF THE NOIREAU AND THE ATTACK ON THE HILLS OF BERJOU AND CAHAN

When 11th Armoured Division resumed its offensive on 14 August its left flank was protected by 43rd Infantry Division commanded by Major-General G. I. Thomas. This Division had gained glory on the slopes of Hill 112, but at what a price, and, more recently, on the slopes of Mont Pincon. Continuing the advance, the three Brigades of 43rd Division leap-frogged with those of 50th (Northumbrian) Division (commanded by Major-General D. A. H. Graham) and drove the enemy from the region south of Mont Pincon between the Druance, Noireau and Orne rivers and from the area between the villages and towns of St. Jean-le-Blanc, Condé-sur-Noireau, Pont-d'Ouilly and Caumont-sur-Orne. At dawn on the 14th, 129 Brigade of 43rd Division seized Proussy where very fierce fighting took place right in the village of Les Haies. Next, 130 Brigade took the lead and seized St. Denis-de-Méré, where many prisoners were taken, then the intersection at Le Fresne and continued to push on to St. Marc-d'Ouilly. In the evening, General Horrocks ordered 43rd Division to force a crossing over the Noireau to the east of Condé. This task was entrusted to 214 Brigade.

The Noireau is a small, tranquil stream that flows into the Orne between deep, wooded valleys. From the point of view of the tourist, this part of the country is very beautiful; however, from a military point of view it is excellent defensive country and one can readily appreciate that, without the aid of the *Résistance*, 214 Brigade would never have been able to cross the stream on its own, especially as the approaches had been heavily mined and covered by fortified positions established on the high ground and on the wooded slopes of Berjou, La Canet and Le Hamel. Incidentally, it is interesting to note that it was not until 12 August that there is any mention in the official British military reports of the wide-ranging activities of the *F.F.I.* But, be that as it may, let us get on with the story of the crossing of the Noireau and the assault on the hills of Berjou and Cahan.

PREPARATIONS FOR THE ATTACK

The attack was planned to start at 6 o'clock in the evening. It was to be preceded by an artillery barrage from guns situated at Grand Beron and to the rear of Les Bruyères-de-Clécy, by mortars of all calibres and by heavy and light machine-guns. The crossing had to be made in two places, one at the factory at Le Rocray and the other near the Berjou railway station at Les Bordeaux.*

Reveille was at 0330 hours on the morning of 15 August and breakfast was 'served' shortly after. However, as so often happens in these cases, it was necessary to wait for several hours while the three battalions of 214 Brigade that were going to take part in the attack, the 5th Duke of Cornwall's Light Infantry, the 7th Somerset Light Infantry and the 1st Worcestershire Regiment, came up to their start lines.

A RECONNAISSANCE TOWARDS LE ROCRAY

As soon as it was light, the 7th Somersets, who had to cross at Le Rocray, sent a reconnaissance group commanded by Captain Baden with Sergeant Martin to find a place where it was easy to cross the stream. Looking at the map, they saw that there was a path that left the Le Fresne — St. Marc-d'Ouilly road and headed towards the stream. This path divided into two branches behind a factory building, one branch going on straight and the other crossing the stream. The distance from there to the next bend in the stream was about 150 metres, all open meadow. On the other

---

*This railway line came from Falaise and joined the Caen — Laval line at Berjou, near the viaduct and the Les Gouttes Tunnel. It fell into disuse shortly after the war.

side of the stream the map showed a railway line that wound its way along the foot of the cliffs.

The patrol went down a sunken path covered overhead by leafy trees and met only one obstacle, near Arclais: a large shed that had been knocked down by the barrage. Sergeant Martin examined it carefully in case it had been booby-trapped and then decided to fix a cable to it and drag it out of the way with the help of a Bren gun carrier. Finally, they came to the last turn in the path before the stream and the carriers were hidden and left under guard.

Captain Baden and Sergeant Martin started to cross the meadow towards the stream. They had hardly gone 30 metres when a low whistle from the Sergeant stopped the Captain in his tracks. Pointing with his finger towards the hill facing them, the Sergeant picked out a German sentry standing there with his rifle on his shoulder. Luckily, at that moment the German was turned three quarters away from them and did not see them. In a few quick strides they were back to the path. They had to crawl all the way back along the path to the factory as the hedges, neither thick nor high, gave them no cover. The path was strewn with mines that were barely visible in the morning mist. It's best that we do not repeat the language used by the two men as they crawled all the way back to the factory!

From there they were able to clearly see German soldiers deepening their trenches and to make out the positions of the machine-guns at the two extremities of the cliff just opposite them. They worked their way back to the houses at the rear of the main factory buildings and there they were met by a young French workman anxious to give them information about the enemy. His assistance was invaluable. He showed them where the Germans had placed mines around the bridge, on the level crossing and at the foot of the cliff. He also showed them which bridges had been blown up and where they could ford the stream.

The 'English vanguard' then went into the factory where they found several barrels of synthetic oil. The buildings were almost empty but they searched them from top to bottom. They could easily watch the stream from the windows and could make out the

Germans digging machine-gun emplacements in the orchard of the Binard farm on the right and along the cliffs to the left. They removed their helmets and their boots and paddled in the water in order to find out how firm the stream bed was. They walked up the stream as far as the bridge at Les Bordeaux and there they found a place where bulldozers could easily make a crossing for the tanks, the artillery and all the other vehicles without having to wait for the construction of a bridge.

Perhaps the Germans did not see them or could not believe what they saw. Perhaps they thought that these harmless poachers were not looking for anything but fish whereas what they were really fishing for was information.

Returning to the factory, Captain Baden decided to take a look at the south side. To do this he slid behind an electric transformer pole a little distance away from the main building. It was lucky he did so because from there he saw what could have been a serious obstacle. This was a canal, three metres wide by three metres deep, with steep, brick sides, running between the stream and the railway line. Thank God, there was almost no water in it. Sergeant Martin had the idea of rolling steel barrels from the factory into the canal, piling them on top of one another to make a causeway across the canal while hoping that the water would flow through the gaps between the barrels without carrying away the make-shift bridge.

The reconnaissance over, the two men sneaked behind the factory and hurried away to make their report. Ah, but wait a bit! The villagers had other plans for them. The young Frenchman who had given them so much valuable information wanted the 'English vanguard' to be photographed with him and his wife and all the rest of the villagers wanted to witness the event, to look at them, to embrace them, to thank them and to wish them well. The noise and the confusion grew. Everyone in the neighbourhood seemed to know of the arrival of the two Englishmen except the Germans. Captain Baden tried hard to get them to stay calm while she who wanted to be photographed and who, incidentally, was very pretty, disappeared indoors to re-appear, with more glamour than modesty, in her Sunday best. She was photographed in front of her house between the two *Tommies*. And mind you, all this was taking place less than 200 metres from the Germans! Finally, after a quick swig of calvados, the two men succeeded in escaping and rejoined their unit.

Captain Baden rejoined the group that had been waiting for him all this time at the last bend in the path and with them returned to the battalion just before two o'clock. He immediately reported to the Colonel. As far as Sergeant Martin was concerned, the Engineer officer promised him two bulldozers and a section of sappers for the stream crossing.

While this was going on, the C.O. of the Somersets also went down with a small recce group to the stream slightly to the left of Le Rocray. They hid behind some farm buildings and stayed there for nearly an hour. They didn't see a single movement by the enemy but they had the greatest difficulty in preventing a crowd of civilians from showing their noisy enthusiasm and thus advertising their presence to the enemy.

Typhoons, attracted by the movements of the enemy on the cliff, swooped over the tree tops, dived across the valley and released their rockets on to the positions the Germans had just finished digging. The C.O. and his group decided to get out of there, fast!

The plan of attack was completed by early afternoon and a quick meal was served to the soldiers. The start line was fixed at about 800 metres from the stream and H-hour was set for 1800 hours by which time it was hoped that the heat of the day would have abated. A very elaborate fire plan was put into effect. The fire of all calibres of mortars was added to the artillery firing from the heights dominating the road from St. Marc-d'Ouilly to Le Fresne. In addition to all this, the 8th Middlesex, with their heavy machine-guns and mortars, were also in support of 43rd Division.

A SUCCESSFUL CROSSING AT LE ROCRAY

'D' Company left first, going directly south across the fields, taking cover as best it could along the hedges and in the corn. A small wooded hill on the left hid it for a while from the sight of the enemy who, nevertheless, began to suspect that an attack was imminent.

He opened up with artillery, mortars and machine-guns. 'D' Company had great difficulty in getting up to the factory and in crossing the wrecked bridge but once they were clear of the buildings fighting resumed with scrimmages with snipers and machine-gunners. They managed to cross the canal dry-footed, set up a bridgehead there and gave the signal to 'C' Company to go into action in its turn.

After waiting in the shelter of the small wooded hill, a shelter that was purely illusory because the enemy knew they were there and sprayed them with heavy fire from both ends of the cliff, the men of 'C' Company started off more or less in the direction of the factory. Just then the Germans chose to send over a hail of shells and mortar bombs on top of them and on top of the factory. The men had to go on without answering the fire because they did not know exactly how far forward their comrades of 'D' Company, who had left before them, had reached.

'B' Company was the next to leave and they, in turn, were covered by 'C' Company who had passed through and beyond the positions held by 'D' Company on the other side of the canal. In order to avoid being taken in enfilade by the German machine-gunners they had to frequently change the direction of their advance as they crossed the railroad track. Zig-zagging in this way, they eventually got to the foot of the cliff and found themselves just below the Battalion's objective, the fields immediately above them. The ground was rocky, criss-crossed with trenches and covered with gorse. The angle of the slope to the top was nearly 45 degrees and the heat was almost stifling.

In its turn, 'B' Company passed through the positions of 'D' Company around the factory and cleared the ground to the right without much trouble, especially the orchards and fields of the Binard farm.

With regard to 'A' Company, it had made a crossing well to the left of Le Rocray and headed independently towards the village of L'Etre-du-Mont.

The support given by the artillery and, in particular, by the mortars and machine-guns of the Middlesex Regiment was decisive. The Germans were literally pinned to the ground and slaughtered. In the two days that followed, several hundreds of their dead were counted on the Brigade front.

The three Companies that had reached their objectives started to dig in for cover against the enemy fire that became more and more intense. These positions were scattered around the factory on a perimetre of about 1000 metres. Enemy losses had been heavy and they had retreated over the fields in the direction of the orchards of Le Val David and La Fosse farms whence they hoped to be able to launch a counter-attack the next day.

From its high ground, 'C' Company was able to see the farm of L'Etre-du-Mont on its left. 'A' Company should have been there but it soon became evident that this was not so. Just before nightfall, a sergeant of 'A' Company learnt that, soon after crossing the stream, his men had become disorganized; some remained on the wooded slopes that overlooked the path from Val-David while others had followed their Company Commander, Major Harvey, in the direction of the farm. The sergeant was ordered to search for and gather in his men, to get them into defensive positions for the night and to send out patrols in the direction of L'Etre-du-Mont. The next day they learnt that Major Harvey had reached the farm and had held it all night with only two men even though some of the buildings were still in German hands.

Down below, in the valley, they made enormous efforts to get the support vehicles across the stream. Sergeant Martin's sappers rolled the barrels into the canal but they soon had water up to their chests because the water was unable to flow freely. Most of the contents had been set on fire by the shelling and every so often a barrel exploded and the sappers had to dive into the water to avoid being roasted. A bulldozer pushed swathes of soil on top of the bridge of barrels, trying to firm it up, but only a few half-tracks and anti-tank guns were able to cross before the make-shift bridge started to come apart under the pressure of the water.

All night long they tried to save the bridge so that the guns and other armaments that were desperately needed could be passed over to the other side and hauled to the top of the cliff. The tank-transporters were ordered to take the ford that had been found by the next battalion in line below the Les Bordeaux bridge.

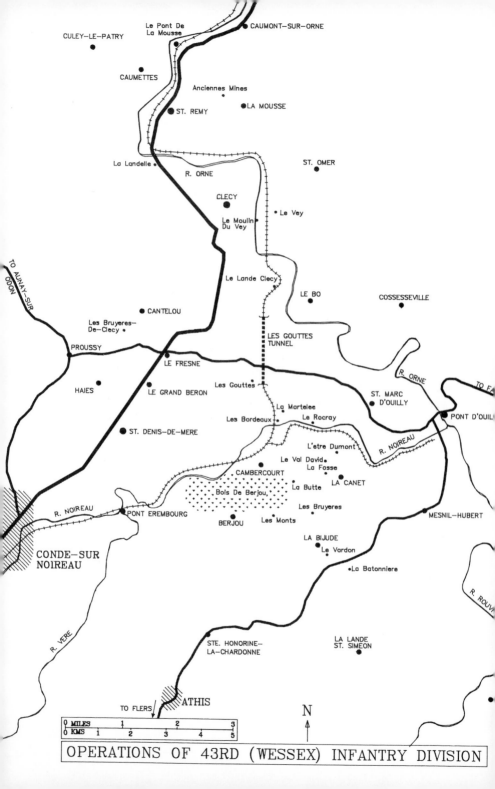

OPERATIONS OF 43RD (WESSEX) INFANTRY DIVISION

PREPARATIONS AT CAMBERCOURT

First, the C.O. of the Worcesters established the start-line his men had to use before setting out for their objective. This was a narrow path that left Cambercourt and led through the woods towards the high ground before reaching the plateau that stretches in the direction of Berjou. Next he picked out the place where they were to cross the stream. Near the Les Bordeaux bridge, destroyed apparently, by the *Résistance,* a group of Engineers, watched by civilians, was busy lifting the *Teller* mines that the Germans had strewn around in large numbers. Sadly, a young man who came forward to give them a hand was blown up, while a German deserter who was crossing the stream in order to give himself up solved all his problems by stepping on another of these atrocious devices.

At this place the stream is about 20 metres wide and about 1 metre deep so it was decided that the men would ford it a few hundred metres above the viaduct and would then take a road up to the path mentioned above. The attack was to be put in by 'A' Company followed by 'B' and then 'C'. All three Companies were to take up positions just below the crest while 'D' Company stayed in reserve with H.Q. Company back in the village of Cambercourt. Very strong artillery support was planned including a large number of smoke shells. H-hour was set for 0630.

The third battalion of 214 Brigade, the D.C.L.I., were to follow the same path to attack in the direction of Les Monts. As soon as the infantry had established their bridge-head, a bridge had to be built so that the armour, anti-tank guns, mortars and transporters could cross over to join in the attack.

A SUCCESSFUL CROSSING AT CAMBERCOURT

In the course of the afternoon the Worcesters assembled near the stream and at 0630 hours precisely the first man of 'A' Company put his foot in the water. The Company had almost completed its crossing when an absolute deluge of mortar bombs crashed down. However, because the Germans had seen the sappers clearing the mines near the bridge it was this spot that they took as their target, thinking that the infantry would be crossing there. Some stretcher-bearers who were near the bridge were caught in the bombardment. 'A' Company met feeble opposition. One or two small groups of Germans carrying white flags came out of the houses at Cambercourt in order to surrender. They were quickly sent to the rear. While the houses were being cleared the artillery barrage that had started at a quarter to six passed over their heads on its way to the hill in front of them where smoke shells had already set the trees on fire in many places. Again, a very large number of *Teller* mines was found at the intersection of the road that climbs towards Berjou. A section of assault engineers that accompanied the leading troops spotted them and, for the most part, made them harmless.

THE ATTACK ON BERJOU WOODS

'A' Company then began to climb the path that twisted through the woods. The slope was so steep and the heat was so great that the men strained under the weight of their equipment. They had climbed for some time when the woods on the left gave way to open fields that formed a reverse slope. Two white Very lights were fired, the pre-arranged signal to tell Headquarters that they had taken their first objective. While the platoons took up their positions the other two Companies emerged from the woods in their turn and dug in in the fields to the left. The three Companies thus found themselves on a flat piece of ground just below the crest with their defences covering a rectilinear front of about400 metres. As they were on a reverse slope, the enemy fire passed over their heads and the men were able to consolidate their positions without too much difficulty.

By this time it was 1930 hours. On the left, artillery and mortar fire and bursts of fire from automatic weapons indicated that the Somersets were having some trouble whereas the Worcesters' sector was

When Scot meets Scot ... Sergeant Laing of the Photographic Service of the British Army, meets Lieutenant Jack Dolgety in Flers. They were both from Forfar, Angus (now Tayside).

I.W.M. #B9352

As these photographs show, Sergeant Laing, who took many of the Imperial War Museum photographs reproduced in this book, had a keen sense of humour and a quick eye for what was topical such as this photograph of a tandem bicycle hauling a trailer with its passenger. In those days even such a humble means of transportation was a luxury!

I.W.M. #B9322

A group of Fleriens of all ages rally round the Tricolour in the middle of the ruins at *Cinq-Becs*.

Many put out flags hidden from the Germans to celebrate their liberation but this young lady of Flers proudly models the apron she secretly stitched together from the flags of France, Great Britain and the United States.

I.W.M. #B9337

A good-natured crowd mobs a solitary British soldier as he hands out sweets, cigarettes and chocolates amid the ruins of *Cinq-Becs*.

Near a building on the Touzé farm at Landigou, an officer of the 1st Hereford-shire Regiment studies his map in preparation for the attack on Durcet and Sainte Opportune. (cf p.185)

I.W.M. #B9348

Infantrymen of the 1st Herefordshire Regiment, supported by Cromwell tanks of the 2nd Northamptonshire Yeomanry, pass the Touzé farm at Landigou on the Paris road. (cf p.185 et seq.)

I.W.M. #B9331

A British tank blew itself up on a mine placed during the night by the Germans at the crossroads at Landigou near the roadside crucifix so the sappers get on with the job of mine-clearing. On the right can be seen the remains of an enemy truck that, a few hours before, had blown itself up on one of its own mines. The body of the truck driver is in the ditch on the left. (cf p.183)

I.W.M. #B9332

Infantrymen wait while, up ahead, the sappers clear the road of mines and civilians from Landigou come to talk to the soldiers. (cf p.183)

43rd (Wessex) Infantry Division liberated Sainte-Honorine-la-Chardonne on 17 August after which they took a few days of well-earned rest. (cf p.189)

I.W.M. #B9358

The fair ladies of Athis welcome their liberators. (cf p.190)

French and British officers hold a conference in Athis while, in the jeep, youngsters play at being soldiers. (cf p.190)

Joseph Collet erects a 'monument' to the Dictator in front of the Vivien bakery
in Athis. The sign reads: *Hitler Kaput* (cf p.190)

At last, the war is over for these refugees and they can return to their farms.
I.W.M. #B9374

The Sisters of *La Misericorde* shepherd their flock through the streets of Athis.
I.W.M. #B9373

At La Carneille the soldiers drink a toast ... (cf p.193)

I.W.M. #B9467

... and bask in the admiration of the local ladies!

At La Carneille, soldiers watch while a horse is shod.

At La Carneille, soldiers watch while one of their comrades tries to persuade a donkey to take him for a ride. Soon after, these same men were in the battle for Le Pont-Huan. (cf p.194 et seq.)

very quiet, as if the Germans had not yet seen them. In fact, it was not till the last hours of daylight that machine-gun fire from the enemy indicated that they had been discovered. The slow reaction led them to believe that the Germans had anticipated an attack along the road rather than by the little-known path. This path was known only to the villagers and the information was passed on to Allied Intelligence by the *Résistance,* to Captain Gauthier, among others, about whom we will write further on.*

NEXT THE D.C.L.I. CROSS OVER — AND CLIMB

The third battalion of 214 Brigade to force a crossing over the Noireau, the 5th Duke of Cornwall's Light Infantry, had been ordered to hold themselves in readiness to support either one of the other two battalions as they made for their objectives, Berjou on the right and Le Hamel on the left. They had to be ready either to lend their weight to the attack or, if the opportunity presented itself, to quickly exploit any success. The C.O. of the Cornwalls made a personal reconnaissance and, bearing his orders in mind, came to the conclusion that he would be in the best possible position to carry them out if he was on the other side of the stream. Knowing of the tasks assigned to his colleagues of the other two battalions, he decided that he could be most effective, in the shortest time, if he was to support the Worcesters.

The C.O. ordered his Battalion to follow the path taken by the Worcesters from Cambercourt to Berjou. The only thing that was different was where they crossed the stream. The viaduct had been partly destroyed and the banks were thickly sown with mines. However, the Battalion managed to cross over by scrambling over the ruins even though they were narrow and dangerous. Once over, the men headed for the railroad station and then took the path that climbs towards Berjou. The Germans undoubtedly realized that fresh troops were crossing the stream because they unleashed a furious mortar bombardment but again they were mistaken in

*See page 285

thinking that the new troops were coming over the stream in the same place as the old and the barrage came down harmlessly far to the right of the Cornwalls.

The woods were on fire on each side of the path. While the smoke covered their movements it made the air difficult to breath. A stormy, oppressive evening followed the beautiful, hot summer day. The men, discarding their battle-dress blouses, were in shirtsleeves. By the time the D.C.L.I. had joined up with the Worcesters the sun was sinking in the west but the Germans, determined to take advantage of the last light, increased their activity and their machine-guns chattered with mounting fury.

Unexpectedly, the Worcesters had taken the crest without meeting too much opposition. They held almost the entire crest except for the highest part, Les Bruyères, that would later give them some trouble. The Cornwalls took up their positions in front of their colleagues. They were no more than 80 to 100 metres from the Germans. With six companies from the two battalions in this small area, it was like Leicester Square on a Sunday afternoon!

As night fell, slowly, little by little, the noise of battle died down while each side prepared its positions for the attack, or counter-attack, the next day. One could hear the noise of picks and shovels on all sides and the heavy breathing of soldiers as they tried to dig slit-trenches in the rocky soil. The night was cold and the men, without their battle-dress blouses and with their shirts soaked with the sweat of climbing and digging, were frozen to the bone.

WILL THE TANKS ARRIVE ON TIME?

Though the night was calm, their worries kept the officers awake. For one thing, they had no hope of artillery support because, in the darkness, the gunners could not set up their long-range wireless sets. For another, though the companies on the crest were sufficient in numbers, they would only be able to handle the inevitable dawn counter-attack by the enemy if they could get the anti-tank guns in position in time. In addition, the situation on the other side of the stream was absolutely chaotic and it was doubtful that they would be able to clear it up in time for the tanks to be in position to support them before dawn. The traffic-jam created by the destroyed bridge and the incredible number of mines strewn all around there had assumed disturbing proportions. Furthermore, at every possible fording place the Germans had peppered the steep banks with all kinds of mines. At the one crossing that was fairly level, an enormous tank-transporter blew up on a mine in the very middle of the road and, as luck would have it, the tow-truck specially equipped to deal with such wrecks also blew up when it arrived on the scene! According to M. Allo, at that time Chief, in this sector, of the Department of the Société Nationale des Chemins de Fer Francais, the English had to lift more than 800 mines that had been laid in a meadow near the Les Bordeaux bridge alone.

In spite of all these difficulties, by perserverance, ability, patience and courage a path was opened. At dawn, threading their way between white ribbon-markers, the anti-tank guns, the half-tracks that had not yet lost their tracks on the mines and the tanks of the Sherwood Rangers (the nickname for the Nottinghamshire Yeomanry) crossed the Noireau and immediately headed towards Berjou in support of the three infantry battalions.

WOULD THE GERMAN COUNTER-ATTACK SUCCEED?

The calm of the early summer morning was broken by German mortars that crashed down on the edge of the wood across from which the troops had climbed the day before. Evidently the enemy thought that the tanks and guns that actually had not yet arrived were sheltering there. Nevertheless, this futile mortar barrage meant that the counter-attack they were about to launch would stand a better chance of success. The first of these attacks came from Les Monts and its full weight fell on the left, on the positions held by the Worcesters. Enemy patrols must have been very active during the night because their mortars and 88's were extremely accurate: they seemed to know the exact positions of their opponents. The Germans even wore British helmets so that they could get up closer to their objectives. Their counter-attack was almost successful and

'C' Company was in serious danger from a large force gathering itself for an attack some 400 metres from them when, due to very aggressive moves by the Cornwalls, the German attack changed direction, to the great relief of the Worcesters for their ammunition was running low. However, a German machine-gun continued to ravage their ranks and as the number of wounded increased the stretcher-bearers started their errands of mercy between the summit and the First Aid Post established at Cambercourt.

The enemy attack now switched to the right of the D.C.L.I. It was so spirited that it temporarily regained control of the path and the pass up which the tanks of the Sherwood Rangers had climbed. Fortunately, the tanks, having spent the night at Cambercourt, had already got through, accompanied by infantry, so the Germans missed the chance of getting themselves in position with their *panzerfausts* and shooting them like rabbits leaving a warren. But all the way up there were numerous fierce scrimmages. The Germans realized that if the tanks succeeded in rejoining the infantry their hope of holding the heights was doomed. With the energy of despair they fought off the tanks but finally they had to admit defeat and withdrew in the direction of the heights of Les Monts and Berjou. Before noon the British tanks and infantry had joined forces again.

BERJOU, LES MONTS, LA BIJUDE

In this way, 214 Brigade accomplished the major part of the task assigned to it, namely, the crossing of the Noireau and the establishment of its three battalions in positions on the hillside from which they could launch their final assaults simultaneously. Each battalion was given a different objective: on the right, the Worcesters were to take Berjou; in the centre, the D.C.L.I. were to head for the heights of Les Mont and Les Bruyères which seemed to be the headquarters of all the enemy forces in that sector; on the left, the Somersets were to take La Canet, then La Bijude and Le Hamel.

THE CAPTURE OF BERJOU

According to Brigade Intelligence, Berjou had been transformed into a minor fortress by the Germans. An entire company was dug in there, supported by no less than 12 tanks or other armoured vehicles. In order to seize the village the Worcesters were to launch a frontal assault, taking as their start line the field hedges on the right of the path by which they had climbed the day before. Two Companies, 'D' on the right and 'B' on the left, were to make up the first wave. They were to be followed at 100 metres by 'A' Company, ready to go to the aid of either of the forerunners, while 'C' Company, keeping the same interval, were to follow up behind, mopping up any of the enemy who had been by-passed by the first two waves. After the infantry had cleared the hedges and sunken lanes of *panzerfausts,* the tanks of the Sherwood Rangers would come to their support on the crest. In addition, the usual artillery barrage would cover the advance of the troops while the heavy mortars would lay down a screen of bombs to cover the right flank of the advance.

After receiving their orders at Brigade Headquarters in Cambercourt, the Company Commanders climbed back up the hill and, in turn, gave out their orders. Soon all was abustle with soldiers leaving their slit-trenches to take up their positions at the start line. Just then they heard the rumble of tank engines and the rattling of tank tracks. A few seconds later the artillery opened fire and the first shells screamed over their heads.

The attack was a model of its kind, probably the most successful since Mouen in June. The infantry, keeping perfect formation, scrambled up the slopes and took the summit in a bound. A plateau of fields and orchards now extended in front of the Worcesters with the village of Berjou, just 400 metres away, directly in front of them. The artillery barrage crashed down a few metres in front of them as they advanced behind its protection while, in their rear, the machine-guns of the Shermans barked viciously. The men knew they were receiving excellent support and it raised their morale accordingly. Every man relished the chance to pay the enemy back in his own coin for the very uncomfortable 24 hours he had inflicted on them. They scorned the lively opposition which, in any case, did not seem to inflict many losses on them and certainly did not slow down the advance nor disorganize it.

It was all too much for the Germans. Those who try to resist were killed or captured but most of them fled from the hurricane of fire that engulfed them as the Worcesters approached. By 1700 hours the village was in their hands. A platoon left in search of the enemy tanks reported nearby by the Sherwood Rangers but all they found and destroyed was a handful of German infantry who attempted to flee in an ambulance. Among the prisoners taken at Berjou were two German officers while another was killed. This was something new for the Worcesters because, up to then, they had never seen any German officers, neither close up nor at a distance, neither dead nor alive.

Although losses in the final assault had been light, one of them was a tragedy deeply felt by the Battalion. R.S.M. Hurd, MM, received a direct hit from a short-fall while, as he always did, he advanced right up close to the barrage. He and 16 other soldiers of his Battalion were buried near the roadside crucifix not far from the village of Berjou.

One should note here that this was the first time since the Invasion that the Battalion had to deal with such a vast quantity of mines. These deadly devices were often capricious. There was one case when a half-track full of soldiers touched a mine. It ripped off a track but left the occupants unharmed while in another case a similar vehicle was totally destroyed, the pieces scattered for hundreds of yards and the lone driver on board killed.

The village was cleared with difficulty because, following their usual practice, the Germans started to shell it with 88's and mortars. This went on until sunset. The evening meal was brought up and would have been eaten with relish had it not been for the fact that every five minutes, with the precision of a clock, from midnight to one o'clock in the morning, a mortar bomb fell on the town and on the positions occupied by the Battalion nearby.

THE 5TH D.C.L.I. TAKES LES MONTS

There is no doubt that Berjou fell into the hands of the Worcesters so easily because the Germans, concentrating their artillery on the heights of Les Monts and Les Bruyères, were unable to go to its defence. Just before the Worcesters launched their attack the Cornwalls went into action against these positions, the key to the enemy's whole defensive system in that sector.

As soon as it was light, the officers of 214 Brigade saw that it was from this very same place that the Germans had launched the counter-attack that had been contained with so much difficulty by the two Battalions. It was also from this same place that the enemy artillery, firing with great accuracy, stonked the vehicles climbing up out of the valley to bring much-needed supplies to the infantry up on the heights. This state of affairs could not have gone on indefinitely and would have thwarted the infantry in their advance towards their objectives. Who knows, it may even have obliged them to go round to the other side of the Noireau. So the decision was taken to eliminate this strong-point as soon as possible and the task was given to the 5th Duke of Cornwall's Light Infantry. No sooner was the plan made than it was put into effect and it is without doubt due to this quick decision and execution that the operation was a complete success. The whole Battalion took part in the attack but the tricky job of getting the enemy out of his lair was given to 'A' Company. When it came to this sort of action, the others admitted, without a trace of jealousy, that 'A' Company was by far the best!

CLEARING THE ROAD FROM BERJOU TO LA BIJUDE

After this success it was time to pause. The men were tired and needed rest. The day before they had left their position in reserve at La Trulandière at dawn in order to join the Worcesters in the ascent of the Berjou woods. That same morning they had stopped a German counter-attack and then given the enemy as good as they had received. Finally, they had routed him decisively and chased him from his strong-points on Les Monts and Les Bruyères. However, there was still a dangerous gap between La Bijude, not yet taken by the Somersets, and Berjou, in the hands of the Worcesters. Berjou and La Bijude are joined by a direct road fed by many side roads and this could have allowed the enemy to bring up reinforcements for another counter-attack. The Cornwalls were the only battalion available so instead of the much-deserved rest they had to mount another operation that lasted all the afternoon of the 16th. Fortunately, the enemy had withdrawn from this sector but the Berjou — La Bijude road and the feeder roads had been so thickly strewn with mines that progress was very slow. It was only late that night that the area was firmly under control of the Worcesters.

HOMAGE TO THOSE WHO FELL

According to the Regimental historian, the crossing of the Noireau and the capture of the overlooking heights, done in such a short time, was a remarkable feat of arms. During the attack, defence, counter-attack and follow-up, the losses suffered by the 1st Worcestershire Regiment had been relatively light: 16 killed, 17 wounded, 2 missing. The tanks of the Sherwood Rangers had given them magnificient support in every action and they too had to record some losses. In passing we must tell of the sacrifice of two of their men. These two left their tank to go to the aid of two of their wounded comrades and, after crawling to them under a hail of bullets, managed to pull them safely under cover near a wayside crucifix. There, the two good Samaritans fell victims to a sniper's bullets. As is common practice, the crucifix, symbol of man's redemption, had been raised on a piece of high ground but in war high ground, even though sanctified by the Cross, only represents a position to be fought over for its tactical value. Snipers claimed many a victim at the feet of these crucifixes.

The two men were buried not far from there, near some farm buildings, in a quiet, sheltered place. A simple ceremony was held and at the end of it the bugles of the Regiment sounded the Last

Post. The poignant, silver notes reverberated in the cool evening air, were carried by a light breeze beyond the wheat fields and the meadows, above the woods and down into the bottom of the valley where the echoes played back the last note, high and yearning, a note of hope and joy, like the trumpet call on the Day of Judgement.

The little group, made up of friends and comrades-in-arms of those who had just been buried, the grave diggers and members of the War Graves Commission, dispersed, each to his duty, their ears still ringing with the last long, long note. They did not know it then but that note virtually sounded the end of the fighting in Normandy.

THE ASCENT OF LE HAMEL

At dawn on 16 August, the positions of the 7th Somerset Light Infantry were as follows: 'A' Company, having cleared the farm at L'Etre-du-Mont (where Major Harvey had spent such an unpleasant night), re-grouped itself in the fields nearby; two Companies, 'C' on the left and 'B' on the right, were on the high ground opposite Le Rocray; 'D' Company occupied the factory area. Each Company sent out fighting patrols to test the enemy defences. They located and destroyed many machine-gun posts along the paths climbing towards Le Hamel, Le Val David and especially towards La Fosse. By noon, the tanks of the Sherwood Rangers, having crossed the stream and having arrived at the factory, awaited orders to go to the support of the infantry. At 1330 hours, 'C' Company, accompanied by a group of tanks that had rejoined them by the Val David path, started out for their first objective, the village of Le Hamel. In order to avoid the enemy artillery, the tanks followed a gully as long as they could and entered the village of La Fosse in strength where they accepted the surrender of the Germans who had been abandoned there by their officers.

M. Ballon recounts: *After having been driven out of our house at La Butte — it had, undoubtedly, been used as a first aid station because we later found a large quantity of blood-stained dress-*

ings there — we descended into La Fosse together with other refugees. The arrival of the British infantry, moving forward as if they feared nothing, made a lasting impression on the civilians. This was in strong contrast to the very obvious demoralization of the Germans. However, some of them fought to the end, like the dead machine-gunner I found a few days later, still at his post, his ammunition exhausted.

Thus, men and tanks arrived in sight of the village, the infantry dashing from one hedge to the next, sometimes ahead of the tanks, sometimes at their side, sometimes behind them. The Sherwood Rangers shelled the houses while the infantry cleared the village. The enemy did not put up any resistance but retreated in haste, abandoning all his equipment.

FIGHTING AT LA CANET*

'C' Company Commander was just saying to himself that if he continued in the direction of the villages of La Forêt and Les Bruyères he would leave his left flank very exposed when his wireless set told him that 'A' Company, climbing up from the farm at L'Etre-du-Mont, had run into serious difficulties near La Canet. He immediately asked for and obtained permission to turn to his left in order to attack the village with one platoon while the others stayed in Le Hamel. Again, tanks and infantry worked together very well. The tanks, firing at anything that moved, got to the centre of La Canet, near the church. They then turned to the right, taking the road to La Bijude, and attacked the Germans entrenched in the orchards just outside the village. The scrimmage lasted about half an hour. Many of the enemy were killed and 15 were taken prisoner.

'A' Company then came up and finished clearing the houses in the village. 'A' and 'C' Company Commanders quickly made a concerted plan to continue the advance towards La Bijude by two dif-

---

La Canet was the old name of the village and the name that appeared on the British campaign maps in 1944. To-day it is known as Cahan.

ferent but parallel routes and to meet half way up the hill. They avoided the direct road to La Bijude for the moment because it was heavily mined. 'A' Company went by a path that takes off from the road to Le Fourneaux while 'C' Company, first returning to Le Hamel where the troops that had been left there had repulsed a counter-attack, and making for Les Bruyères, turned to the left in order to get back to the main road at the wayside crucifix. Here they met up again with their colleagues of 'A' Company. All this was done with the support of tanks to which the infantry gave the task of dealing with the ubiquitous snipers.

MINES, MINES EVERYWHERE

As always, the paths and roads were heavily mined. Because the sappers were busy in the valley, the *Teller* mines had to be cleared by the infantry who very soon learnt how to become competent engineers and all went well without accidents.

On leaving the area of the wayside crucifix they had to reconnoitre a path to the right and, on the left, the road to La Bijude. A patrol went to the right and very soon returned with 20 prisoners. Night fell. Other patrols continued to harass the Germans all night long and there were further scrimmages. The next morning civilians found a wounded soldier of 'C' Company lying in the field and took care of him.

La Bijude and the surrounding villages, Le Bas Hamel, Le Vardon and La Batonnière, were strongly held until the dawn of the 17th but at 0800 hours 'C' Company entered them without opposition. The villages were stuffed with mines. They took 10 more prisoners. By 1000 hours all was over, the sappers started clearing the mines and patrols made contact with the Cornwalls who, at that time, were between La Bijude and Berjou.

LOCAL MEMORIES

(Recounted by M. Bessac with the help of M. Laignel)

AT THE ROCRAY FACTORY

The Rocray factory had been completely idle since 6 June. The Director, M. Bonneau, who lived in Condé, had followed most of the population of Condé to Bouilly. The only staff members at the factory were those who lived in Le Rocray. Since 6 June our main occupation had been to search for food in the surrounding countryside where a few shopkeepers of Pont-d'Ouilly had withdrawn. However, Germans had been billetted on us and not only did we have to put up with them but we also had to make sure that they did not carry off the tools and equipment from the factory. Inevitably, there were unpleasant incidents and some sticky situations but we got out of them thanks to M. Guyon and M. Laignel who both spoke German quite well.

On the evening of 6 June we decided to sleep in a natural depression (a dry stream-bed) in the side of the hill behind our houses. While many stayed there until the very end, others returned to sleep in their own beds. Thanks to the factory generators, we were lucky to have electricity and in each house that had a wireless set we were able to tune in and get the news of the advance of the English. We realized they were coming in our direction. This was confirmed by the sound of the approaching battle and on Thursday, 10 August, we heard the whistling of shells. On Sunday, 13 August, in the morning, while returning from St. Marc-d'Ouilly by the high ground, we watched the English artillery shelling the road from Condé to Caen. The shells fell at Le Fresne and very near the Vallée cheese factory at Le Grand Béron. The fire drew nearer and nearer and grew more and more intense until 15 August.

PREPARATIONS

On Thursday, the 10th, we decided to dig proper dugouts, each in his own garden, by the side of the path to Arclais in case — which was quite improbable of course — the fighting should take place around us. These shelters would allow us to stay in Rocray in safety. A German pioneer subaltern who was billetted on me warned me that we were going to be ordered to get out. On an impulse, I showed him the dugout I had built for the five of us, the Charrier family and ourselves. He inspected it thoroughly, with the eye of an expert, and then he said to me, "You are one of us." He was right: I had served in the Engineers during the 1914—18 war.

He saw that I knew what I was doing and I did not hesitate to assure him that all the other shelters were the same. Fortunately, he did not bother to inspect them. In any case, he had other things on his mind. He had been given the job of preparing the bridges on the Noireau, from Cambercourt to Cahan, for demolition and also of mining the road from Condé to Pont-d'Ouilly and the path from Arclais to La Martellée. The two bridges at Rocray, the bridge over the Noireau and canal and the foot-bridge over the sluices had been mined late on the evening of 14 August.

I can still see myself, accompanied by M. Laignel, dismantling the drinking water pipes running under the main bridge in order to save them from destruction. We worked on the same scaffolding side by side with the Germans while they set their explosives in place under the deck of the bridge. Each of us did his own thing!

At the request of M. Guyon, the Germans had given us permission to move the fire-fighting pump from the factory to the left bank of the Noireau, near to the houses. We had everything under control. Most of the inhabitants of Rocray, and especially the women, watched all these preparations with apprehension. As the local 'expert' I assured them that there was nothing to worry about; there may be just a little bang but no danger at all. That is what should have happened but what I overlooked was that at that time the Germans, being short of explosives of the right kind, had used others that they were not familiar with and did not know how to use.

DESTRUCTION OF THE BRIDGES

The evening of 14 August

First the foot-bridge over the sluice was destroyed at about 2000 hours. The detonation was enormous for such a small job and mud was thrown about everywhere. It was easy to see what was going to happen to the other bridges. I was, therefore, anxious to warn everyone that we could expect something even bigger and that it would be wise to take shelter. When night fell we took to our dugouts. We had barely got in when a German officer summoned us in these words. "Frenchmen?" As no one replied, the voice repeated. "French civilians, will you please reply." *Someone replied.* "Yes, what is it?" *I thought it was mistaken of him to reply and that the German was going to force us to evacuate but he did not do so. The officer went on in a loud voice.* "Frenchmen, we are going to destroy the bridges. Go back to your houses, open the doors and windows and then return immediately to your shelters. We know that they are well built so you have nothing to fear."

Obviously, we had to obey his order; it was in our own interest. The first bridge was blown up a quarter of an hour later. What a bang! What a blast! The pieces rained down on all the roofs. A quarter of an hour after that it was the turn of the other bridge. The blast seemed to be even stronger and pieces of metal showered down very near us. When all was over each of us went to his house to check on the damage. It was not insignificant. Shattered windows and doors, a few blown out, collapsed walls, debris and furniture strewn about all over the place. As we had no lights by which to clean up, there was nothing for us to do but wait for daybreak and we spent the night in our dugouts.

THE FIRST ENGLISH ARRIVE

The morning of 15 August

The day started with a calm that lasted the best part of the morning. But it was an uneasy calm, more so for us because we could clearly see the Germans moving about on the high ground to the south of us and on the edge of the woods. We thought they might even be watching us. In Rocray itself there was quite a bit of activity that morning. We were all busy cleaning up our houses, temporarily repairing the broken doors and windows and so on.

At about 1100 hours we saw two men in English uniforms coming up the twisting Arclais road; they were two officers on a reconnaissance. They approached slowly, looking around in all directions. They seemed very nervous. I think it was Mme. Laignel who saw them first. Taken completely by surprise, she screamed to her husband anxiously, "Albert! Albert! Albert!" M. Laignel ran to her but first warned the Englishmen that the Germans were nearby, on the opposite slope of the hill, in fact. Soon other Rocray inhabitants appeared and expressed their delight noisily. I can still see one of the English officers as he asked us to keep quiet and saying, "Shush" as he made the gesture of putting his finger to his lips.

At this moment, Mme. Laignel, who had disappeared to pretty herself up, re-appeared to be photographed between the two Englishmen. They then left by the same road by which they had come. Their visit was very brief, only about 30 minutes. The gathering took place in front of M. Laignel's house, number 5, which is in an alley just facing the access road. At that time the alley was still sheltered by a few large fir trees that hid it from the sight of the Germans.

During the very short time the English officers were at Le Rocray, M. Laignel was able to give them some valuable information about the Germans that he had found out by making a trip to the Binard farm on the other side of the Noireau — the German side — on the Condé—Pont-d'Ouilly road. As a subterfuge, he had furnished himself with two jugs which he pretended he wished to fill with cider from the abandoned farm. He discovered that the house was filled with Germans who were surprised to find him there. It was not easy to allay their suspicions but he managed it and returned with the jugs, filled. On the way he noted that the road near the farm was mined and also that there were German soldiers in a field on the side of the hill. The two Englishmen were very grateful for all this detailed information.

THE CROSSING OF THE NOIREAU

The afternoon of 15 August

At about 1500 hours the noise of airplanes coming in low broke the calm of the day. Suddenly we had front-row seats at the performance of the R.A.F. planes attacking the enemy positions with machine-gun fire, rockets and light bombs. It was a beautiful display of fireworks, brief but effective. Taken by surprise, the Germans ran in all directions but many were killed on the spot. This action was followed up by well-directed artillery fire to which the Germans replied feebly but it forced us to return to our shelters.

It was at this moment that a farm worker named Jean Blanc, coming at a good pace from La Martellée and heading towards Arclais, in his shirt sleeves, his coat over his arm, shouted out to us in passing, "They're coming! The English have arrived!"

A little later, at about 1800 hours, the first English troops arrived at Rocray and began to cross the stream. They didn't have much difficulty because the Germans, in blowing up the footbridge over the sluice had, at the same time, damaged the sluice gate and this let the water out, leaving the overflow runway dry. Unfortunately, the crossing was in sight of the Germans opposite it and they covered it with machine-gun fire. One Englishman was wounded by a bullet in the groin. He was taken to my house where we stretched him out in the dining room and gave him first aid. In the meanwhile, an English machine-gunner, sheltered by the trees of the alley, replied to the German fire and silenced it.

After crossing the Noireau without trouble, 4 Englishmen were wounded on the right bank. M. Laignel helped the stretcher-bearers carry them and took two of them with him to his house. One of them was a seriously-wounded Lieutenant whom he placed on a chaise-longue by the front door. A little later the stretcher-bearers brought in a German Captain who had been run through by a bayonet in the vicinity of M. Binard's farm. The English Lieutenant, seeing the serious condition of the German Captain, got up and gave him his place on the chaise-longue.

German shells exploded on the hill behind the houses. As it was late, I was afraid that the English would not be able to come up in sufficient force to establish themselves in strength on the right bank of the Noireau but I was agreeably surprised when I saw that supplies were already coming across the stream below the factory. The deep canal that fed the turbines had been filled with empty barrels. The barrels, mostly metal, had been pierced by pickaxes in order to allow the water to flow through them. Supplies continued to come across without interruption and by nightfall we felt safe. We had waited for this moment for so many months and at last we were rewarded.

EVACUATION OF LE ROCRAY
THE LES GOUTTES TUNNEL

The evening of 15 August

The Germans continued laying down harassing fire on the hill behind Le Rocray. A few shells, short-falls, fell close to the houses. So, together with M. Guyon, we suggested to everyone that we should take shelter in the Les Gouttes tunnel, at least for that night. They all agreed so off we went in pitch darkness along a path that had been mined from one end to the other but we made it without incident. The Les Gouttes tunnel, also called the Berjou tunnel, is so called in the area because it runs under the village of Les Gouttes between the railway stations of Berjou and La Lande-Clécy. It is 1800 metres long. Before the Invasion it had been used to

shelter Goering's train when he came to Normandy on an inspect-
ion tour. We knew that the tunnel was full of people who had been
there for several days but there was still room for us. We brought
nothing with us so we had to spend the night sleeping on the rails,
on the wooden ties of the railroad tracks and on the stone ballast.
Naturally, it was difficult to sleep even though we were very tired
but at least it was the same for all of us.

A VISIT TO LE ROCRAY

The morning of 16 August

On 16 August, at about six o'clock in the morning, M. Guyon and
I, curious to know what had happened during the night, return-
ed to Le Rocray. When we got there we noticed flames coming
from a warehouse on the left bank of the stream, near the office
buildings. A shell had set fire to a stockpile of charcoal. The fire-
fighting pump that we had moved to the right bank of the Noireau
during the night of the 14th was much too far away to be of any
use to us because we did not have sufficient lengths of hose. So
we picked up some buckets and crossed the Noireau at the outflow
of the canal that feeds the turbines. This part of the canal that
runs between the main buildings of the factory was spanned by
a concrete slab designed to carry trucks up to 20 tons in weight.
The Germans, who had orders to blow up all the **bridges**, *had*
left it intact because, after all, it did not have a super-structure
and, therefore, was not a bridge!
When we arrived at the warehouse the charcoal and anything
else around it that could burn had burnt itself out. There was not
much left for us to do. Then we noticed that a pile of firewood
in the kitchen of the canteen attached to the warehouse had also
started to burn. Armed with our buckets of water we pushed open
the door — and found ourselves face to face with an English soldier.
He was seated on a box, warming himself, his legs stretched out,
in a very relaxed attitude. He held a small bottle in his hand,
balancing it on his thigh, and as soon as we opened the door he

greeted us with, "Have a drink of whisky", and offered us his bottle. Each of us had to take a swig, one after the other. The Englishman was very insistent and tipped up the bottom of the bottle to make sure we each had a good gulp. Finally, we put out the fire with the water buckets and by using the factory fire extinguishers that were still serviceable.

Now that the English had discovered the famous non-bridge that spanned that stretch of the canal, supplies started to arrive with much less trouble than before. The path between the factory buildings was marked out with white ribbons.

We thought that all the Germans had left but there were still some laggards around. M. Laignel went off to gather potatoes that had been uncovered in the factory garden by the bulldozer that had scrped out the ford over the Noireau but his harvest was interrupted by machine-guns bullets that whistled past his ears.

During the night a few shells had hit the houses. A mare had been killed by a mine in the field between the courtyard and the Noireau. That, added to the incident with the potatoes, decided us to return to the tunnel.

LEAVING THE TUNNEL A SECOND TIME

This time the departure was better organized. For a long time we had planned how to evacuate ourselves and since 6 June we had had the chance to get hold of some bicycle trailers or the parts to make them. And so a convoy of seven trailers left the tunnel, again taking the well-known path that was still not entirely cleared of mines. M. Laignel stayed behind in Le Rocray.

Because the atmosphere inside the tunnel was so stale and the air so unpleasant, we, together with the Morineau and Charrier families, decided to take up positions outside the tunnel, close to the entrance, at the side of the path that runs from Les Gouttes to La Martellée. We stayed there all through the 16th, to the great delight of M. Morineau who was a heavy smoker. He had been deprived of all tobacco for some weeks but now he took a cigarette from every British soldier who passed. Sometimes they even gave *him an entire pack.*

As it was very hot we all slept the night of 16/17 August under the stars. M. Guyon and the other families with children preferred to sleep right inside the tunnel.

THE SECOND VISIT TO LE ROCRAY ON 17 AUGUST WE RETURN TO STAY

On the morning of 17 August some of us went to see what had happened in Le Rocray. This time everything was quiet. The traffic, controlled by the British Military Police, continued to flow through the factory. German prisoners were being interrogated in a courtyard. A large tent had been raised in a field between the canal and the railroad track. We saw that, at last, it would be safe to leave the tunnel and we went off in search of the families and their luggage.

While we were away the women prepared breakfast. It was a make-shift meal, of course, but, nevertheless, we did it justice. After that we all set off. We were unable to return via La Martellée because at the time the road was being cleared of mines and the English had stopped all traffic on it. So we returned across the fields, dragging our trailers, and that was not easy. However, it all went off without incident and that evening we had the great satisfaction of taking our first meal in liberated territory.

THE ENGLISH STAY A WHILE IN LE ROCRAY

The English stayed in Le Rocray for 5 days. One evening they gave a variety show in the largest of the rooms (now the room in which the weavers trim their work) and it was filled with soldiers. We were all officially invited to this show. I think it was on 19 August.

There seemed to be everything imaginable in the large tent, offices, shops, a first aid station, etc. We were allowed to visit it. One evening my wife saw some chocolate bars there. We had not seen chocolate for ages. Mlle. Huguette Charrier, who was then

15 years old, was with us. She had learnt English at school and would have liked to try it out on the English soldiers but she was shy and did not know how to begin. I suggested that she ask them for chocolates as my wife was dying for some. She could not bring herself to do this because she feared a refusal so I told her to say that my wife had dysentery! She did this and immediately my wife was given a chocolate bar. After that, the conversation that started in this way between the young girl and the English soldier went on for quite a long time.

MEMORIES OF THE LES MONTS FARM

At that time M. Ballon occupied the Les Monts farm situated on the very top of the highest land near Berjou. On the morning of 15 August they were turned out to make room for a German head-quarters that installed itself there. The Ballons withdrew into the Capet woods near La Renaudière and dug themselves a shelter. In the evening the older M. Ballon went back to the farm to look for some cider. The German headquarters had withdrawn to Vardon and had been replaced by front-line troops who also occupied the Cimetière woods and Les Bruyères. Smoke shells had started fires all over the place. M. Chauffray, a former postman, went off to look for a safer shelter. He came across the first English soldiers on the path from the wayside crucifix to Capet and they advised him to take everyone into the tunnel. Leading the way, one of the soldiers said, in excellent French, "Hey, Father Ballon, where are you going?" Astonished that an Englishman should know him he tried to find out more about it but the person who addressed him continued on his way, leading the column of infantry. Later he was given to understand that it was probaly René Grosse, the local barber.

Only Grandfather Clement did not want to go to the tunnel. He preferred to return to his house in the village and passed through the German lines in the Cimetière woods. He was immediately encircled by shells that exploded all around him. An explosion tore the sleeve from his precious raincoat. Although he knew that the shells were English, he swore a mighty oath — at the Germans!

MEMORIES OF LE VARDON AND OF LA BIJUDE

The Germans had built an enormous gasoline dépôt outside the village of Haut Vardon, near La Bijude, just on the fringe of the fighting. Fortunately for the inhabitants, the Allied aircraft did not spot it. Just before the English arrived, the Germans placed guns there that were in action from 12 to 16 August. The Devardon family was ordered to evacuate its house so that the German headquarters, that had withdrawn from Les Monts, could spread out its maps of the area. In the evening of 16 August the inhabitants noticed German infantry withdrawing in Indian file along the paths so that they could avoid their own mines. Two days before, these same soldiers, on their way to Berjou, had said to M. Ramard, "Just some new attacks; we'll soon beat them back."

The night was calm. Early in the morning of the 17th M. Michel and M. Roger Paris left for the village of La Butte; they found the English there. They told them that the Germans had left and that they could advance with impunity but warned them that mines had been placed everywhere. While this was going on, Mlle. Michel, who had left to milk the cows, had a surprise: she found an Englishman in her field. He had been wounded in the legs. He wore the badge of the Somerset Light Infantry. Soon everyone in the village knew all about it and everyone wanted to do something to help the wounded man. Using a ladder as a stretcher, they carried him to the home of M. Tison where a strong cup of coffee, well laced with calvados, revived him. He told Mlle. Devardon, who spoke English, that he had been on a reconnaissance during the night, that he had been wounded in the legs and that his companions were about a kilometre to the rear. M. Michel then left to go to Cahan to tell them of the situation in La Bijude and the surrounding area. When the wounded man was picked up by his comrades they gave his boots to M. Ramard as a souvenir, in exchange for milk.

MEMORIES OF LES BRUYÈRES

The village of Les Bruyères near Cahan, where the well-known Guerin family lived, had taken in its share of refugees, as had many others. Among the refugees were the Decavel and Leray families of Condé who brought a guest of honour with them. He was the pilot of an English fighter plane who had been shot down near the village of La Mare near Caligny and had parachuted to safety.

M. and Mme. Leray recall: *My wife and I saved a tandem bicycle and trailer from the ruins and we were cycling back from Tinchebray where we had collected some things for we had no clothes left. Near Chapelle-du-Chêne we saw an aeroplane crash after it had been hit by anti-aircraft fire but it seemed to us that the pilot came down in the neighbourhood of La Croix-à-la-Main. As we came to the crossroad at Les Rivières we saw him coming out of a field. He was still tangled up in his parachute but he wanted to go along with us. Some people by the riverside, who had seen what happened, beckoned us to come to their house where they dressed him in civilian clothers and shaved off his moustache. The Germans came looking for him. In a panic he ran to hide in a wheat field. The alarm passed and he took his place in the convoy of refugees. Near Berjou a German staff car stopped the cyclists and ordered them to move a drunkard who was lying on the road and barring the way.*

Later, using a photograph taken by Dujardin, M. Ricordeau forged an identification card for the airman.

Other Allied airmen were also hidden in those parts. One day, it must have been 14 July, three of them were invited to a feast in honour of our national day. To the toast of "À La Marseillaise!", they stoutly replied, "God save the King!".

'Maurice' was the name the pilot took in order to appear to be one of us. Some days before 15 August an important German radio station had been installed at Bruyères. Maurice decided to play games with the Germans. He disappeared one day and was gone for a long time. When he finally returned he came from the direction of the radio station, smoking a cigar given to him by the Germans. His hosts anxiously asked him what he had been up to and

he replied, "I have just taken the surrender of the German Air Force!"

On the morning of 15 August a German motorcyclist arrived at Bruyères and announced that the English were in the tunnel. The signal staff quickly packed up and left. The refugees from Condé also left but they did not go in the same direction. Frequently risking their lives in passing through German positions where the fields had been mined, they set out down towards Les Gouttes with the airman who was delighted at the prospect of rejoining his compatriots. Those who stayed at Les Bruyères passed the night of the 16/17 in their shelters. In the small hours of the morning they were surprised at the arrival of an Englishman who told them, in good French, that they could now leave their shelters because the fighting was over. Surprised to hear him speak their language so well, the Guerins questioned him. "I am French", he said, "originally from Malo-les-Bains. I guided the English through the woods and along the country lanes." Just then the farm dog started to bark, as it did every time it saw a uniform, and, thinking that there were still some Germans prowling around, the guide disappeared. The Guerin family never saw him again.

MEMORIES OF CAMBERCOURT

Madame Blais, whose husband was Mayor of Berjou at the time, remembers 15 August very well. *On that day my husband left to go to Mass in the tunnel. He was very careful of mines. When he returned he told me he had met some Englishmen. We thought there would be fighting in our neighbourhood because at dawn we had seen the Germans preparing defensive positions in the village. Then we saw them leave towards Berjou, taking their dead and wounded with them in small carts. I will always remember one of the wounded; he had his arm ripped off and was wearing a tourniquet made of a twist of straw. We thought the press-house would be the safest place for us to shelter in. An artillery bombardment started in the afternoon. During a lull we left the building to see what was happening and saw English soldiers, crouching*

*as they crept along the walls and hedges. A soldier, a bullet hole
in his helmet, lay dead, stretched out on the ground in front of
a shed. Another, lying on the path up the slope, seemed to be asleep
if it were not for the ghastly wound in his side. We went back into
the press-house and were joined by some English soldiers. They
seemed to be quite oblivious to the noise and the danger of the
battle that had started up again. They began to play cards on the
floor. When an N.C.O. gave them orders they gathered up the
cards and went off to meet Death with a joke on their lips.*

MEMORIES OF THE LES GOUTTES TUNNEL

The town of Berjou did not receive orders to evacuate. As a matter of fact, it is difficult to see how an evacuation order could have
been received because all telephone lines had been cut and from
the middle of July the town had been right behind the front line.

The course of events was as follows. From the middle of July,
M. Ricordeau, a teacher and secretary to the Municipal Council,
had hidden and given shelter to an Australian airman, Norman
K. Baker, whose fighter plane had been shot down. His story will
be told further on.* Later, two more airmen were hidden by the
Marischael family at Bas-Hamel. Of these, one was a bomber commander. He carried a map with him, drawn up at headquarters,
on which the areas to be bombed were marked in red. The areas
included the hills surrounding Berjou and the town itself. However,
the bombardment was not to be an aerial bombardment but an
artillery barrage that was going to cover every square metre of the
designated area.

In the evening the three Allied airmen sat on a bench at the
rear of the school garden. They watched as the Germans sent convoys of horse-drawn vehicles, heavily camouflaged with branches,
to supply the front with munitions and food.

One day — it was about 10 August — Norman Baker showed
the bomber commander's secret map to M. Ricordeau and told

*See Appendix C, page 294

him that it was absolutely necessary for the population to leave because the township was going to be shelled at any moment. One way or other, they had to let everyone know and get them away. This was not easy to do because no one felt in immediate danger. Many said that they would not leave their homes and, of course, it was impossible for M. Ricordeau to divulge his source of information.

Little by little the front came nearer and nearer. A few English shells whistled overhead. (Even so a German officer continued to tell them, the locals, that they had pushed the English back into the sea). A battery of German artillery installed itself near the orchard of Leon Chauffray's farm and opened fire. He, forced to accept the inevitable and deafened by the noise, decided to leave with his family.

M. Ricordeau decided to tell the inhabitants of the town that he had received orders from the Prefecture to evacuate the community. This information was quickly passed from mouth to mouth. Many people from Cambercourt took refuge in the tunnel while some of the town's inhabitants left in the direction of the communities to the south of the Canton of Athis. Unfortunately, a few delayed too long. They were caught in the artillery barrage and suffered heavily; many dead were left to be mourned. The Piel family, bakers, and the Marie family each lost a child.

The Abbé Génissel stayed behind in his parsonage, together with his nephew, a seminarist. In the final days they had the company of a German sentry who slept on the floor because there were only two beds. The rest of their possessions had been buried and the furniture bricked up in a shed.

The Abbé recalls: *On Sunday, 13 August, I went down into the tunnel to say Mass for the hundred or so people who had taken refuge there and who, I thought, might want some spiritual comfort. The people had settled down in the tunnel quite well. M. Blochliger, manager of the local dairy, did his best to look after all those poor unfortunate people; he even brought a cask of wine! Others had brought rabbits, and chickens that clucked during the service. A confessional was improvised, a bicycle wheel serving as the grill. As far as the altar was concerned, it was placed on the bed of a cart that had been pushed into the tunnel for this purpose.*

In passing, one should remember that in 1941 Goering's special armoured train was parked in the tunnel. It had been white-washed for the occasion by the Todt organization. They also installed light, a second track, some further tracks for shunting etc. Sentries were placed every kilometre from Cerisy to Berjou. The train remained in the tunnel about a month. Railway traffic was interrupted and busses had to tranship travellers between La Lande-Clécy and Berjou. Every time Goering left his train or returned to it in his green convertible car exceptional security measures were enforced.

THEY ARE GOING TO BLOW UP THE TUNNEL!

On the morning of 14 August, with the tunnel sheltering about twelve hundred persons, German engineers arrived to dig holes for explosives with which to blow up the entrance. There was panic among the refugees. M. Blochliger, who spoke German, tried to reason with the Commander of the detachment but he refused to listen; he had received his orders and he intended to carry them out. The Abbé Génissel then talked over the situation with M. Blochliger as they searched for a way to prevent such a massacre. Learning that there was a high-level headquarters in the chateau of M. de Saint-Pol, they hurried there hoping to speak to the General. But he had other things on his mind. His troops, charged with provisioning 84 Army Corps, had just been chased from Le Mans by the American advance and the American Airforce had destroyed almost all his vehicles. Not only was he unable to bring up weapons, munitions, food, medical supplies etc. but he also sensed that, hour by hour, as the fighting drew nearer, it was going to be more and more difficult for him to escape the jaws of the pincer that was closing in on the German armies.

The two emissaries were so persistent that finally a Colonel agreed to listen to them. During his stay at the chateau, this officer, Colonel Jung, had at least treated the Saint-Pol family fairly even though the circumstances were not the most felicitous. Later he was captured at Saint-Lambert-sur-Dives on 19 August by the

Canadian Argyll and Sutherland Highlanders and was sent to the United States as a prisoner. On his release, as happened to all senior officers, he had to be cleared by a de-Nazification court before he could resume his law practice. At that time he was able to produce a certificate attesting to the fact that he had prevented the mining of the tunnel and thus saved many innocent lives. He was acquitted.

M. Blochliger and Abbé Génissel told Colonel Jung that the tunnel was filled with refugees, mostly women, children and the sick, who could not leave its shelter without risking certain death. The Colonel was sympathetic. He promised the petitioners that orders would be given that the tunnel was not to be blown up on condition that it remain neutral and not be used by the *Résistance* or the Allied armies. A proclamation signed by him and drawn up in German and English stating that the tunnel was reserved for refugees was taken back by the two Frenchmen and displayed at the entrance.

The joy of the two emissaries was so great that they all but forgot to thank the Colonel for what he had just done for them. M. Blochliger asked him, "What can we do for you in return?" The officer looked at Abbé Génissel and replied, "Pray to God that He will protect me in the same way that I have protected your refugees."

When recounting this story to the author, L'Abbé Génissel added: *I interceded on his behalf with the Virgin Mary at Mass the next day, 15 August.*

As I was late taking confessions on the evening of the 14th, I spent the night in the house of the Chauffray family in Cambercourt. Early the next morning, wanting to celebrate Mass at Berjou for those who had stayed there, I crossed the Noireau and climbed towards the village by the shortcut. Germans were entrenched in the woods and on the slopes and the nearer I got to the village the more of them there were. The parsonage, as with many other houses in the town, had been turned into a fort and I could pick out several machine-gun nests. The side of bacon that I had not hidden had been eaten by hungry soldiers. I rang the church bell at about 7.30 and conducted the service in honour of the Virgin.

Two families were present, the Marie family — their son gave the responses; he was killed later that afternoon — and a few members of the Piel family.

The baker had continued making bread right up to the last minute. He filled a sack for me and I put it on my back for the people in the tunnel. I went towards Cambercourt, bowed down under the load, glancing from right to left, when suddenly I saw a round clod of earth. I was about to put my foot on it when I jumped aside. I broke out in a cold sweat and said a prayer as I carefully picked my way between the deadly mines. If I had touched one I would have been finished. At the level crossing, a German cart had blown itself up on one of its own mines. A German soldier had been killed together with one of the horses while the other horse still stood in the traces, terribly wounded and covered with blood. The poor animal had to be put out of its misery.

After I had said Mass in the tunnel, I ate breakfast. In the afternoon, accompanied by some friends, I went to the neighbouring village of Ardrilly for news. The path was strewn with mines. When we arrived there we saw the English infantry coming down towards the stream and towards Le Rocray in small groups, firing all the way into the hedges, along the hill slopes, in the fields and in the woods. Smoke shells fell around us. We turned back along the path. When we returned to the tunnel we saw English officers there some of whom were talking with members of the Résistance. We were liberated! Though every face showed joy, there were some who, seeing armed civilians of the Résistance around, were not quite sure that all was over yet.

THE FLAG OF BERJOU

On the morning of 18 August, M. Blais, Mayor of Berjou, went to the Town Hall to tell M. Ricordeau, teacher, and Secretary to the Municipality, that the English Brigadier who had installed his Headquarters in the railway station of Berjou—Cambercourt would like to have the village's flag presented to him. The two men decided that a delegation of officials would present the flag to the Brigadier in the afternoon. Accordingly, three of them, M. Alexandre Blais, the Mayor, M. Fernand Delaunay, the Agricultural Officer and M. Roland Ricordeau presented themselves at the Berjou railway station with the village's flag rolled up in a sheath of oil-cloth.

It was tea time. The delegation was received with great cordiality and friendliness. They spoke of the difficult time that the population had just lived through. They thanked their valiant liberators whole-heartedly. They unfurled the flag and ceremoniously placed it in the waiting-room that had been raised to the dignity of an international meeting place. There were several French-Canadian officers at the Headquarters and they acted as interpreters.

Tea was served in an atmosphere of friendliness and congratulations.

At the end, the Brigadier stood up and everyone stood up with him. He made a short speech stressing the traditional friendship between England and France and of their common fight against fascism. He solemnly promised that the flag would accompany him during all the fighting to come and, looking directly at the representatives of the town, he vowed to take it all the way to Berlin and then to return it to Berjou. The delegation then withdrew, thanking the Brigadier and wishing him well for the rest of the campaign.

The Brigadier kept his word. The flag of Berjou went all the way to Berlin. After the Armistice, Captain Gauthier, a French-Canadian Intelligence Office, whose story is told in a following chapter*, returned it to Berjou. And so, after this memorable journey, it came back to its rightful place in the Town Hall. Today, stitched into its folds, it carries the insignia of Brigadier Essame's 214 Brigade.

Nowadays, this precious relic only leaves the Town Hall on special occasions. The last time it was taken from the Town Hall was to lead the funeral cortège of the former Mayor of Berjou, M. Blais.

*See page 285.

THE RESISTANCE HELPS 43RD DIVISION

While doing research for this book among the War Office files in London, the author came across a document from Brigadier Essame, the Commander of 214 Brigade of 43rd British Infantry Division, mentioning the invaluable information provided by a *Résistance* group under the orders of Raymond Pierre (Croix de Guerre with bronze star). Before going into an extensive account of their adventures and the actions they took part in that contributed in no small measure to the success, among many other operations, of the crossing of the Noireau and the battle of Berjou, it is as well to mention exactly how this group came to be formed.

RAYMOND PIERRE'S STORY

I began to form and took command of an armed Résistance group early in 1944. We called the group the Robert Déan detachment of France-Tireurs Partisans in memory of Robert Déan, the son of a former municipal councillor of Caen, who was executed as a hostage at a very early age at Chateaubriant. The arrest of Michel de Bouard, Dean of the Faculty of Letters at Caen University, whom I had recruited into the National Front organization and who became its regional leader and my betrayal to the Gestapo forced me to flee from Caen.

I went to Clécy where my mother lived. There I was able to take advantage of two 'covers' that enabled me to get on with the formation of my group. The first 'cover' was given to me by a friend who was employed in the Ministry of Information at Caen that had been infiltrated by the Résistance. (Its Director was eventually deported). Thanks to him I was able to get myself officially named the local delegate of the Department of Information of the Vichy Government. The second 'cover' was the close relationship I had enjoyed since childhood with the Prieur family, proprietors of the Hotel Le Moulin du Vey, a place so popular with the Germans that the Prieur family were thought to be collaborators.

After being active in the F.T.P.F. for several months, I brought together a small group of young people in Clécy who were itching to get into action. The brothers Jaques and Paul Leboucher were most active in the group and Victor Bertrand was also involved. We were in it 'part-time', i.e. for the moment we combined our Résistance activites with our normal life. Our most important task was to assist the full-time groups such as those of Pontécoulant. To our small group we added some local recruits like Chauffray who, unfortunately, was posted to a group in Caen and was arrested and shot at the time of the Invasion. We also recruited other young men who had fled from their homes in order to escape the police or the Gestapo.

WITH THE BRITISH

Thury-Harcourt was burning when we made contact with the British troops. Since 6 June we had devoted ourselves full-time to the Résistance. Various full-time Résistance members such as Pierrot and the Lassus brothers of Malo-les-Bains, now joined the part-timers. At the start, these full-time members were dispersed in groups of four. One of these groups was in the village of Pouclée, another on the Ile des Aulneaux at the foot of Pain de Sucre, and another at Rochetaillis. After the bombardment and evacuation of Clécy I stayed in the village of Fontaine for some time. During this period we were mainly engaged in acts of sabotage, as related in the last chapter. We had plastic explosives, detonators, incendiary pencils and some 'black boxes' but very few weapons. The weapons that had been hidden since 1940, mainly rifles, were not of much use. Furthermore, our main storage dèpôt in the old quarry of Les Fours à Chaux at Clécy had fallen into the hands of Brigadier Stehlin of the Clécy gendarmerie.

One of our preoccupations was, therefore, to equip ourselves with light machine-guns, automatic rifles and ammunition. Arms supplied from London were parachuted into La Mayenne county but we did not receive them directly. We got hold of them in various ways thanks, mainly, to the better-equipped groups who supplied

Building a Bailey bridge over the Orne at Putanges proved to be very difficult because of the inaccessible and awkward site. (cf p.202 et seq.)

The first tank goes over carefully to test the strength of the bridge.

A Sherman tank in the middle of the Bailey bridge at Putanges.

I.W.M. #B9463

The bridge has stood the test! 29 Brigade of 11th Armoured Division can now cross the Orne at Putanges and continue the pursuit of the enemy towards Argentan, Gacé and L'Aigle.

I.W.M. #B9466

A 'Sexton' of 11th Armoured Division crossing the Seine. The 'Sexton', a self-propelled gun, was designed and produced in Canada and comprised a British 25-pounder mounted on the chassis of a Ram cruiser tank, a Canadian design based on the Sherman. The Ram tank did not see service.
I.W.M. #B9807

The self-propelled gun is followed by other vehicles of 11th Armoured Division. When keeping regulation distances between vehicles an Armoured Division convoy extended for 100 kilometres.

I.W.M. #B9478

A truck of 11th Armoured Division towing a 2-wheeled 180-gallon water tank complete with filtration equipment along a street in Putanges.

I.W.M #B9476

Inspecting a disabled German Mark IV tank in Putanges.

I.W.M. #B9475

While the approaches to the Putanges bridge were heavily damaged and set on fire by the bombardment the church at Pont-Ecrepin was undamaged.

I.W.M. #B9480

A 'Firefly' of the 23rd Hussars in the market place in Putanges waiting its turn to cross the bridge. The 'Firefly' was a Sherman tank fitted with a 17-pounder gun

I.W.M. #B9477

Two members of the French Forces of the Interior pose in front of the Putanges Town Hall. (cf p.203)
I.W.M. #B9539

At Ecouché other *Résistance* fighters are delighted to be able to go into action at the side of soldiers of the 2nd Free French Armoured Division.

I.W.M. #B9540

A patrol of the Inns of Court at the intersection of Highway 24 and the road from Saint-André to Saint-Hilare-de-Briouze. (cf p.182)

I.W.M. #B9427

Half-tracks of 2nd French Armoured Division not far from Ecouché. (cf p.203)

I.W.M. #B9421

Men of the 4th King's Shropshire Light Infantry march through Ecouché on their way to attack Montgaroult and Sentilly. (cf p.212)

I.W.M. #B9456

Soldiers hitch a ride in a German staff car captured near Argentan as it is towed away. (cf p.219)

I.W.M. #B9531

Self-propelled guns of the 13th Royal Horse Artillery take up positions in a wheat field near Argentan. (cf p.206 et seq.)

I.W.M. #B9530

Infantry and tanks of 11th Armoured Division are glad to take a rest while the Americans liberate Argentan. Once that is done they can resume their advance towards Gacé and L'Aigle. (cf p.219 et seq.)

I.W.M. #B9528

The war is over for these Germans as their captivity begins.

I.W.M. #B9527

German prisoners under a fierce and watchful guard!

I.W.M. #B9626

Now that Argentan has been liberated the column can make its way towards the town. A 6-pounder anti-tank gun of one of the infantry battalions in convoy. (cf p.207)

A solitary British soldier inspects the ruins behind the church of Saint-Germain in Argentan. (cf p.219)

Tanks of 11th Armoured Division go through Le Bourg-Saint-Léonard on their way to Exmes and Gacé. (cf p.219 et seq.)

I.W.M. #B9599

The 3rd Monmouthshire Regiment and the 23rd Hussars take part in the liberation of L'Aigle. (cf p.230 et seq.)

I.W.M. #B9653

Motorised infantry of the 8th Rifle Brigade near the entrance to the concentration camp at Belsen. (cf p.238)

I.W.M. #BU3927

Major Wigan and Major Blacker (later Sir Cecil Blacker, Adjutant-General of the British Army) of the 23rd Hussars, seated first and second from the left, celebrate Victory in Europe on the evening of 8 May 1945. (cf p.205 and p.233 et seq.)

Jodl, Speer and Doenitz are arrested at Flensburg by troops of 11th Armoured Division during Operation BLACKOUT. (cf p.238)

I.W.M. #BU6711

Lieutenant-General 'Jorrocks' Horrocks, Commander of XXX Corps (on the left), promises Major-General 'Pip' Roberts the moon for his night advance on Amiens! (cf p.233)

us from their stocks. Carrying these weapons was a risky business and many of our comrades were arrested. One day my wife and I were returning on a tandem bicycle from St. Germain-du-Crioult. We had an automatic rifle wrapped in a blanket and hidden in the luggage rack in the rear. We got a flat tire while riding down the hill into the village of Canteloup, near Clécy, just as a column of German infantry passed us as they marched up the hill. I'll always retain the bad memory of the long minutes we spent on that narrow path while we had to suffer the contagion of the Germans as they brushed against us and our automatic rifle.

If my memory does not fail me, I think it was about the middle of July that we decided to make our headquarters in the galleries of the iron mine at St. Remy where many families, mine among them, were taking refuge. We carried our supplies of arms and ammuniton there. We took up positions in one of the galleries called 'The Old #4' so that, if the Germans came, we could defend ourselves. We slept in small caves running off the main chamber. Branches formed the mattresses of our beds. Some families placed themselves in that part of the gallery nearest the entrance. In fact, we were all mixed up together. Our position was a good one not only because the altitude gave us a commanding view of the countryside but also because it offered us excellent mobility of movement in case we had to get out fast. This was because, although the entrance to the mine was at the bottom of the hill, from the St. Rémy—Thury-Harcourt road, one could get out of it at just about any other elevation of the hill, including the summit. Most of us knew the layout of the galleries very well, some, like Victor Bertrand, because they were miners at St. Rémy, while others, like myself, because they had worked there some time in order to escape from the Service du Travail Obligatoire (the Forced Labour Service). Finally, we had the whole-hearted sympathy and support, as far as he could give it to us, of M. Vogel, the Manager of the mine.

On 13 August my companions, Jean-Pierre Aumont, Marcel Angot and René Lassus, who had left to carry out sabotage activities in the Culey-le-Party area, made our first contact with the British troops as they came down the left bank of the River Orne when the right bank, on which we were still encamped, was still in the hands of the Germans. Lassus, in high spirits, returned to us accompanied by an English sergeant and two soldiers whom he had guided across the Orne at the hamlet of Caumettes and had then brought into the mine. We gave them a warm welcome. We pointed out where the Germans had built an observation post and a machine-gun emplacement at the entrance of one of the galleries on a hill near ours. I gave them what information I had and asked them to tell their Commander that we were completely at his disposal to carry out any mission he would like to entrust to us. They said they would like to take back some prisoners. That was no problem, we told them, nothing easier!

Up to that time we had not taken any prisoners for the sole reason that we would have had to guard them and we had better things to do. The same applied to deserters. One of our comrades had offered to bring us 50 or 60 Poles, conscripts in the German army, who would like to desert. I refused because they would have been a burden to us and would have created a needless risk.

Everyone wanted to go on the hunt for Germans. For this mission I chose, firstly, Pierrot, a survivor of the Pontecoulant disaster* who was the most aggressive of us all. For the second, I gave way to the importunities of a young man, full of enthusiasm, René Grosse, called 'René the Hairdresser', who had been with us for only a very short time but who burned with the desire to do something. (Unfortunately, he later fell victim to a German). They returned empty-handed, without prisoners, and we had no time to try again. Everyone wanted to guide the English back to their lines. I had to exercise my authority to make sure that only Lassus went back with them. I couldn't afford to let the whole section go over to the English just when our presence behind the German lines could be most useful.

That same day, another companion, Roger Lemouland, made contact with an armoured English patrol to whom he served as a guide while they made a reconnaissance of the right bank of the

---

*Pontecoulant, a small village near Clécy, was the scene of a 'shoot-out' between the *Maquis*, who had an arms dépôt there, and the Clécy gendarmerie led by Brigadier Stehlin, a collaborator with the Gestapo. One gendarme was killed and a *Partisan* was wounded, arrested and probably later shot.

Orne between Caumont and Pont-de-la-Mousse. There was a brief scrimmage there with the Germans. The English withdrew but the next day they occupied the heights at Caumont. That evening, Lassus, in high spirits as usual, returned to us, this time accompanied by Captain Gauthier, a French-Canadian. Everyone was delighted with this because up to then I had been the only person who could speak to the English. We immediately got down to business. I brought all my men together and, with the aid of the map, we gave Captain Gauthier all the information we had gathered about that sector. Each man gave details of what he remembered from his last outing, the positions of the Germans, the state of the roads and the bridges, the morale of the enemy etc. Captain Gauthier was absolutely delighted. I asked him if he wanted any prisoners. He told me that it wasn't worth it; he now had enough information.

The Captain brought us up to date on the general progress of the English troops and he asked us to concentrate on getting some specific intelligence. We agreed wholeheartedly and he then told me what he wanted to know. Most urgent of all was a reconnaissance of the bridge at La Landelle. We did that at once and before he left he had the results. He also asked me to lend him the services of Aumont, Angot and Lemouland and to place them directly under English orders. I agreed. He then offered us supplies. I asked him specially for flash-lights, and for bicycles because the tires of ours were shredded. It was arranged that I would meet him at 12 o'clock at the hamlet of Caumettes with the information he had requested. Just as he was about to leave to go back to his unit, still accompanied by Lassus, and while my men were starting to disperse, he had second thoughts and asked me to recall them. "There's something I forgot", he said. "Tell me which villages you do not want us to shell." Each of us, of course, asked him not to shell his own particular village, St. Rémy, Clécy, Le Vey, Le Bo and, in particular, Le Fresne. "All right, I promise you that none of those villages will be shelled", and he kept his word.

At dawn the next day, 14 August, I sent out three groups to gather the information Captain Gauthier had asked me for. Jacques Leboucher and a companion took the sector of Cossesseville—

Pont-d'Ouilly—St. Marc-d'Ouilly. Georges Groult and Paul Leboucher went to the sector running north of the valley of the Noireau. Victor Bertrand and Raymond Mellion went to the valley of the Noireau between Condé and Pont-d'Ouilly. As for myself, I decided that the best way I could use the morning was to go on a reconnaissance with Pierrot in the direction of La Mousse and St. Omer with the intention of making use of the splendid observation post afforded by the rocks of La Houle that overlook Le Pain de Sucre. (Sugar-loaf Hill).

We left on foot, skirting round the hill on which the Germans still had an observation post, and came to the path that runs from Croix-Blanche to La Mousse. There we came across two Germans sitting on the bank bordering the path. We had taken the precaution of carrying empty haversacks so that we could say we were out in search of food. We were not far from the place where, the day before, Pierrot had shot a German prisoner. (Later we learnt from the people at La Mousse that he had only been wounded). We fell into conversation with the two Germans, trying to assess their morale. Just then a German staff car appeared with a senior officer and his driver. The car stopped. The officer asked us what we were doing there. We told him that we were looking for potatoes for our families who had taken refuge in the mine. He told us to get into the car and took us up a narrow path to the right in the direction of Pain de Sucre. We finally stopped in amongst Germans who had just installed an artillery battery there. Abruptly, the senior officer made us get out, spoke to the Lieutenant who commanded the battery for a few minutes and then drove off, leaving us in the hands of the Lieutenant. He ordered us to sit on the ground and went off to attend to his battery duties. There were dozens of Germans all around us. We realized then that we were prisoners. We waited patiently. The Lieutenant did not say a word to us. After a while Pierrot took an identification paper from his pocket bearing the stamp of the Commandant of Vire in which he was described as a police deputy and said to me, "I am going to show him this and see what happens." The Lieutenant looked at the document and returned it to him without a word. Rather nervously, we continued to wait. The Lieutenant sat down with a group of N.C.O.'s and started to eat. We watched them. Just then two Germans arrived by a small path that climbs up from the valley below, accompanied by two young men whom they had just arrested. We knew the young men. They were from the mine and they had been out in a genuine search for food. They were carrying pails of milk. They were dazed and frightened. We greeted them warmly and threw ourselves on their rations, emptying the milk from the pails. The scene seemed to disarm the Germans who watched us with amusement. We played the fool. When the Germans had finished eating, the Lieutenant approached us. He still had a suspicious look but after a while he said, in German, "Get out of here." Both Pierrot and I understood him; he did not have to tell us a second time! As unhurriedly and calmly as possible the four of us beat it. What a relief that was for Pierrot and me. If we had been arrested I would not have been able to keep my rendez-vous with Captain Gauthier. We decided that we had better get back at once. While we were on the path we tried to pin-point exactly where the guns of the battery had been placed and also where some more guns were that we had seen on the reverse slope of Pain de Sucre during our forced stay there.

I was at the rendezvous at Caumettes at noon. Lassus guided me across the Orne. Jacques Leboucher and one of the members of his team left a little before us having given me all the information that they had been able to gather. We took an Airforce officer with us, Group-Captain James, who had lived for some time hidden on a farm and who had been brought to us that morning. He had a bottle of calvados with him. I introduced him to Captain Gauthier. Group-Captain James uncorked his bottle and offered it to the French-Canadian. Thinking it was cider, Captain Gauthier took a good swig of it. His face became crimson and he nearly passed out! When he had recovered I gave him Jacques Leboucher's intelligence and told him that the others had not yet returned. I also told him about the adventure Pierrot and I had had that morning and I pointed out on the map the exact positions of the battery and the other emplacements that we had seen. He told me that at precisely 1400 hours all these positions together with the other positions on the hill near us would be shelled by

British guns. Finally, he led me to a truck and, opening the rear, said to me with a self-satisfied air, "There are the supplies you asked for." I looked in. Indeed, there were the things we had asked for, cigarettes, flash lights and bicycles. But the bicycles, black in colour, with heavy frames and large raised handle-bars, were obviously English. I said to the Captain, "You don't think I am going to send my men out to ride around in the midst of the Germans on those bicycles, do you? They are obviously English bicycles. They will be noticed immediately." Crestfallen, he replied, "You're right. I didn't think of that. I'll try and find you some others." We arranged to meet again at the same place at 1800 hours and then Lassus and I left to return to the mine, taking with us all the gifts from the brave Captain that we could carry.

As 1400 hours, the time set for the bombardment, drew near we and the refugees were taking a meal very close to the entrance of the Old Quarter. A wood fire burnt under a cooking pot that hung from a tripod. At ten minutes to two o'clock I said to one of the fellows, "I think we should get everyone back into the gallery. One never knows. If they fire short we run the risk of being hit." They did not need any persuasion and we all went back into the gallery, taking the cooking utensils with us. At exactly 1400 hours the first shells came rushing in. They were smoke shells. Several exploded near the entrance to the gallery. Everyone rushed further back into the mine. The shells started to fall further away but it was a while before anyone dared to look outside to see if they had landed among the Germans opposite us. Then someone said, "They are landing on the battery, on Pain de Sucre." After about a quarter of an hour the shelling stopped. We stuck our noses outside. The trees and rocks were pock-marked with craters. At the very place where we had lit the fire and placed our cooking pots there was now a shell hole, not a very big one, the kind made by a smoke shell. Someone said, "Those English! You'd think they were aiming at us! But where are the Germans? Have they gone?" I ordered two of my men to go and see what had happened. When they returned they told us that they did not meet a single German, that there was no trace of the battery and that no one was left among the rocks of Pain de Sucre. The Germans had left! We were liberated — but for a while no one believed it.

However, I had too many other things to worry about to spend time on this. Paul Leboucher and Georges Groult, Victor Bertrand and Raymond Mellion had not returned. I was very anxious about them. I mentioned this to Captain Gauthier when we met at 1800 hours. I asked him to let me know immediately if any word came in about them. He told me that, thanks to the information we had given them, 214 British Light Infantry Brigade was now ready to launch an attack across the Noireau and he asked me to furnish them with two guides for each of the three battalions. I told him that I would lose no time in finding some men who knew the region. We set the next rendezvous for 0800 hours at St. Rémy at which time he would give me further instructions.

At the rendezvous the next day, the first thing he did was to give me some good news. Paul Leboucher, George Groult and Raymond Mellion had been found. They were with the English troops. They had had some trouble with the Germans but, nevertheless, they did some good work, bringing in valuable information. Now only Victor Bertrand was missing and I was pretty sure he too would be found. "Have you found me some guides?" asked Captain Gauthier. I replied that I had been able to find only two who knew the valley of the Noireau: René Grosse, who is from Ste. Honorine-la-Chardonne and Brégis, from Condé, I believe. But I had heard that there were some members of a Résistance group from Condé in the Gouttes Tunnel and I counted on finding the extra four guides among them. We were told that all six men must be in place by the afternoon at the mouth of the Tunnel that opens on to the valley of the Noireau and that they would be met there by English soldiers. There was one difficulty: communication; none of my comrades spoke English. As a way round the problem, we gave each battalion a number — one, two, three — and also a Franco-English code-name. They were 'Sandwich' for one; 'Beer' (pronounced as in 'byrrh') for two; 'Rendezvous' for three.

The bridge at La Landelle had been destroyed so we had to ford the Orne on foot and go on to the crossroad at the bottom of Bellevue hill near Clécy. A jeep waited for us near the roadside crucifix there. Captain Gauthier gave me a passport in case we were stopped on the way by English soldiers. I said 'au revoir' to him but in fact it was 'adieu'; we never saw each other again.

The three of us left, Grosse, Brégis and I. We found the jeep at the roadside crucifix with an English sergeant and private soldier in it. Instead of taking the main highway to Condé we took a minor road, the D133A, and, going by Proussy, rejoined the highway at St. Denis-de-Méré. English soldiers stopped us at the intersection. "Where do you think you're going?" There was a discussion. "By St. Denis-de-Méré? Impossible! There's fighting all around there. By Le Fresne? There may still be Germans there. That is why we did not come by the main road." Finally, the soldiers told us to go to Rendez-vous-des-Chasseurs via Le Fresne by the Le Fresne— Pont-d'Ouilly road and to wait there. They escorted us and all went well. We arrived at Rendez-vous-des-Chasseurs. We quenched our thirst with a barrel of cider and found ourselves in the middle of a battle. Artillery from both sides pounded away and we heard the rattling of machine-guns all around us. An English officer appeared and told me that it was out of the question to get into the tunnel by the La Lande—Clécy entrance as that would take too much time. We would have to go over the tunnel through the village of Gouttes and he gave us an escort of two soldiers. We followed them on foot for about two kilometres. None of the party, neither the English nor we, were very happy with this idea. While going through Les Gouttes we heard machine-guns firing from all corners of the fields but fortunately we were often able to take sunken lanes and so felt sheltered to some extent. However, when we finally arrived at the mouth of the tunnel shells began to fall among us. We were about 10 metres above the railroad track at that point so we crawled, some of us flat on our stomaches, some flat on our backs, down the slope as fast as possible and then dashed into the tunnel for shelter.

The tunnel was crammed full of refugees. I started to look for the Résistance members from Condé. Just then, three uniformed French officers wearing kepis came out of the darkness. They were members of the Free French from London. They had walked along the entire 1800 metres of the tunnel. There were cheers, shouts of welcome and cries of joy. We pressed around them, we con-

*gratulated them, we hugged them. It was impossible for me to find
anyone in this crowd. All I could do was to wait patiently. One
of the officers jumped up or was hoisted up on to a table that was
placed across the tracks and he started to sing the Marseillaise.
Everyone joined in. It was very moving but, all the same, I had
to think about finding my guides. The commotion went on until,
finally, I managed to catch the attention of one of the two officers.
I introduced myself and politely, but firmly, told him that the
demonstration would have to calm down. At first he did not take
this very well but when he understood my reasons he helped me
quieten the crowd. I was then able to move among them and soon
found the Résistance members from Condé. I knew one of them,
Disler, a baker's son. He told me that he was ready for action and
undertook to find three others who knew the area well. I recognized
the three of them but I never knew their names though it is very
likely that Le Moulec, a Breton, was one of them.*

*When I got the four of them together with Grosse and Brégis
I told them what they had to do. I appointed them, two by two,
to each of the three battalions and I gave them the passwords. All
this time the two English soldiers were still there. Finally, I left
them all together. All that remained was for someone to pick them
up but the time for that had not been set precisely. As far as I
was concerned, my job was over. I was anxious to find Paul
Leboucher, Georges Groult, Raymond Mellion and, especially, Victor Bertrand. I left the tunnel by the small railway station at La
Lande-Clécy and come out into the last hours of a beautiful afternoon on 15 August.*

*Jacques and Paul Leboucher had gone back to their farm at
Le Vey. Raymond Mellion turned up the next day; Victor Bertrand the day after that. They had had a nerve-racking experience.
On the way to Condé they had been stopped just short of Clécy
by some Germans who, knowing that the English had been informed
of their movements and their positions, accused them furiously of
being spies and said they were going to shoot them. Luckily for
them, the Germans were in such a state of fear, excitement and
disorganization as they tried to avoid being cut off that the Frenchmen managed to escape. Having escaped once, Raymond Mellion*

was recaptured a little later by some other Germans. He managed to escape again just as the soldiers were forming a firing squad to execute him. At last he joined up with the English.

Victor Bertrand had also fallen into the hands of the Germans; he was taken to Cossesseville where he spent the night of 14/15 August. The next day he was taken to Mesnil-Hubert where they gave him a shovel and a pickaxe and told him to dig his grave. Six Germans waited around him. By a miracle, two of them, then two more and finally a fifth man were successively called away by a Lieutenant. That left only one man to guard him. The German squatted down with his rifle between his legs. Victor did not hesitate. He was an experienced hard-rock miner, handy with a pickaxe. He threw himself on the German, buried the pickaxe in his head and fled. The day after that, going by Ségrie-Fontaine, he met up with the English who had just crossed the Noireau and gave them a lot of useful information.

The attack on the Noireau was a complete success. The English were delighted that their losses were so light. The guides for the three battalions were all safe and sound and had performed magnificiently. That is what a Colonel and two other officers of 214 Brigade told me on 18 August when they came looking for me at Clécy. The Colonel added that Brigadier Essame wanted to see us all immediately. Even so, we took the time to detour to the village of La Fontaine in order to unearth a case of champagne and to finish off a few bottles from it. For some of us it was more difficult to rejoin the group. Aumont, Angot and Lemouland, and Pierrot also, had been 'adopted' by English units and had already left with them to follow the fighting. Wearing British uniforms, they went as far as Holland. Pierrot was at the Battle of Arnhem. Lemouland wrote to tell me that he was with First Canadian Army in the fighting at Falaise, Pont-Audemer and Le Havre, then in the north of France, in Belgium and in Holland, right up to 11 November 1944 before being inducted, on 16 November, into the 1st Regiment de Chasseurs Parachutistes at Lisieux.

Those who remained resumed their normal lives with their families. Finally, there were only the six of us left, the two Leboucher brothers, Raymond Mellion, the Lassus brothers and myself. A Colonel took us all in his jeep to Brigade Headquarters near Berjou. We slept there in a tent, fêted, fussed over and spoilt with all sorts of marks of appreciation. The next day we were presented to Brigadier Essame who formally thanked us and gave me the following letter attesting to the services we had given him.

THE WAR OFFICE
LONDON, S.W.1

To Whom It May Concern

The bearer of this letter, M. Raymond Pierre, has been of the very greatest assistance to the Brigade under my command. Under his brilliant leadership (as Raymond 1929 of the *Maquis*) his French *Résistance* force which was located at St. Rémy carried out active patrolling deep into the enemy lines and supplied me with accurate and detailed information of the enemy's dispositions and minefields and the state of the crossings of the Orne and Noireau rivers. When my Brigade assaulted across the River Noireau, this information was of the very greatest assistance and contributed in no small measure to the success of the operation. His force also supplied to the battalions under my command guides with intimate knowledge of the local roads and tracks and location of the enemy mines.

M. Pierre should be treated as a proved and gallant ally and I hope that every effort will be made to put him in touch with the French forces of General de Gaulle, which he and his men are anxious to join. He is now accompanied by the following members of his patrol force:

René Lassus 1988
Julien Lassus 1989
Jacques Leboucher 1926
Paul Leboucher 1991
Raymond Mellion 1990

In the Field
19 August 1944

Signed: H. Essame, Brigadier
Commander, 214 Infantry Brigade

THE ADVENTURES OF NORMAN BAKER BEHIND THE GERMAN LINES IN NORMANDY

During the afternoon of 17 August the Germans, who were preparing battle positions nearby, forced the civilians to leave La Bomberie. The local people went only a few hundred metres down the road and there they passed the night under the peaceful stars — while machine-gun tracer bullets criss-crossed over their heads. Among the villagers was an Australian airman who was particularly happy when, at the end of the battle, he was finally able to rejoin the Allied troops. He was glad, not only because his adventures had come to a happy ending for himself but, more especially, because the risks taken by those who had hidden him were over at last. Here is the story of his adventure — or rather, the series of adventures — as he recounted them on one of his return visits to France after the war.

In February 1943, after completing a long period of training in Australia, Norman Baker was sent to Great Britain via the United States. He had just turned 22. It was at Scunthorpe, in Lincolnshire, that he first began to fly Spitfires. In August of the same year he was posted to 453 Australian Spitfire Squadron. At the time the Squadron's job was to escort Flying Fortresses and other bombers when they attacked enemy targets in Europe. They also attacked V1 launching sites and the enemy's lines of communication. His Squadron was based, successively, near Christchurch (near Bournemouth), at Perranporth in Cornwall and then in the Shetlands. In January 1944 he first met Pierre Clostermann at Detling, near Maidstone, in Kent. (Clostermann and his friend, Jacques Remlinger, were to become famous with the illustrious 602 City of Glasgow Squadron).

These young men became so expert at attacking ground targets with machine-guns and light bombs that, under suitable conditions, they could place their bombs (they usually carried either

2 — 250-lb. bombs or 1 — 500-lb. bomb though sometimes they carried all three for a total of 1000 lbs.) no more than 20 metres from the target.

They were next transferred to the British 2nd Tactical Air Force which had the job of covering Montgomery's 21st Army Group during the Normandy operations. At first they operated from an airfield at Ford, near Brighton. Their missions consisted of flying attack sorties and machine-gunning behind the German lines. By D + 3 a landing strip had been prepared on the rolling countryside above Arromanches and it was there that the R.A.A.F. fighters would replenish their fuel and ammunition after having made a pre-dawn crossing of the English Channel from Ford. By about D + 12 453 Australian Squadron transferred itself entirely with all its supplies, mechanics, workshops etc. to Arromanches and started operating from there.

It was from this base that Norman Baker set off on the hot and stormy afternoon of 7 July, flying a sortie to the south of Mont de Cerisy. His orders were to attack and destroy anything that moved in that sector, especially transports and troops. For the past month or so he had often flown over this part of Normandy. Flying high over the country he soon picked out the familiar silhouette of Mont de Cerisy and a quick glance round the horizon fixed the positions of Tinchebray, Mortain, La Ferté-Macé, Briouze and Flers. In this part of the Bocage, although there are many roads, they are often difficult to trace from above because, for the most part, they disappear under the canopies of the leafy trees that border them. Knowing this, it was not unusual for the Germans to take a chance and move their vehicles along the roads in broad daylight.

The Squadron, consisting of 3 Flights of 4 planes each, was just going to wind up its first sortie without having seen anything of note when suddenly, to the west of Briouze, Baker saw a truck racing at full speed along a straight, exposed section of road, making for Flers. As he was leading his Flight he immediately dived in pursuit of the truck. Flying at tree-top level, he came up to it as close as possible so as not to lose it and did not open fire until the very last moment. Hit dead on, the truck caught fire and exploded just as Baker's plane flew over it. Norman heard the characteristic sound of bullets hitting his Spitfire but at first thought that debris from the truck had hit him as he passed over it. Climbing to regain altitude, he turned back to make sure that his comrades had flown safely through the cloud of debris thrown up by the explosion. He inspected his plane and only then saw that he had been hit by machine-gun bullets from anti-aircraft guns in positions on the edge of the road. He had not noticed them in the excitement of the chase. Thinking that this was a newly-established, unreported flak position he continued to climb up to about 7000 feet while wondering what he should do next. He soon realized that his beautiful Mark IX.B Spitfire was not behaving normally. The dashboard instruments showed that the engine temperature was rising rapidly. The cooling system had evidently been damaged. The sound of the engine began to change. His airspeed dropped. Now he was in trouble. He had to get back to the Allied lines at any price. If he did not ...

Two planes of his Flight stayed with him while the rest of the Squadron left. There was not much they could do for him except give him encouragement. Very soon the needle of the thermometer on the instrument panel stuck at the end of the dial. The engine oil started to burn. The exhaust smoke became blacker and blacker and the plane started to lose altitude. Baker used his wireless to tell his Headquarters what was happening: "I can go no further. I'll have to put it down." "O.K., do what you think best." Flames had now replaced the smoke on each side of his cockpit. He was going to have to act fast.

In a flash, as if in a re-run movie, Norman reviewed all the most dangerous operations he had ever taken part in. There was the attack on the V1 launching site in April near the forest of Crécy when, after the planes of 602 Squadron made the first run at the target, he dived in his turn with the rest of 453 Australian Squadron down to 700 feet, right into the middle of what looked like a sheaf of white-flecked 20mm tracer bullets. The base was destroyed but one of his friends, hit dead on when he dived on the target, did not have time to get out of his plane and crashed with it. Then there was the low-level reconnaissance flight carried out by his Flight a few days later during which, following the course of the Seine, they had flown the gauntlet of anti-aircraft guns firing from both sides of the valley. Another friend was lost that evening. There were many other incidents but to-day, because of an unlucky bullet that came from he knew not where, it was going to be his turn.

Fortunately, as he was a good pilot, all these memories flashing before him at that critical moment did not inhibit his reflexes. Just a few hundred feet below him there was a large field and he decided to crash-land in it rather than attempt a landing on wheels. That could have been dangerous to try because of the risk of an unseen ditch, or a patch of rough ground or an unnoticed dip in the field. Besides, he did not want to hand over a plane to the enemy in good flying condition.

He skimmed over the roofs of the farms of La Morlandière, just cleared an apple orchard and then pushed the nose of the plane down.

The moment the plane touched the ground he felt himself thrown forward with brutal force. He thought his Spitfire was going to fall apart with the violent jolting. The screaming noise of tortured metal deafened him. Clods of earth, gouged up by the bent propellers, flew up on all sides and oil and soil smeared the windscreen. Finally, after a last shudder, the plane came to rest — and then there was silence. After the excitement of the successful belly-landing Norman took a few seconds to gather his thoughts. His coolness and his skill had enabled him to escape death but what would happen to him now? In England he had often been told that the French population helped Allied pilots to avoid capture and that the *Résistance* had organized ways of getting them back. However, now, stuck in the middle of a field, he felt very lonely and fearful and wondered what was going to happen next.

His thoughts were rudely interrupted by the smell of smoke reminding him that his plane was on fire. After all this he was not going to let himself be trapped in the plane to be burnt alive. The thought of this re-vitalized his instincts and once again he became cool and precise in his actions to free himself from the plane. With a turn of the hand he unlatched the cover of the cockpit and opened it. He unfastened the oxygen hose, disconnected the wireless cables, unbuckled his seat belt and leapt out of the plane to land on terra firma. He snatched his helmet off and ran away from the plane, fearing that it would burst into flames at any moment.

With a thunderous roar, one of his friends in the Flight, David Murray, came hedge-hopping low over the field. Norman gave him a wave of the hand to tell him that he was alright and his fellow fighter-pilot acknowledged it as he watched from above.

* * *

That evening, because a storm threatened, they were hurrying to bring in the last of the hay on Albert Poulain's farm. For the past month they had become accustomed to the sound of Allied planes as they flew their sorties — indeed, they saw practically no other planes — but the sound of this plane flying just over the barn caught their attention. There was no doubt that it was in trouble. A few seconds later someone cried out that it had crash-landed in the large field.

This was not the first time a plane had crashed at La Morlandière. The Germans had often used this same field to land the small planes that carried couriers to their Headquarters at the nearby Chateau of Mont de Cerisy. In August, 1943, two of their officers who, the day before, had taken part in a typically drunken German party in M. Corbière's rooms at the Chateau, borrowed a courier plane. Their first attempt to take off was unsuccessful; the second attempt cost them their lives because the plane caught the tops of the trees and crashed in flames.

Leaving his work companions in the hay loft, Marcel Hellouin ran in the direction of the crash while the remaining two Spitfires continued to circle above their downed comrade. The fear of being seen by the Germans at Le Mont forced him to approach the field along one of the hedges. When he was opposite the fighter-pilot he called out, "Monsieur, come here quickly." At first Norman started to run towards him but as he crossed the slope he suddenly remembered that in the hurry of escaping from the burning plane he had forgotten to carry out the most important duty when making a forced landing in enemy territory, i.e. to destroy the I.F.F. apparatus. This ultra-secret apparatus, Identification Friend or Foe, was a radio device used by the Allies to distinguish their own planes from the enemy's.

Marcel Hellouin saw the pilot return to his plane while at the same time he heard the noise of the German trucks climbing the hill from Le Vivier; the Germans in Cerisy had seen the crash. He could not understand what was going on. What was the pilot up to, climbing back on a wing, bending over into the interior of the cockpit and hitting something that set off a weak explosion in the plane. While Norman came running back towards him he saw a thin wisp of blue smoke rise out of the cockpit. Hardly had Norman joined him than, on the other side of the hedge, the Germans entered the field from the Caligny road.

Without losing any more time Marcel Hellouin led the pilot across the wheat field in the direction of an old path near which the inhabitants of La Morlandière had dug a shelter. They were out of breath when they arrived there. They heard the cries of the Germans who were looking for the pilot and the hails of bullets they fired at random in order to persuade him to show himself and give himself up. Feeling safe for the moment, the two men tried to take stock of the situation. *"As my French is terrible and as the English of my guide was not much better we did not get far,"* said Norman. *"From the signs he made I gathered that Marcel Hellouin wanted to give me something to eat and also something inconspicuous to wear so that I could pass unnoticed. I showed him the small bags of dehydrated food and French money we always carried with us when we left on missions over France and I gladly accepted his coat. However, I was very concerned about what would happen to him if the Germans found me with him so I was glad when, after indicating that he would return in a short while, I saw him leave in the direction of the farm house."*

Just then the threatening storm burst and the rain came down in buckets. The Germans called off their search and took shelter in Albert Poulain's house. They asked if anyone knew which way the pilot had gone; needless to say, they were given the wrong direction.

On returning to his farm, Marcel Hellouin was questioned in

his turn. Showing remarkable composure, he did not even flinch when one of the soldiers said to him, "You were with the airman. We saw you through binoculars from Mont de Cerisy and recognise you. Tell us where he is hiding." When they saw that even the threat of taking him away and shooting him did not frighten him nor induce him to confess, the Germans gave up. They discussed among themselves whether it was worth searching the entire farm or not and then left, leaving only a sentry to guard the wrecked plane. Later, some youngsters, unable to control their inquisitiveness nor their desire for souvenirs, were caught and led to the chateau in the village. There they were held in custody for a few hours and then released, somewhat chastened but probably in more fear of the good spanking they were going to get from their fathers!

* * *

All alone in his hiding place Norman thought about his situation and decided that it would be best for himself, and also for the villagers who had seen him and for the person who had helped him, to get away from there as soon as possible. His decision was quickly made; as soon as the rain stopped he would leave. And so, at the first break in the storm he took off. Leaving the path that seemed to meander in the general direction of the place where he had crashed, he came out into a field and found himself in the middle of a herd of cows that had taken shelter from the storm under a large oak tree near the hedge he had just left. Curious by nature and not at all frightened by this sudden apparition, the animals approached him and sniffed him with their wet noses. Animals were familiar to Norman as he had been brought up on his parents' sheep farm and he immediately saw how he could take advantage of the situation. The field in which he was and which he had to cross sloped gently upwards. He felt sure that, if he could get to the high point of the field, he would be able to see the Germans who were looking for him and so he headed for the high ground, driving the animals before him as any good farmer would do at milking time. When he got to the top of the sloping field our peasant-pilot allowed the herd to start grazing again while he looked around him. He saw some figures coming and going around the plane but his pursurers seemed to have given up the hunt. He got back on the road, climbed over some banks, crossed some more fields and arrived at the railway track that runs from Caen to Laval. He skirted the railway track in order to take advantage of the high hedges that provided cover from anyone watching from Mont de Cerisy. There were more fields to cross, then a farm where the people, busy with milking, did not see him. Finally he took a path that led him out on to the road from Caligny to Flers.

Darkness came on and a ground fog rising from the earth saturated by the storm gave warning of a cold and damp night to follow. Norman began to look around for a comfortable barn in which he could sleep. The noise of an approaching vehicle interrupted his search. There was no gap in the thick hedges so he could not leave the road to hide from the occupants of the *Volkswagen* who were soon abreast of him. It seemed to him that the Germans looked at him very suspiciously while he calmly scrutinized them with a great deal of curiosity: after all, it was the first time he had ever been so close to the enemy — and it was not to be the last time!

The car went on its way and a much-relieved Norman continued his walk. A hundred metres further on he saw a man coming towards him. The man was wearing a cloth cap and when he saw Norman he stopped and began to roll a cigarette. Norman slowed his walk, wondering whether the man was going to speak to him or not but when he came abreast of him he decided, instead, to address him. "Pardon, Monsieur," he said to the other in French, "I am the airman who crashed nearby." The man smiled know-ingly and replied, "Yes, yes, I know. Come with me, you'd better hide yourself." He led Norman into a small thicket at the entrance to the path to the Lebailly wood-working factory. When they were hidden from passing field-gray uniforms the man in the cap introduced himself. "Je suis Russe," he said. "I am Baker, from Melbourne," replied Norman and added, "good day, Monsieur Russe," assuming that the stranger had given his name. "No, no," replied the other, "I am a Russian, from Leningrad." The two men burst into laughter and shook each other warmly by the hand.

The explanation for this amazing incident was that, a few days after the Invasion, some Russian prisoners who were working for the Todt Organization escaped the surveillance of their gaolers and fled to the village of Hoguet near Caligny. There they were housed, fed and employed on the farm of M. Rabâche, the Mayor of Caligny, who planned to hide them until the Allies arrived. This meeting on the soil of Normandy of Ivan the Russian and Norman the Australian was really a remarkable coincidence.

Ivan sent one of his compatriots to alert Arthur Lebailly. M. Lebailly then went in search of a Parisian who had avoided a forced labour draft and who also was in hiding at Le Hoguet. The Parisian spoke English well. By now it was completely dark. The two men left their hiding place and eventually Norman got into Arthur's house through a ground-floor window. At the time there was a large number of hapless refugees sheltering in the village and it was judged more prudent to allow as few people as possible into the secret. In the course of conversation with the interpreter Norman learnt that he had chosen the most dangerous sector of the front in which to crash because, not far from there, in the direction of Vassy, was Rommel's Headquarters. Wryly, Norman said he would just as soon forego the honour of being introduced to the famous General.

After a good meal, Norman quickly fell asleep in his host's bed despite the excitement of the day while the latter slept on the floor. It was a short night for Norman because they had to get up at daybreak and leave on bicycles in order to get to Athis before the village awoke. Arthur Lebailly, who accompanied Norman, had taken the precaution of strapping some hay-making tools to their bicycles so as to allay the suspicions of anyone they met. The journey went off without incident and on arrival at Athis Arthur immediately brought his cousin Fred Brisset into the picture. Fred took them into his room, opened a cupboard and started to twiddle the dial of a hidden wireless set run on batteries stolen from the Germans. For the first time since his crash Norman was able to listen to a news broadcast in English from the B.B.C.

* * *

While this was going on the two cousins discussed the situation. Fred was one link in the chain of an organization tht took care of Allied airmen. His job was to maintain contact with just one person, the only other person he knew in the organization. In turn, this person had a contact in Caen. Unfortunately, just at that time the bombardment and fighting around Caen had scattered the members of the network. While waiting for contact to be re-established it was decided that Norman should go to the house of Fred's parents who lived in the little village of Ste. Honorine-la-Guillaume. *"I was immediately welcomed there as a 'very important person' and treated like a member of the family,"* recalls Norman, *"and for two weeks I lacked for nothing. The interpreter I had met at Caligny told me that it had been decided that I would be passed off as a refugee who had been so badly shell-shocked by the bombardment of Condé that I had lost the use of my ears and my tongue. As far as the Germans and the neighbours were concerned I was, therefore, deaf and dumb. I spent the time working for my host, clearing the hedges in the fields and helping him build a small cart with the wheels of an old bicycle so that he would have something on which to carry a few belongings in case he had to be evacuated.*

One day I went with my host to a neighbouring village in order to repair a clock there. That was the day he got the idea of manufacturing home-made mines to destroy car tires. We placed gunpowder in shoe-polish boxes together with a shotgun cartridge detonated by a nail embedded in the lid. It worked quite well but the gunpowder was not powerful enough to destroy the tires. July 14 was a particularly memorable day because it was also the birthday of my hostess. Cider and calvados flowed freely. After the meal my host played 'Mademoiselle from Armentieres' on the violin and then, before anyone could stop him, he astonished the Germans with a rendition of the Marseillaise on his horn."

Round about 20 July Norman and his host were picking cherries when a cart came by led by a man and a young, fair-haired woman. They were René Lechevallier and Mlle. France. They warned them that the Gestapo were looking for Fred to check out a report from a German deserter of hidden small-arms and that it would be better for the airman to leave his hiding place before the Germans came to interrogate Fred's parents. Without even returning to the house, Norman followed his new guides, still carrying his basket of cherries. Along the way he amused himself by bombarding the rump of the horse with cherry stones. As for René Lechevallier, he lost no opportunity to play pranks on the Germans. Whenever he saw a sign pointing the way to a Headquarters or a storage dépôt he would take a hammer from under the seat, stop the cart, prise up the sign and nail it back pointing in the opposite direction. Eventually they arrived at Berjou where the school teachers, M. and Mme. Ricordeau, took Norman in.

The school adjoined the teachers' living quarters and for several days it was filled with German troops who were either coming back from the front or going up to it. What amused Norman the most was to sleep in a bedroom right next to one occupied by a German Colonel. He continued to be a shell-shocked day-labourer working for the Ricordeau family. For greater security, a false identity card was forged for him. Every day he worked in the garden, chopped wood, gathered grass for the rabbits and accompanied his hosts when they went to find food in neighbouring farms. Each time a German spoke to him he would point his finger to his mouth and ears and shake his head. This cut short any attempt at conversation. The soldiers, always scrounging for food, would give him tobacco in exchange for butter. One day the situation became really comical. M. Ricordeau's assistant, M. Bourg, who spoke German fairly well, decided that Norman needed a haircut. He mentioned this to some SS troops who had replaced the others and learnt that one of them was a barber. The man told him that he could cut any kind of hair style and that he had even cut the hair of Field-Marshal Rommel. So, in exchange for some butter, Norman was sat down in the middle of a dozen of the SS who patiently waited their turn while the German Field-Marshal's barber trimmed the Australian Flying Officer's hair with razor and scissors.

Occasionally, Norman went to Theil or to Bruyères to visit two of his colleagues there. Once they visited him at Berjou. But in spite of everything the time dragged. The efforts of René Lechevallier and Mlle. France to repatriate him ran into serious difficulties. Finally, when they learnt that British troops had occupied the area near Vire and Vassy, they decided that the time had come to try to get through the front lines. On 3 August, Lechevallier, Mlle. France, an R.A.F. Sergeant, a Colonel of the Free French Forces and Norman left Berjou on bicycles. When they arrived at St. Germain-du-Crioult they made for Vire. As they approached Viessoix some Germans dug into trenches on the downward slope in front of the village shouted at them to stop. René Lechevallier urged them, "Keep going, don't pay any attention to them."

They next saw three English tanks that had been knocked out by anti-tank fire and found a supply of cigarettes in them. Although they knew they were very close to the British lines they decided that it was more prudent not to go any further that evening because night was coming on. They passed the night in a house partially demolished by shell-fire. They got back on the road at dawn but now the Germans they met were more and more nervous and more and more hostile. Each time they were stopped they were sent back to the rear and eventually found themselves back at Maisoncelles without having been able to get through the lines. There was nothing for it but to turn back despondently and try again the next day.

When they returned to Berjou they found that the town had been evacuated so they took Norman to Bas-Hamel where, once again, he found himself right in the middle of the Germans. As a precaution, he was placed in a room at one end of the chateau and hardly moved from there. To pass the time he read English novels and played records on an old gramophone. One day, while he was listening to a Maurice Chevalier record with his friends, there was a peremptory knock on the door. It was a young German orderly. "You will have to play the music more softly; my General cannot hear himself speak on the phone." And that is how Norman discovered that he was not the only distinguished guest at the Chateau. The General who did not like music was General Schraub.

A little later, Norman, alone in his room, heard a knock at the door. "Entrez," he said. It was one of the few French words he knew how to speak. It was an awkward moment when the German officer, looking suspiciously at this young man dressed in overalls, asked him, "Can you tell me where I can find Madame M.?" Norman thought fast and then took the risk of saying in his best French, "Je ne sais pas, Capitaine." He then smiled and, walking in front of the German, made a sign to him to follow. He led the Captain along a long hall and then down a staircase that went into a part of the building that he had never been in before; he hoped that he would meet Mlle. France or some other member of the family. At the bottom of the stairs he met Annie, the youngest of the sisters. She was five years old and on that day his fate rested in her hands. Although she had never met the Australian before she immediately guessed who he was. When she saw the German walking behind the airman she became frightened but Norman, his back to the German, reassured her with a smile and a wink and said to her, again in his best French, "Where is Madame M.?" Annie understood at once. Forcing a smile, she turned to the German and said to him, "Follow me and I will take you to her." Thus, thanks to the presence of mind of a little French girl, no more than 5 years old, Norman escaped a prisoner-of-war camp and his hosts escaped torture and death.

* * *

Le Bas-Hamel, occupied as it was by a General and his staff and guarded by sentries and the Military Police, was really a most unsatisfactory place in which to hide an Allied airman. The front was very near and with the ceaseless military activity round the important Headquarters the village was like a busy bee hive. René Lechevallier and Mlle. France decided to try to get through the lines once again. They had to leave at night. Norman remembers: *I was scheduled to go with someone very important (later it turned out that he was a very senior secret-service agent) but at about one o'clock in the morning he told me that, as it was absolutely vital that he succeed in getting through to the Allies, he could not take any unnecessary risks and that, therefore, he could not take me with him.* A new attempt was scheduled for the following night but, again, without success because the guide could not come. The very next day René Lechevallier and Mlle. France entrusted Norman to two young students of Caen University with instructions to take him to La Bertinière where he had passed the first two weeks after his crash landing. The three men left the Chateau through the gate guarded by sentries and headed in the direction of Sainte-Honorine-la-Guillaume.

Barely had they left the avenue leading to the Chateau when a Military Police car caught up with them. The occupants, a Captain and a Sergeant, stared at them as they passed. The car went on about 50 metres and left the road to enter a field. The trio was relieved, thinking that the Germans had left the road in order to go back to their camp but when they arrived at the gate to the field they were surprised to see that the two policemen had simply hidden their car and were waiting for them with revolvers in their hands. The two students were unaware that Norman had an identity card and so were alarmed by the sight of the two men. They presented their papers and began to explain that their companion had lost his. Their explanations did not seem to satisfy the Germans and the Sergeant who, up to then, had said nothing, barked at Norman, "Your identity card?" As if he had not a care in the world Norman took his card from his pocket and held it out to the Captain who gave it a quick glance and handed it back to him. He then glanced at the identity cards of the two students but, thinking that they had been trying to play games with him in pretending that Norman had no papers, he sent each of them on his way with a sharply-administered box on the ear before climbing back into the car.

On arriving at La Bertinière, Norman was dismayed to see that the house that had sheltered him from 8 to 20 July was in ruins. He learnt that in the evening of the previous day many bombs had fallen on the village and that one of them had completely destroyed the house and buried its owner under the ruins. It took a long time to dig him out and he was lucky to escape unhurt. What he regretted most was the loss of his violin and his horn!

That evening, Norman and his companions slept with thirty others in a barn a short distance from the road along which the enemy columns were fleeing in retreat. The English were not very far behind. Early on the morning of 17 August the Germans took up positions in the village and the nearby area, blew up the bridges and prepared to defend themselves. In the afternoon the civilians were driven out of La Bomberie and took refuge in the woods above the hamlet. Soon after seven o'clock in the evening bullets began to whistle through the trees and shells started to explode all around them. For part of the night a German mortar platoon fired several rounds from the wood, changing position after each shot in order to avoid being pin-pointed. This, of course, made the woods a prime target for the English guns and they did not stop shelling the area until the Germans ran short of ammunition and withdrew. Even the nonchalant Australian had to admit that it was a 'warm night.'

Someone returned to the village at dawn and brought back a bucket of milk — and some news that excited Norman: 'The English are in the large Touzé field!' Norman rushed off in the direction they indicated, running up the slopes and scrambling through the hedges. When he arrived at the field and looked down into it he saw an unforgettable sight: there they were, a wonderful, strong army, well disciplined and powerful, in such contrast to the beaten, retreating Germans. While the Germans were exhausted, disheveled, dirty, unshaven and disorganized, the Tommies whom he saw around the tanks and other vehicles, drawn up as if on parade even after a night's hard fighting, were in great heart and in great humour. Some were polishing their boots and some were shaving, others were making tea and others were writing letters while listening to the latest news on the B.B.C. Norman approached a Sergeant and started telling him his story but was quickly interrupted: "Ah, you're an Aussie? Come and have a cup of tea."

Norman had dreamed of just such a cup of tea. He had often asked himself if he would ever again enjoy this typical British beverage. Now this wonderful 'cuppa' marked the end of his Normandy wanderings among those who had sheltered him at peril to their lives. There were many touching farewells and then Norman was sent back with an escort of the Fife and Forfar Yeomanry, first to 29 Brigade Headquarters, then to 11th Armoured Division and finally to Bayeux. From there he was hurried back to England where he collected his personal belongings and where they gave him a new uniform. But before leaving Normandy he just had time to go to say 'hello' to his pals at 453 Australian Squadron at Base B.19 near Caen, or rather, to those who were still alive, for their losses had continued to mount. The Squadron strength was normally maintained at 26 pilots. In the previous 11 weeks, 14 of them had been shot down but of them 5 had, like Norman, escaped death and captivity.

*   *   *

Norman rejoined his Squadron at Douai but as soon as 11th Armoured Division captured Antwerp they were moved to that city. After the Arnhem disaster they were sent to Norwich, in Norfolk, and from there they carried out many reconnaissance flights and bombing and strafing missions on the V2 launching sites near The Hague. On one of these missions Norman was hit by flak. From this base they also gave support to the Army in Holland, Belgium and, later, in Germany.

In March 1945 Norman was sent on leave. When he returned they wanted to make him the Royal Australian Air Force Fighter Command Liaison Officer at Fighter Command Headquarters in Britain but he declined. He felt that the war in Europe would soon be over so he asked for and obtained repatriation to Australia so that he could continue to fight against the Japanese. He ended up as a senior instructor of Spitfire pilots in New South Wales when the first atomic bombs put an end to the war. By that time he had logged about 700 hours of wartime flying and had chalked up close to 250 combat missions.

On 17 April 1947 General Juin awarded Flight-Lieutenant Norman K. Baker the *Croix de Guerre* with silver star for 'exceptional war services rendered during the liberation of France.'

Since then Norman has returned to France several times in order to re-visit those whom he could never forget. On one of his visits he made a 'pilgrimage', on foot, following the same route from Cerisy to Le Hoguet that he had taken when dodging the Germans.

To the great surprise of those who accompanied him, he led them unhesitatingly and without a single mistake across the same fields, paths and slopes that he had crossed almost twenty years before. During this nostalgic 'walk-about' Norman had what was probably one of the most delightful surprises of his visit. After the Liberation, the wreckage of his plane had been dissected, literally piece by piece, by souvenir hunters who tore it apart and made off with anything that could be ripped off and carried away. As the group of 'pilgrims' was crossing Marcel Rabâche's farm near La Bazoque, the farmer came out to ask what was going on. When they told him he begged Norman to wait a few minutes while he went back to his house. He soon returned with — believe it or not — the joy stick of Norman's Spitfire which he ceremoniously presented back to the pilot!

* * *

Every year in Australia there is a reunion of the pilots who escaped and who are now members of the Royal Air Force Escaping Society. They observe a minute's silence in memory of those who helped them and then someone recites the following invocation:

> We remember those who helped us. These people, from every walk of life, rose up in the midst of oppression and tyranny and exhibited enormous compassion and fellow-feeling for us, the lost and stranded. They were inbued with a hatred of injustice and a will to contribute to Nazi defeat. Without hesitation they set out on this dangerous course which often led to torture and to death. Their unity of purpose cut right across religion, race and politics. The qualities which they displayed are those of which the world will always be in need.
>
> How fortunate we are to have been able to enrich our understanding of human values in time of danger and to have been brought into such close contact with the charity and sacrifice of ordinary people.

The factory at Le Rocray (cf p.242 et seq.) in September 1987. This photograph was taken from the location of the German positions on the hill overlooking the factory.

Collection of Tom Bates

Albert Laignel (cf p.243 et seq.) and Jean Brisset, author of *La Charge du Taureau,* at the factory at Le Rocray in September 1987.

Collection of Tom Bates

Raymond Pierre (cf p.281 et seq.) in 1944 in the uniform of a 2nd Lieutenant in the 1st Normandy Infantry Battalion, F.F.I. The small photograph shows M. Pierre in 1987.

The disused Les Gouttes tunnell (cf p.242 et seq.) from the Les Gouttes end in June 1986.

Collection of Tom Bates

Flying Officer Norman Baker, Royal Australian Air Force, leaving his Spitfire after returning from an early-morning dive-bombing and straffing attack on a V2 launching site in the woods north of La Hague. (cf p.275 et seq.)

Collection of Norman Baker

This photograph was taken in 1982 from the same position on Mont de Cerisy from which the Germans saw Norman Baker's crippled Spitfire crash-land in the large field in the middle of the picture. (cf p.297)

Kimbal Baker, Photographer, Melbourne

Annie in 1945 (cf p.306)

Collection of René Lechevallier

Mlle. France and René Lechevallier in 1945. (cf p.303 et seq.)

Collection of René Lechevallier

In June 1979 the Tibbetts brothers, Joseph and Samuel, re-visited the grave of their friend, Corporal Baines of the Inns of Court, in the cemetery at La Selle la Forge. (cf p.182)

L'Orne Combattante

Former Sergeant Reay, DCM, of the 3rd Royal Tank Regiment, lighting the Flame of Remembrance at the Divisional Memorial at Le Pont-de-Vère in June 1984 accompanied by Trooper Woodward of the same Regiment. (cf p.318)

L'Orne Combattante

The late Major Joe How, MC, 3rd Monmouthshire Regiment, the Regimental Historian and the author of two outstanding books about the Normandy campaign, *Normandy, the British Breakout* and *Hill 112*, with his hand on the shoulder of Jean Brisset of Flers, the author of *La Charge du Taureau*, in June 1984.

L'Orne Combattante

In June 1984, Jean Menard, who built the museum at St. Martin-des-Bésaces (cf p.317) uses the diorama to show 'Pip' Roberts how he, the General, won the battle in 1944! Mrs. Annie Roberts, the General's wife, is by his side.
L'Orne Combattante

At the Souleuvre bridge ceremony in June 1984, the former Brigadier Jack Churcher of 159 Infantry Brigade, explains to 'Pip' Roberts, his Commanding Officer, how the Division captured the bridge on 31 July 1944! (cf p.318)

L'Orne Combattante

The bridge over the River Souleuvre looking north along the road down which Lt. Powle and his troop made their dash through the German lines to capture the undamaged bridge. (cf p.74 et seq.)

Collection of Tom Bates

The former Lieutenant Richard (Dicky) Powle of the 2nd Household Cavalry, the leader of the troop that captured the Souleuvre bridge the first time on 31 July 1944, was invited to 'open the bridge for the second time' in June 1984. He was assisted by M. René Sauvade (*M. Moustache*), the Chief of Protocol for the 1984 Reunion ceremonies. (cf p.318)

L'Orne Combattante

In August 1944 the 4th King's Shropshire Light Infantry and the Inns of Court Regiment were the first into Vassy (cf p.135). In June 1979 they returned to march through the town on their way to — one more banquet!

L'Orne Combattante

The band of the 3rd Royal Tank Regiment march through the *Place Genéral de Gaulle* in Flers in 1984. (cf p.318)

L'Orne Combattante

At the Town Memorial in Flers, June 1984.
Left to Right:
Front row: M. Douard, Mayor of Flers, 'Pip' Roberts, Bill Close, 'Claude' Davey.
Second row: John Collinge, Canon Norman Woodhall, Horace Todman.
L'Orne Combattante

In June 1984, "former Corporal Ted Chapman, VC, of the 3rd Monmouthshire Regiment (cf pp.199, 237-8) was the Guard of Honour for the Division's Roll of Honour that is usually kept in the Memorial Room at the Town Hall in Flers Castle. It was he, still every inch a soldier, who offered the book to the Divisional Chaplain, Canon Norman Woodhall, for the benediction."

L'Orne Combattante

The stele at Aubusson unveiled in June 1987 to the memory and honour of 11th British Armoured Division.

M. Bedouelle

TAURUS PURSUANT

A HISTORY OF 11ᵀᴴ ARMOURED DIVISION

TAURUS PURSUANT

A HISTORY OF 11ᵀᴴ ARMOURED DIVISION

EPILOGUE

In the Foreword, Tom Bates has explained how the English translation of my book, *La Charge du Taureau,* came to be written. Now he has asked me to write this additional chapter, which did not appear in the original, to tell how the book came to be written in the first place and to bring events up to date. This is the chapter. Please accept it as the Epilogue to the story about the men of 11th Armoured Division and the other heroes of those heroic days.

When the battle for the *bocage* was over, the Guards Armoured Division found itself in the area between Flers and Condé-sur-Noireau. There, one day in August 1944, I met two guardsmen and invited them home to meet my family. They saw an harmonium in the corner of our living room. While one of them played the foot-pedalled instrument, the other sang with a wonderful trained voice. It turned out that he had been a tenor with the Sadlers Wells Opera Company. A few days later they left when the war moved on to Belgium. All I knew about them were their names and their Battalion but I could not forget them. It took me 23 years to find out what had happened to them. Gerald Hamblin, the singer, had been killed at Nijmegen on 20 September, 1944, fighting towards the relief of Arnhem. William Chappell, the musician, was still alive and living in Nottingham.

It was during the long search for the two men that I got the idea of writing about the battles that had taken place around Caligny, the village where I lived. I started with a few articles for a local newspaper and these eventually were expanded into *La Charge du Taureau.*

As Major 'Claude' Davey, formerly of the 3rd Monmouthshire Regiment, said later: *I think that when we look back down the years we see only two chapters in our lives. The first was the war which we were glad to see the back of! The second, in the aftermath of war, was living or trying to live a new life and in so doing we all drifted apart. And then one day in 1970, 25 years after the war and right out of the blue, something happened which changed everything for me and for many others... In 1969, articles on the battles which had led to the liberation of that part of the bocage were published in the local newspaper called 'Orne Combattante'. In the final article the author asked if it would not be a fine thing if his town, the town of Flers, could invite some of the Veterans of 11th Armoured Division who had liberated the town and the surrounding villages to come for a weekend to join the townsfolk in celebrating the 25th Anniversary of their Liberation.*

The author also proposed that a twinning be made between Flers and a British town, preferably a town which had supplied men to the Division.

My tentative suggestions were immediately taken up by Monsieur Leverrier, President of the French Old Comrades Association and by a local priest, Father Amiard, a truly remarkable man to whom this book is dedicated. Father Amiard was a great patriot and a steadfast friend of Britain. Some of his courageous deeds during the Liberation are described in this book. By 1969 he had retired after teaching English for many years but, nevertheless, he played a leading role in the organization of the first Old Comrades meeting in Flers. This took place on two days in May 1970. It was he who suggested to the Flers Committee that French families should offer accomodation to the visitors in their homes and this, together with his unflagging enthusiasm, his tactful mediation when necessary and his transparent goodness, ensured the success of the Reunion.

In those two days the Normans, generally so cautious and reserved, greeted their middle-aged guests with warm hospitality and overwhelmed them with marks of their long-remembered gratitude.

Many of the Old Comrades who attended the ceremonies wrote back to express their feelings, as did Colonel Reeves of the 4th King's Shropshire Light Infantry: *We shall retain the happiest recollections of all that was arranged for us; our being met at Maison des Jeunes, the visits to the battlefields and the stories of the war, the personality —very dear—of the Count when he addressed us, the lovely countryside, the children with flowers, the old lady of the village who accompanied us up the hill, the cemeteries so beautifully kept, that Sunday morning visit to the Castle, that wonderfully conducted service in St. Germain church and, of course, the banquet.*

'Claude' Davey wrote: *It was a moving experience we shall never forget. We must say 'thank you' also to all the families who opened their doors and their hearts to us. I have a feeling now that the Anniversary was not the end of an event but rather the beginning of very many lasting friendships. Indeed, I very much share the words of your President, M. Leverrier, in his speech at the banquet: "All of us wholeheartedly hope that this meeting will contribute in its modest way to create a stronger fellowship between our two peoples, to awaken mutual understanding so that our children may know a better age, without war, without sorrow or fright, without grief and hatred."*

And Ken Ball, formerly of the 2nd Northamptonshire Yeomanry: *The celebrations have left such an effect on us that we are going to treasure our memories of Flers and its people. We cherish the thought that we came as strangers and left as friends.*

In his speech at the banquet M. Halbout, M.P., the Mayor of Flers, mentioned the words 'monument' and 'twinning' for the first time. They were not uttered in vain; the two projects were to be taken up soon after.

General Roberts was unable to attend the Flers ceremonies in 1970 because at the time, as one of the protagonists in Operation GOODWOOD, he was needed for the exercise conducted by the Staff College over that battlefield. However, he was kept informed of the plans and proposals from the town of Flers. In October 1970 he endorsed the idea that a monument be erected at Pont-de-Vère to all the men of 11th Armoured Division who gave their lives in Normandy and elsewhere in North-West Europe.

Early in 1971 an 11th Armoured Division Old Comrades Committee was formed to deal with the two projects proposed by the town of Flers, namely, the twinning with a town in England that had associations with the Division and a permanent memorial to the Division. Former Majors Close (3rd Royal Tank Regiment), Davey and Todman (3rd Monmouthshire Regiment) were elected, respectively, Chairman, Secretary and Treasurer of the Committee. Father Amiard dubbed them 'The Three Musketeers' while he, who represented the Flers committee, was called by them 'The Flying Padre' in reference to the *Aéro Club des Cèdres* he had founded in 1927 to encourage an interest in flying model aeroplanes. As the dear man said, "This affair with 11th Armoured Division is the sun that shines on my old age!" In fact, heavy duties fell on his shoulders but he handled them with skill and tact and earned the respect and gratitude of everyone.

In September 1972, the Secretary of the Divisional Committee sent out an appeal in the form of a letter signed by General Roberts to all who served in 11th Armoured Division to let them know that the village of St. George-des-Groseillers, on the northern outskirts of Flers, had purchased a site on which the Divisional monument could be erected. The village wished to donate the land free of charge for that purpose. Furthermore, the town of Flers had voted £15,000 for site preparation and landscaping. All that remained was for the Division to raise the £3,000 or £4,000 needed for the monument itself. The money soon came pouring in from all over Great Britain and the unveiling date was set for 9 June 1974.

In the meanwhile, the Divisional Committee had short-listed three British towns they considered suitable for twinning with Flers. The town of Warminster, in Wiltshire, was finally chosen. Corresponding in size and population to Flers, it is situated on the fringe of Salisbury Plain where all British armoured forces trained during the war and so was well known to the veterans of 11th Armoured Division. The 'Three Musketeers' and the 'Flying Padre' made the necessary approaches to the civic authorities on each side and agreement was reached. The twinning ceremonies took place in Flers on 13th May 1973 and in Warminster on 1 July of the same year. The *Charte de Jumelage* was signed by M. Halbout and Mr. Middleton and reads as follows: *We hereby resolve that our two towns shall henceforth join together in a common endeavour to improve communications between our people, to encourage the study of the French and English languages and cultures, to foster close ties between our English and French schools and societies and to provide a sound basis for personal friendships as a practical contribution to international understanding. As witness our hands, this Thirteenth Day of May, 1973.*

During the course of the twinning ceremonies in Flers, Major Davey, the Secretary of the Divisional Committee and the person who, everyone agreed, was mainly responsible for the success of the negotiations, was asked to unveil a plaque naming one of the main streets of Flers, *Rue de la 11ème Division Blindée Britannique*. To his great surprise, for it had been kept a close secret up to then, he was, at the same time, awarded the Medal of Merit of the *Union Nationale des Combattants*.

As Major Davey wrote in June 1973: *The ripples from the small stone we threw into the pond are growing all the time!*

One month later a letter was sent to all members of the Division to inform them that 'the response of Divisional Old Comrades had assured the success of the project for the construction of the Memorial near Flers, Normandy in 1974; that the Memorial had been ordered and that it was to be made of the same pink granite from Perros-Guirec in Brittany that had been used for De Gaulle's Croix de Lorraine at Colombey-les-deux-Eglises; that General Roberts, accompanied by Major Close, had visited Flers in June for preliminary discussions about the arrangements for the unveiling ceremony next year; that it had been agreed that the ceremony will be held on Sunday, 9 June 1974; that arrangements had also been made for the Cambrai Staff Band and a contingent from the 3rd Royal Tank Regiment to attend; that the families in Flers will accomodate as many Old Comrades as possible ...'

About 400 Old Comrades came to Flers for the unveiling ceremonies, many with their wives. The ceremonies started on Saturday, 8 June with all the Old Comrades marching through the town to the Castle where they were met by the town authorities. General Roberts, Major Close and Major Todman were then awarded the *Union Nationale des Combattants* Medal of Merit by M. Leverrier, the President of the Flers branch.

Next they visited the Divisional Memorial Room at the Castle — another idea of Father Amiard — which contains the Divisional Roll of Honour.

That night there was a picnic and a fireworks display in the grounds of the Castle and down by the lake.

The dedication ceremony was held on Sunday morning in the presence of dignitaries from both sides. The religious service, the unveiling of the Monument, the laying of wreaths, the speeches and the final March Past all gave the ceremony a deeply-moving solemnity especially for those who remembered that it was in this very place that many of their comrades who had fallen at Pont-de-Vère and on the slopes of Aubusson had first been buried before being re-interred later in the permanent cemetery at Tilly-sur-Seulles.

On the way back to Flers the procession stopped at St. Georges-des-Groseillers to unveil a street plaque named for the many Canadian prisoners killed there by Allied planes in a tragic, mistaken attack in June 1944.

After that, however, spirits were raised by a typical Norman banquet which lasted for four hours and was attended by 1500 people. That was an unforgettable experience!

Father Amiard may have been excused for thinking that he could, at last, take things a little easy now that, after four years' work, the Monument and the Divisional Memorial Room at the Castle were realities. But that was not to be. Councillors from the towns around Flers that had been liberated either before or after that city had been invited to attend the ceremonies at Pont-de-Vère. They were all so impressed with the fervour of the ceremonies and the homage to those who had fallen that each of them wanted to organize some expression of remembrance in his town. It was arranged by Major Davey, accompanied by the Chief of Protocol, the formidable M. René Sauvade, affectionately known as 'Moustache', and gently assisted by Father Amiard, that each year two Regiments of the Division would be invited in turn to re-visit Normandy. This would give the towns a chance to re-name a street or a village square or a bridge after the Division. Those details were easy to arrange but what was difficult was to persuade each town to take its turn for each of them was convinced that it had the right of precedence!

Thus, from 1976 to 1983 a *Rue de la 11ème Division Blindée Britannique* was named at Vassy, Athis and St. Martin-des-Besaces. General Roberts unveiled a plaque at Putanges commemorating the date of the crossing of the River Orne by the Division's 29 Armoured Brigade on 19 August 1944 while another plaque was placed at Pont Huan, a place well remembered by the 3rd Monmouthshire Regiment. At Pont-de-Vère a free-standing granite stele, containing a Visitors' Book, and a plaque showing the Order of Battle of the Division were added to the Monument. They too were inaugurated by General Roberts.

Meanwhile, just as in 1944, there was great activity in St. Martin-des-Besaces. While reading *La Charge du Taureau,* Jean Menard of that town had come to realize how strategically vital a part his town had played in the launching of Operation BLUECOAT, the capture of the bridge over the Souleuvre river and the dash for the Vire — Vassy road. Determined that his town's place in history should never be forgotten, he built a museum that features an impressive diorama illustrating how the town was captured from the Germans. That display and the many documents and photographs supplied by the Imperial War Museum make the museum at St. Martin-des-Besaces an important stop on the tour of the Normandy battlefields and a vivid memorial to those who fought and died there.

In 1976 Father Amiard celebrated his 'Golden Jubilee', the 50th anniversary of his ordination as a priest. After all those years of service his energies were drained and his health was failing. He left his residence at the Cedars, the school at which he had taught English to three generations of pupils, and moved to a home for the aged. There, as his life slowly came to its end, he enjoyed the visits of his many friends, both English and French. One of his last meetings was a lunch at the *Maison de Retraite* for 'Pip' Roberts and Annie, his wife, with the 'Three Musketeers', Rose Coombs and Mike Willis (both from the Imperial War Museum) and other privileged friends present.

The feast of the Ascension had always been an important day in the life of Father Amiard, not only because of its significance in the church calendar but also because this was the holiday on which, from 1930 to 1960, he had always organized a race meeting of the Cedars Model Planes Challenge, named after the *Aéro Club des Cèdres,* the club he had founded in 1927 following one of his many visits to England. So it was fitting that it was on Ascension Day 1983, at the age of 84, that his spirit finally soared away.

The 40th anniversary of D-Day and the subsequent battles in North-West Europe were commemorated all over Normandy. It was a specially important anniversary in Flers because it coincided with the 10th anniversary of the unveiling of the Divisional Monument. Four hundred Old Comrades, again many with their wives, came to attend the celebrations. The first was held at the famous Souleuvre bridge. General Roberts was there to describe the battle and to explain the special tactical importance of 'Dicky's Bridge'. He then invited the former Lieutenant Richard Powle of the 2nd Household Cavalry, the leader of the troop that had captured the bridge the first time, to 'open the bridge for the second time!' Next he unveiled a bronze plaque naming the bridge *Le Pont du Taureau*.

Back at Flers in the afternoon, the band of the 3rd Royal Tank Regiment, the only regiment of the 'Charging Bulls' still in existence, led the march of the Old Comrades from the Town Hall, through the streets of the town to the Castle and back to the Town Hall where a civic reception was held. At the special request of the French Committee, former Corporal Ted Chapman, VC of the 3rd Monmouthshire Regiment, was the Guard of Honour for the Division's Roll of Honour that is usually kept in the Memorial Room at the Town Hall. It was he, still every inch a soldier, who offered the book to the Divisional Chaplain, Canon Norman Woodhall, for the benediction.

On Sunday, 3 June, a moving ceremony took place at the Divisional Memorial at Pont-de-Vère. Among the thousands who were present were General Roberts and General Churcher, the former Commander of the Divisions's 159 Infantry Brigade, Mr. Edward Moore, the Chairman of the Warminster Twinning Committee and Mr. Curtis, Chairman of the Warminster Town Council. The service was conducted by Canon Woodhall assisted by the Reverend Christopher Mackonochie, the Chaplain of the 3rd Royal Tank Regiment. Amid a brilliant panoply of colourful flags from the patriotic associations of all the surrounding towns and villages, grizzled ex-Sergeant Reay, DCM and young Trooper Woodward, both of the 3rd Royal Tank Regiment, together lit the Flame of Remembrance in memory of the 2000 soldiers of the Division whose names are on the Roll of Honour.

On the French side, two among many are worthy of special note. One was René Sauvade, the formidable-looking but ever popular

'M. Moustache' who, as Chief of Protocol, was responsible for the smooth running of the ceremonies. The other was Michel Morel who had started his military career in 1944 as a 17-year-old escapee from the German occupation police. He had persuaded an officer in 11th Armoured Division to accept his enrollment and served with such distinction as to earn the award of the British Military Medal and a Citation from 'Pip' Roberts. His subsequent exploits in all France's global trouble spots earned him many other awards but his proudest honour was to act as the Divisional Standard Bearer at all the ceremonies.

And now let me use the words of Major 'Claude' Davey to end this Epilogue.

So ended an amazing 14-year chapter in Franco-British relations based on the cameraderie of French and British Old Comrades and French families. What was done in that time was unique in any history of the aftermath of war... When we were invited back to Normandy to celebrate with the town of Flers the 25th anniversary of their liberation it would have been easy to have said 'sorry we can't come', meaning, 'we can't be bothered.' Had we done that we would never have known what we were going to miss over the remainder of our lives and we would never have gained such an expanding circle of friends. There would have been no twinning of Flers with Warminster, there would have been no annual visits of Old Comrades to Flers and the surrounding villages — those marvellous trips which, in truth, were adventures.

There must surely be a moral in this history since 1970. It must be that if anyone offers you the hand of friendship, if anyone seeks your support, if anyone asks you to share in a joint venture, never turn away because you will never know what opportunities might develop from the tiniest of beginnings.

BIBLIOGRAPHY

Belfield, Eversley & Essame, Hubert. *The Battle for Normandy.* London, Batsford, 1965.

Bell, Noël. *From the Beaches to the Baltic (History of 'G' Company, 8th Rifle Brigade).* Aldershot, Gale Polden, 1946.

Bevan, D. G. *The 1st and 2nd Northamptonshire Yeomanry, 1939-1946.* Brunswick, Germany, J. H. Meyer, 1946.

Brownlie, W. Steel. *The Proud Trooper (The Story of the Ayrshire Yeomanry).* London, Collins, 1964.

Carver, R. M. P. *History of the 7th Armoured Division (The 'Desert Rats').*

Cazenove, H. de L. *The Northamptonshire Yeomanry, 1794-1964.* Privately published by the author.

Courage, G. *History of the 15/19 The King's Royal Hussars, 1939-1945.* Aldershot, Gale Polden, 1949.

Cunliffe, M. *History of the Royal Warwickshire Regiment, 1919-1955.* London, Clowes, 1956.

Dunstan, Simon. *Great Battle Tanks.* Weybridge, Surrey, Ian Allan, 1979.

Eisenhower, Dwight, D. *Report by the Supreme Commander to the Combined Chiefs of Staff on the Operations in Europe of the Allied Expeditionary Force, 6 June 1944 to 8 May 1945.* London, H. M. Stationery Office, 1946.

Ellis, L. F. *Victory in the West, Volume I, The Battle of Normandy.* London, H. M. Stationery Office, 1962.

Essame, Hubert. *History of the 4th Battalion, The Somerset Light Infantry, June 1944 to May 1945.* Privately published, 1945.

Essame, Hubert. *The 43rd (Wessex) Infantry Division at War.* Germany, British Army of the Rhine, 1952.

Essame, Hubert. *Normandy Bridgehead.* London, Macdonald, 1971.

Godfrey, E. G. & Goldsmith, R. F. K. *The Duke of Cornwall's Light Infantry.* Aldershot, Gale Polden, 1966.

Gunning, Hugh. *Borderers in Battle: The War Story of the King's Own Scottish Borderers, 1939-1945.* Berwick-on-Tweed, Martin's Press, 1948.

Hastings, R. H. W. S. *The Rifle Brigade, 1939-1945.* Aldershot, Gale Polden, 1950.

How, J. J. *History of the South Wales Borderers and the Monmouthshire Regiment: Part IV, The 3rd Battalion, The Monmouthshire Regiment.* Pontypool, Hughes & Son, 1954.

Kemp, P. K. *History of the Royal Norfolk Regiment, 1919-1951, Volume III.* Norwich, Soman Wherry Press, 1953

Kemp, P. K. *History of the 4th Battalion, The King's Shropshire Light Infantry.* Shrewsbury, Wilding & Son, 1955.

Kemp, P. K. *The Middlesex Regiment (Duke of Cambridge's Own) 1919-1952.* Aldershot, Gale Polden, 1956.

Macksey, Kenneth. *To The Green Fields Beyond (The Royal Tank Regiment).* Kingsteignton, Frank Ltd., 1965.

McMath, J. S. *The 5th Battalion, The Wiltshire Regiment in North-West Europe.* London, Whitefriars Press, 1947.

Meredith, J. L. J. *From Normandy to Hanover (The 7th Battalion The Somerset Light Infantry).* Hanover, 1945.

Moberley, R. B. *The 2nd Battalion, The Middlesex Regiment (The Duke of Cambridge's Own), Campaign in Europe, 6 June, 1944 to 7 May, 1945.* Cairo, Schindler, 1946.

Mullaly, B. R. *The South Lancashire Regiment, The Prince of Wales' Volunteers.* Bristol, White Swan Press, 1953.

Nicholson, W. N. L. *History of the Suffolk Regiment 1928-1946.* Ipswich, East Anglian Magazine, 1948.

Palamountain, E. W. I. *Taurus Pursuant (11th Armoured Division).* Germany, British Army of the Rhine, 1946.

Parsons, Robbins & Gilson. *The Maroon Square. The 1st Battalion, The Wiltshire Regiment in North-West Europe, 1939-1945.* Franey Company, 1947.

Roberts, G. P. B. *From the Desert to the Baltic.* London, William Kimber, 1987.

Scarfe, Norman. *Assault Division (3rd British Infantry Division).* London, Collins, 1947.

Sellar, R. J. B. *The Fife and Forfar Yeomanry, 1919-1956.* Edinburgh, William Blackwood & Son.

Traggart, A. F. *Needs Must (The Inns of Court Regiment).* London, Mildner & Sons, 1949.

Watkins, G. J. B. *From Normandy to the Weser (The War History of the 4th Battalion, the Dorsetshire Regiment, June 1944 to May 1945).* Dorchester, Dorset Press, 1952.

Watson, D. Y. *The 1st Battalion, The Worcestershire Regiment in North-West Europe.* Worcester, Trinity Press, 1948.

Historical Records of the Herefordshire Light Infantry and its Predecessors. Shrewsbury, Livesey, 1962.

History of the 3rd Reconnaissance Regiment (Northumberland Fusiliers) in the Invasion and subsequent campaign in North-West Europe, 1944-1945. Privately published, 1946.

The Story of the 23rd Hussars. Husum, Germany, 1946.

INDEX

PRINTED IN GREAT BRITAIN BY

Tas Offset Printing Services
Wensum Point, 32 Whiffler Road, Norwich, Norfolk NR3 2AZ

NORMANDY THE SEARCH FOR SIDNEY

By Tom Bates

This book, the second of the 'Normandy Trilogy', will be published in 1989. It tells how, 40 years after D – Day, two former soldiers of the 1st Battalion, the Royal Norfolk Regiment, ex-Corporal Ernie Seaman, MM and ex-Private Bill Holden, returned to Normandy with the author to help him find the exact place where Corporal Sidney Bates, their comrade in the 1st Battalion, made the stand at the Battle of Perrier Ridge on 6 August 1944 that earned him the posthumous award of the Victoria Cross.

The book also tells how, while 'searching for Sidney' in Normandy in 1984 the author, who served with XIV Army in Burma in 1944, became involved in two D – Day stories that concerned the former Suzanne Prevel of Colleville-sur-Orne who is now Madame Lenauld of Colleville-Montgomery.

It is hoped that the publication of these two stories, both of which add to the Invasion saga, will help Madame Lenauld find the final resting place of the British soldier who died in the arms of her fiancé, Jean Lenauld, on D – Day. She has been searching for the grave of her 'soldat inconnu' ever since then because she took a vow on that day that she would tend his grave for the rest of her life.

The book will be illustrated by numerous photographs, many in colour, and will also contain several maps. It will be printed by Tas Offset Printing Services of Norwich, Norfolk, the printing business established after the war by Bill Holden, the former anti-tank gunner of the 1st Battalion, the Royal Norfolk Regiment.

SIDNEY BATES, VC
'A TRUE CAMBERWELL BOY'

By Tom Bates

This book, the third of the 'Normandy Trilogy', is scheduled for publication in 1990.

By then it will have been nearly 10 years in the making. It will tell the story of the 23-year-old South Londoner who gave his life to save his comrades of the 1st Battalion, the Royal Norfolk Regiment in one of the most savage battles of the Normandy campaign in August 1944.

The book will tell how, encouraged by Sidney's surviving family and helped by a series of lucky discoveries, the author, who is not related to Sidney Bates, traced the pedigree of this cockney boy back to the 18th century — and maybe further back !

With the cooperation of the Regimental Association of the Royal Norfolk Regiment and assisted by surviving comrades-in-arms, of all ranks, of the former Corporal of their 1st Battalion, the story is told from the point of view of the 'common' soldier.

It draws on official and unofficial sources to trace the brief history of this working-class civilian soldier from the time he volunteered in June 1940, just after the disaster of the Dunkirk defeat, to August 1944 when he gave his life just before the climax of the Normandy victory.

An Epilogue brings the story up to date. It recounts how Sidney's Victoria Cross medal was acquired by the Regiment after it had disappeared for more than 40 years and how a battlefield monument was erected to commemorate the 'true Camberwell boy' and his comrades.

This book also will be printed by Bill Holden who fought with Sidney Bates in the 1st Battalion, the Royal Norfolk Regiment. It is his way of paying tribute to his former comrades and of closing the circle of remembrance.

SOBRIQUETS & NICKNAMES IN THE BRITISH ARMED FORCES

Compiled by Tom Bates

It was originally intended that this collection of sobriquets and nicknames should be an Appendix to *Normandy—The Search for Sidney*. During the 1984 pilgrimage to Normandy with Ernie Seaman and Bill Holden the author noticed that nearly everyone they referred to in their accounts of their war-time experiences had a nickname. Very seldom did they refer to a man by his real name if, indeed, they had ever known it. It was always his nickname they used when talking about him and it was this name that, 40 years after the events, gave a man a certain immortality.

However, once the author started compiling the list it grew and grew. Contributions came in from all directions. Every book of war-time reminiscences he read produced a further crop of nicknames and, when they could be contacted, the authors of those books were always helpful about explaining how or why the 'sobs' or 'nicks'* had been bestowed — if they knew or remembered.

In 1985, the magazine, *The Military Chest* (since replaced by *Fighting Forces),* was kind enough to print a short excerpt from the list and that elicited many more names from its readers. Soon, what was to have been an Appendix was larger than the book itself! And so the idea for another book was born.

The scope of the collection has been enlarged. Nicknames from before World War II have been added, many of them 'historical', and it has been decided to illustrate the book with photographs of the recipients of the sobriquets and nicknames wherever possible.

Nicknames from the Royal Navy and the Royal Air Force have widened the coverage of the book and have justified its more expansive title. Although at present (1988) the book is predominantly an 'Army list' it is hoped that by the time it is published (scheduled for 1991) it will include many more entries from the other services and also from the women's branches of the services.

Contributions to the list, especially when supported by photographs, will be welcomed and acknowledged. They can be sent to the author at either of the two addresses given below. If requested, all photographs will be returned to the owners.

BATES BOOKS
Tas Offset Printing Services
Wensum Point, 32 Whiffler Road,
Norwich   Norfolk NR3 2AZ,
England.

BATES BOOKS
120 Hillcrest Road
Berkeley
California 94705
United States of America

*NICKNAME: A name or appellation added to, or substituted for, the proper name of a person, place, etc, usually given in ridicule or pleasantry.
SOBRIQUET: An epithet, a nickname. (*O.E.D.*)
Following the tongue-in-cheek convention that, whereas the men 'sweated', the officers 'perspired', the 'sobs' are for the officers and the 'nicks' for the men!

NOTES

NOTES

NOTES

NOTES

NOTES

NOTES

NOTES

NOTES

NOTES

NOTES

NOTES

NOTES